Hope you enjoyed your visit
as much as we enjoyed
having you

David and Mary.

a
Wild
and
Open Sea

a
Wild
and
Open Sea

The Story of the
Pentland Firth

James Miller

First published 1994
by The Orkney Press Ltd
12 Craigiefield Park, St Ola
Kirkwall, Orkney KW15 1TE

Typeset by Corina Knight
Designed by Iain Ashman
Printed in Great Britain
by The Kirkwall Press

ISBN 0 907618 33 2

The publishers wish to acknowledge
the financial support of
Orkney Islands Council and
The Scottish Arts Council
in the publication of this book

The drawing of the yole on page 9 is
from a painting by George Manson

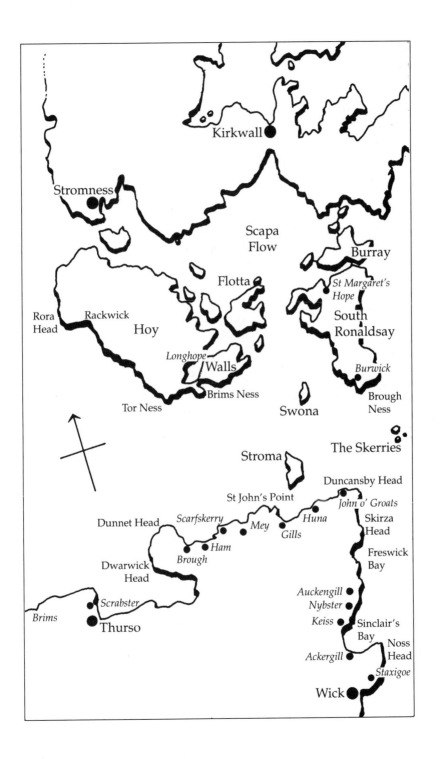

Kirkwall

Stromness

Scapa
Flow

Burray

*St Margaret's
Hope*

Flotta

Rora
Head

Rackwick

Hoy

South
Ronaldsay

Longhope

Walls

Burwick

Brims Ness

Tor Ness

Swona

Brough
Ness

The Skerries

Stroma

Duncansby Head

St John's Point

John o' Groats

Dunnet Head

Scarfskerry

Mey

Huna

Skirza
Head

Ham

Gills

Dwarwick
Head

Brough

Freswick
Bay

Auckengill

Brims

Scrabster

Nybster

Thurso

Keiss

Sinclair's
Bay

Noss
Head

Ackergill

Staxigoe

Wick

To the memory of my parents
and to the
communities of the Firth

Contents

Introduction

I was born in the village of Keiss in Caithness in a house overlooking the sea. Its grey expanse was my first horizon but closer acquaintance with it came gradually, and an early excursion on my own, down the winding flight of steps to the harbour, earned me only a well-skelped backside in public. The shame burned stronger than my mother's blows. She knew the sea could take me, as it had taken my grandfather.

I had gone down to meet our father's fishing boat, *Rose*. She was 28 feet long and he steered her in through the jaws of the harbour on as many days as weather and seasons would allow, her hold hissing and creaking with crabs plucked from the seabed.

Often I loved the sea, but at other times I hated its cold, colourless malevolence. It held no compassion, only movement and the mocking strength of a brutal, unremitting tyrant. But it was as if it were a member of the family – turning your back was no use.

'I dinna care aboot the owld boat,' I remember saying once, in a fit of petulance.

My mother was very angry: 'That boat's put the bread in your mouth and the claes on your back.'

Our stretch of sea was Sinclair's Bay, a graceful loop of shore with cliffs at either end and miles of pale yellow sand in the centre. Our house stood above the harbour on the north side of the bay and, sitting up in my bed, I could watch at night the lighthouse winking on Noss Head.

There were often other lights out on the water, for ships anchored in our bay to escape pounding gales. Sometimes Noss Head's guiding eye disappeared in fog and we fell asleep to the mournful, deep baying of the foghorn. With the wind in the north-east, white water stormed the harbour walls and salt spray rose to douse our windows. There was always something happening on the sea.

One night my brother and I watched the lights of a boat move slowly but steadily towards the beach. A flare went up. Our father shook his head. In the morning a trawler lay stranded in the surf. The trawler was called the *Jean Stephens*. The crew walked ashore at low tide, leaving their vessel to rust to pieces. For years the raw, red hull and round, knobbled bulk of the boilers formed a landmark for beachcombers.

According to the written records, a blizzard was blowing that night in January 1958. I don't remember the snow, only the cold, sorning, spray-laden wind that came off the breakers when we went to the beach in the morning to see the wreck.

It was said that the skipper had taken Noss Head for Duncansby Head and, until his error dawned on him, thought he was happily steaming towards the Atlantic. He was not the first to make that mistake. Duncansby Head is 11 miles north of Noss and is where the east coast of Caithness bends sharply to mark the start of the north coast. Duncansby Head is the eastern signpost for the Pentland Firth, the northern gate from Europe to the Atlantic.

Another wreck formed the objective of another dimly remembered excursion. I know now that the date was in September 1953. I was five years old. We went, the whole family, one grey Sunday afternoon along the cliffs to the north of the village until we reached the point of Nybster, the place we call the Dog's Nose, from its shape and not because it's often cold and wet there. From the Nose we could see in the distance the waves breaking over the remains of the *Hassett*. She was a Grimsby trawler; five of her crew had been washed overboard and lost, and the survivors had been heard singing 'Land of Hope and Glory' as they waited for the breeches-buoy to take them off.

So I grew up with the sea, with its rhythms and its sounds, its smell and its strange inhabitants. I learned a little about boats, navigation, the points of the compass, the patterns of the tides and their dangers. I heard stories of wrecks and storms, of sailing ships and destroyers. I have long had it in mind to write a history of the Pentland Firth and this is the result. It is also, in a sense, a history of my ancestors and therefore of me. From as many sources as I have been able to plunder, I have gathered information and tried to fit it all together to make a story that, I hope, will prove of some interest and value. The direct connections between many of the events recorded here and my immediate forebears must remain a mystery; I suspect that this is the case for all families other than the lucky, powerful few to whom genealogies and bloodlines have always been important.

The people who live along the shores of the Firth are people of the sea. They have knowledge of a shifting world, of tides and creatures beyond the imagining of landsmen. This made them in the past both superstitious and open-minded. They are an intelligent, friendly people, intolerant of fools, steady but still quick to laugh, resourceful

11

and thrifty. A quiet enthusiasm is preferred to a loud voice. The sea brought the world to their door and, in turn, they went out to all the corners of the oceans. Captains and seamen from the shores of the Firth rose to prominence in the navies of many countries. There is not space here to tell all their stories, but remember, for example, Charles Calder from Dunnet who began a seafaring life as a boy on the Wick schooner *Bella* and went on to be the first man to pilot ships of 20,000, 30,000 and 40,000 tons through the Suez Canal;[1] and the first ship to pass south through the new Canal on 18 November 1869 was the *Dido* under the command of John Groat from Longhope.[2] At one time, in the village of Rackwick on Hoy, a man and his three sons each held a master mariner's ticket. [3] It is, therefore, no surprise to find the great novelist of the sea, Joseph Conrad, having the captain of the *Narcissus* 'born on the shores of the Pentland Firth'.[4]

For the sake of brevity, I have limited the geographical sphere of interest of the book to the Firth proper and immediately adjoining coasts: on the Caithness side I have focused on the stretch between Holborn Head and Noss Head, and on the Orkney side from Stromness southabout to South Ronaldsay. This excludes much about Wick and Kirkwall, but readers can find more of their history in some of the books in the Bibliography.

I have also been conscious throughout of telling a male-dominated story. Seafaring has been essentially a male business, at least as events have been recorded, and it is easy to forget the wives, daughters and mothers waiting at home - as they still wait.

Slackwater

The Pentland Firth on the Hondius Atlas, Amsterdam 1636

Twice every day, the tide surges through the Pentland Firth from the Atlantic to the North Sea and back again, creating some of the worst turbulence that mariners regularly have to negotiate. The currents frequently surpass 10 knots, a force that can treat a ship like a plaything. In the laconic words of the *North Coast of Scotland Pilot*, all vessels should 'be thoroughly secured before entering Pentland Firth, even in the calmest weather'.

The Firth itself is not large. From Dunnet Head, which can serve as its westerly entrance, to Clettack Skerry, the most easterly of the jumble of rocks and islets that make up the Pentland Skerries, it is a distance of 17 miles. From Dunnet Head north to Tor Ness on the island of Hoy is barely eight miles. At the eastern end of the Firth, about six and a half miles separate Brough Ness on South Ronaldsay from Duncansby. Through this gap between Orkney and Caithness, both tide and shipping have to pass, as if along a river in the sea. Many captains and shipowners preferred in the past to make long detours north of Orkney or south by the English Channel to avoid the roosts and eddies of the Firth. Today a sizeable proportion of the shipping between northern Europe and North América passes through the waterway. As well as the freighters, liners, bulk carriers, trawlers and coasters, there are tankers, some sailing on, some heading to or from the oil terminal on the island of Flotta in Scapa Flow. The number of vessels using the Firth is estimated to reach almost 6000 in each year (see Appendix 2).

At Duncansby Head the Caithness coast bends sharply southward to form a wall of rock stretching with few interruptions right to the county's land boundary with Sutherland. Near the Firth, Freswick Bay and Sinclair's Bay offer a few miles of gentle beach; and to the west of the Firth, things are similar, with Dunnet Bay and Thurso Bay holding large sweeps of sand.

The coastal scenery of Caithness and Orkney, with its three-dimensional tapestry of geos, stacks, gloups and caves, is renowned. This carving of the rocks is the sea's artistry and, as the sea is the chief protagonist in this book - some would say its villain - it is right to look at this point at the power the sea can deploy. Without some understanding of this, the reader cannot properly appreciate the Firth.

When the wind blows over the sea, it transfers energy to the water to make waves in a complicated process not fully understood by oceanographers, although from the tangle of equations and computer models that they have so far produced, some simple rules can be extracted. Waves have length - the distance between successive crests; height - the vertical distance from crest to trough; and period or frequency - the time it takes successive crests to pass a given point. These properties are related to each other. Waves also have energy. This energy increases as the waves become higher roughly as the square of the height, i.e. a 2-foot wave will have four times more energy and a 4-foot wave sixteen times more energy than a 1-foot wave.[1]

The height of the waves depends particularly on three aspects of the wind: the windspeed; the duration - the time for which the wind has been blowing; and the fetch - the distance of open water over which the wind has already passed before reaching the observer. A 40-knot gale that has been blasting from the north-west across the Atlantic can raise larger waves than a similar gale blowing up from the east across the narrower North Sea.

Wave patterns are extremely complex. They defy ready analysis, even by advanced computer programmes, as windspeed is constantly fluctuating and waves travel at different speeds, sometimes reinforcing each other, at other times cancelling each other out; but again some rough empirical rules, known to seafarers from experience, seem to hold good. An established gale - a Force 8, gusting between 34 and 40 knots - can produce in a fully arisen open sea waves about 10 seconds apart with an average height of almost 30 feet, but 10 per cent of the waves will reach higher, up to nearly 60 feet. In winter the wind in the area of the Firth rises to Force 7 on perhaps 15 days in every month, and to Force 8 on seven days per month. Force 10 is frequently reached, but Force 12 is reckoned to occur once every five years. Westerlies are fairly short-lived, but high pressure sitting over Scandinavia can result in south-easterly storms persisting for up to a week. The size and power of waves also depend on whether the wind is blowing against or with the direction of the tide.

Another aspect of the weather in the Firth brings danger to the seafarer - fog. This is most frequent in the summer months when warm air blowing from the south-east passes over the colder sea, and piles up banks of condensation along eastward shores. Heavy rain or drizzle can seriously reduce visibility in the Firth, but fog is the more crippling and has often caused ships to go aground.[2]

As waves approach shorelines they tend to slow but their heights increase. This is due to friction from the seabed, and leads to breaking.

Waves break when the crest is moving faster than the trough. It is as if the wave trips and falls on its face. On a steep beach the crest plunges forward, trapping air inside its curling fall, air that is squeezed slightly, only to burst out again, throwing spume before it. Spilling breakers, where the frothing crest tumbles down the advancing wave slope, are characteristic of gently sloping beaches.

Since waves slow down in shallow water, a wave coming in from the open sea can alter when it comes in to shore near a headland. The part of the wave towards the headland, where the shore is nearing, will slow down, while the rest of the wave, out in deeper water, will continue at greater speed. The effect is to bend the wave around the headland, almost as if it is following the contour of the coastline, and so for instance in particular seas a wave can turn around a headland and into a bay behind it - an effect called *refraction*. In other circumstances waves can rebound or *reflect* from the shore, producing confused choppy water when they interfere with other incoming waves.

17

The power released when a wave hits the coast is awesome, and consistently underestimated by those who have not experienced the wrath of the sea. A wave 10 feet high and 150 feet long can smash into the coast, or a ship for that matter, with a shock pressure of over 1200 lb/sq ft. The maximum pressure may last for only a fraction of a second, but it is repeated, hammer blow after hammer blow, in a heavy storm. In severe conditions, the shock pressure in the Atlantic can rise to over 6000 lb/sq ft.

Added to this when the sea attacks the coast are four other weapons: corrosion, corrasion, attrition and hydraulic action. The corrosion, caused by chemical action between the sea's salts and the rocks, is the least obvious. Corrasion is nothing other than sandblasting, as the waves pick up and hurl grit and sand against the shore. Attrition occurs when the sea cuts under rocks so that they break and fall under their own weight. Hydraulic action takes place when the water traps and compresses air in cavities and cracks; like a pneumatic ram, the compressed air forces its way forward, opening cracks wider and further.

All of this energy and action over the centuries has eroded the cliffs around the Firth into the shapes we see now. The regular strata of the sandstone rocks are susceptible to a continuing pattern of erosion that has produced the characteristic features found around the coast. Any weak point in a cliff, due, say, to a cleft or a fault line, will be attacked and widened and deepened - the most common result is what we call a *geo*, pronounced 'gyo' with a hard 'g'. This word was originally Norse (see Appendix 1) as are most of the terms in use in Caithness and Orkney for coastal features, and has no exact English equivalent (geographers have borrowed *geo* as a technical term). Geos can be as wide as a small harbour - and some are used as such - or so narrow you can touch both sides at one time; they can slope from top to bottom, allowing a way down a cliff, or drop sheer to the dark water in the shade below.

When the sea has tunnelled into a cliff face to produce a cave, continued pummelling and hydraulic action may drive a hole up through the cave roof to the open air at the landward end. Such a feature is called a *gloup* ,and the roof of the cave on the seaward side will gradually be reduced to form a natural arch. When this too falls, another geo comes into being. At the tip of a headland or ness a hole can be driven through from one side to the other at sea level. This opening is called a *thirl door* or *tirl door*, and as it grows upward it too forms a natural arch. When the arch falls, a pillar of rock is left standing clear from the cliff behind to form a stack or a clett. Rocks worn down to sea level comprise a skerry.

The first indication of the proximity of the Firth to the seaman approaching from the Atlantic is the high lump of the island of Hoy, a grey mountain rising on the skyline. As he draws nearer, in clear weather, the cliffs become visible. From the Kame of Hoy to Tor Ness, almost 14 miles of red rock face the ocean like a rampart. A good way to see these cliffs, for those who do not have their own boat or the time and strong boots needed to walk the coast, is from the daily Scrabster/Stromness ferry, the mv *St Ola*. In thick weather I have sailed by them and seen nothing but an impenetrable curtain of haar, but when the air is clear, and especially with a westering sun, the wall glows red and the massive scale and detail of cleft and geo is easily picked out.

On her course northward from Scrabster, the *St Ola* comes close to Hoy at the island's south-west corner, Rora Head, but away to the east is the straight 600-foot face of The Berry and the rounded profile of the 500-foot Sneuk. Between these two prominences and to the east of them towards Tor Ness, the cliffs fall to modest-seeming heights. Those to the west of the Sneuk run at around the 300-foot mark until they drop sharply to the sandy curve of Rackwick, the 'bay of wreckage', before rising again to 500 feet at the Too of the Head and then dipping to 300 feet at Rora Head.

Rora Head's western face is smooth and sheer. Hard frosts a few years ago sliced pieces from the cliff to leave the gleaming, unblemished surface now visible. At the   19 foot of the Head, the dark mouths of caves, some of which lead right through the rock, can be seen. A mile to the north of Rora Head stands the far-famed Old Man of Hoy, a 450-foot finger of sandstone protected from the sea's full erosive power by its basalt base. In the early nineteenth century, the Old Man had two 'feet', a natural arch at the base, and a more 'humpbacked' silhouette, but the landward leg has long since been amputated by the elements and the figure trimmed. George Low described the stack in 1774 as 'having something of the appearance of a man with a large burden on his back'.

The rock rampart of Hoy rises gradually from the Old Man to the riven vertical of St John's Head (1136 ft) and the partly detached mass of Brae Brough. The cliffs here take on a deep red colour in the sun, with green bands where ledges allow grass to flourish. The height of the cliffs falls gradually to the north of St John's Head until the last headland, the Kame of Hoy, drops like a knife-blade at an angle of 45 degrees from 950 feet. Beyond, the grassy steps of the Bay of the Stairs and the narrower, steep Bay of the Tongue - both geos rather than bays - mark the quick descent to the low-lying north corner of Hoy and the opening of the Sound leading into Stromness.

Eight miles to the south of Tor Ness, the peninsula of Dunnet Head reaches out like a broad claw. The cliffs here do not reach the height of those on Hoy, but Easter Head, to give the tip of the peninsula its proper but hardly ever-used name, is a perpendicular face of some 330 feet. To the east, the Caithness coast continues low and rocky, punctuated by creeks, geos and bays, until the land heaves upward again to the 200-foot knuckle of Duncansby Head. Halfway between lies the prominent St John's Point, an exposed headland which seems higher than its 50 feet. On either side of the Point, a geo cuts into the grassy heath and, beyond the clumps of sea pink fringing the cliff edge, rocks run offshore in a reef. When the tide ebbs here, a mottled swathe of sea curves away like a scimitar blade in the birth pangs of the Men of Mey race.

Duncansby Head offers a textbook lesson in coastal rock formations within a reasonable walking distance. Between the shell-sand beach at Sannick and the lighthouse is the gaping hole of the Gloup. Below its precipitous sides, to be approached with caution, the sea can be glimpsed through the cave mouth, and on stormy days spume and spray drive up through the opening like smoke. Impressive though this Gloup is, there are larger ones on Stroma, where an illicit whisky still was once hidden, and on South Ronaldsay at Halcro Head, where the roof opening is fully 100 yards from the cliff edge.

To the east of the Duncansby Gloup, Longgeo cuts into the cliff like a slice taken from a cake, but the largest geo in the vicinity is the Long Geo of Slaites to the south of the lighthouse. The sea is carving a stack away from the land here; called Humlies Hole, the top of the stack is still joined to the mother cliff behind, but one day this crumbling stone umbilicus will be cut. At one time, the opening of Humlies Hole probably resembled that of the Thirl Door, further to the south at the end of the beach of Queenicliff. A number of stacks rise offshore at Duncansby, probably the most photographed stacks in Scotland; the highest, the Muckle Stack, reaches a height of 297 feet.

Returning to the Orkney shore, to the east of Tor Ness the coast curves towards Brims Ness and the island of South Walls. A road links the island of Hoy to South Walls. This was built early this century over a natural causeway or ayre which formerly could be crossed only at low tide. Heavy winter swells deposit tangles on the road, which divides Aith Hope, open to the Firth, from the inner end of Longhope. On the Aith Hope side there is a short stretch of sandy beach, but on the other is shingle, its orangey-fawn colour characteristic of Orkney stone.

The southern coast of South Walls is a further sculpture of geos and headlands, between 50 and 100 feet or more, and it ends in the east in the lump of Cantick Head with its lighthouse. Offshore lies the small island of Switha, and to the north the rounded bulk of Flotta. East again is the Sound of Hoxa, the southern gateway to

Scapa Flow, dividing Flotta from South Ronaldsay. South Ronaldsay itself is a long hilly island; its southern tip, the low-lying Brough Ness to the east of the sweep of Burwick Bay, forms with Duncansby Head the eastern jaws of the Firth.

The islands of Swona and Stroma stand athwart the Firth like two giant stepping stones. Stroma is the larger of the two and divides the passage into the Inner Sound - between it and Caithness - and the Outer Sound, the main channel for shipping, two and a half miles wide. The Pentland Skerries lie to the east. The largest of the group, the Muckle Skerry, rises to about 50 feet above sea level and has a lighthouse.

A Wild and Open Sea

These northern waters set about bare, windy coasts have impressed writers since the earliest times. John of Fordun wrote in about 1380 that Scotland was bounded on the north 'by the Pentland Firth, where a fearfully danger-ous whirlpool sucks in and belches back the waters every hour.'[3] At that time, Orkney and Shetland were still parts of the kingdom of Norway. The early geographers rarely visited much of the country they described. They relied on the reports of travellers, and blithely repeated the mistakes of other writers. In 1570, when Bishop John Leslie was in England at the time of the imprisonment of Queen Mary, he began a description of his homeland. It was published first in Rome in 1578, and was translated into Scots by Father James Ratisbon of Dalrymple in 1596. This is how the Bishop described the north:

> *Hier the thrie craigis of the utmost parte of al the cost*
> *make twa bosumis, or Lochis. The first of*
> *thame in Strathnaver to name is Houbron, notable*
> *in mekledom: the other twa in Cathnesse ar Hoy*
> *and Dunesbe called, of quhilkes Ptolomie names*
> *this Dume. This is the last and hindmest hil in Scotland,*

22

*and thairfor the schortest, bot the maist dangerous sailing
ower to the Iles of Orknay be Pintland Firthe.*

The reputation of the Firth was well and widely known.
Those who ventured to relate the experience of crossing it
did so in such a high-blown manner that it is a wonder
anyone was foolhardy enough to follow them. This is
what William Lithgow, one of the most widely travelled
men of his time, had to say in 1628:

*Forsaking Cathnes, I embraced the trembling surges (at
Dungsby) of struggling Neptune, which ingorgeth
Pentland or Pictland frith, with nine contrarious tides;
each tide overthwarting another with repugnant courses,
have such violent streams, and combustious waves, that if
these dangerous firths be not rightly taken in passing
over, the passengers shall quickly lose sight of life and
land for ever ...*

Fourteen years before, Lithgow had been shipwrecked
in the Mediterranean on a voyage from Greece to
Constantinople, when 'every man looked with the stamp
of death on his pale visage' - and it reads as if the Firth
reminded him vividly of his earlier experience.

In contrast, but also in confirmation, there are the
words of the late Dr Sydney Peace, a former honorary
secretary of the Longhope lifeboat, on the sea conditions
prevailing in the Firth on the night of 17 March 1969 when
the lifeboat *TGB* was lost:

*Imagine the confusion - waves of irregular height and
shape, spray flying all over the place, chased every now
and then by charging masses of solid water. Sooner or
later a tidal build-up would thrust itself against an
oncoming hill of sea. The result would be a rearing
monster of power surging upwards like a liquid cliff. I am
not surprised that men reported waves of sixty feet in
height that night in that place.*[4]

There is a timelessness about the Firth coasts. With the wind whipping at your clothes and the light dancing off the sea and the smell of salt in the air, you experience sensations shared with every human who has stood here before you. Was it always thus?

Standing on Dunnet Head and looking northward to Hoy, it is easy to suppose that the island was once connected to the mainland. The sawn-off, red walls of rock, one below your feet, the other a few miles away, look the same, like two ends of a broached dyke. Geologists seem wary about providing an answer to questions about the age of the Firth. Being good scientists, they are unwilling to risk their reputations on flimsy evidence. Without going into detail on the complex sequence of changes in sea and land levels before, during and just after the last Ice Age, suffice it to say that Orkney may have been connected to Caithness about 10,000 years ago. It seems that this land bridge did not last long, the Atlantic drowning it before animals and plants had much chance to cross.[5]

The question of when the first humans launched themselves across the Firth to reach Orkney is a matter for speculation.[6] Radiocarbon dating of material remains from archaeological sits in Orkney suggests it took place 4000-3500 BC. As to where - take your pick, but common sense leads me to think that the crossing may have taken place in stages, first to Stroma and then to Swona and South Ronaldsay. Flint tools, which may predate the crossing, have been found at Freswick. These early peoples were probably familiar with the Caithness shore for some time before they ventured further; the coast provided plenty for small hunting communities.

The middens excavated and painstakingly sieved by archaeologists reveal fish and shellfish bones. One tomb, first discovered in 1958 by Ronald Simison at Isbister on the tip of South Ronaldsay, has provided a clue to the spiritual dimension of this distant world. Ninety per cent of the animal bones associated with the human remains in the Isbister tomb are of the sea eagle. It seems that this great bird was of totemic or religious significance. On the

24

basis of this and other evidence, John W. Hedges has built up a convincing picture of life in neolithic Orkney. No comparable archaeological work has been done on the Caithness side; the evidence has not survived as well on the southern shore of the Firth, but we can be fairly certain that life there was not so different.

In Rome some time around 56 BC, a young geographer called Diodorus Siculus sat down to write an account of the known world. He recorded a description of Britain taken from the report of a Phoenician sailor called Pytheas who, over two centuries before, had sailed along the coasts of the island. The concept of this distant, unknown place was shaky: Britain was described as triangular, the three points of the triangle being Cantium, Belerium and, extending out into the open sea, Orca, where waves of immense size were noted.[7] There is some evidence that the north of Scotland may have enjoyed a warmer, less stormy climate around 2000 BC and possibly at other times since, for example around AD 1000. If this was the case, perhaps the Firth was kinder to seafarers and may have allowed more daring voyages in these periods.[8]

An early record of another voyage in the area comes from the account of the campaigns of the Roman general Agricola in Scotland in AD 81-84 by his son-in-law Tacitus. In AD 83, as Agricola's army advanced north of the Tay, a cohort of auxiliary troops, the Usipi from the Rhine, mutinied, killed a centurion and escaped in three small warships. To return to Germany the mutineers sailed around the north coast and thence across the North Sea where, Tacitus records with some satisfaction, 'they lost their ships through bad seamanship'.

In the following year, after the defeat of the Celts at the battle of Mons Graupius, Agricola dispatched his admiral to sail around the north end of Britain. The explorers enjoyed favourable weather and returned without mishap to their base. Scholars disagree on how far the Roman fleet went - some argue they reached Cape Wrath. Tacitus says that they 'discovered and subjugated the Orkney Islands, hitherto unknown'.

The northern shores 'are beaten by a wild and open sea,' he wrote; and he described a 'huge and shapeless tract of country, jutting out to form what is actually the most distant coastline and finally tapering into a kind of wedge'. Cape Wrath or Caithness? The fleet also sighted what they called Thule before the approach of winter made them turn back. The location of Thule has always intrigued mariners; in this case, the Romans probably saw Shetland, though Iceland or the Faroes have also been suggested as the original of this semi-mythical land.

What the native Orkney and Caithness folk had to say about being 'subjugated' by the Romans has not been recorded. But who were they? What kind of ships did they possess? They were Celts of some kind, the race that later became known as the Picts and, if their seamanship was as good as that of the Celtic peoples Julius Caesar encountered on the shores of Gaul, they were skilled sailors indeed.

The strength of the ships manned by the tribes in what is now Brittany perplexed the Romans, and it took Caesar some time and effort to overcome them during his conquest of Gaul. They were built and rigged differently from Roman ships, and had a shallow draught but 'exceptionally' high bows and sterns to cope with the heavy Atlantic seas. The hulls were of oak, fastened with iron nails, and the sails were made from raw hides or thin leather. Though they were slower than Roman galleys, the Celtic ships were more seaworthy.

The oldest known plank-built boats in Europe were discovered in the mud of the Humber estuary at Ferriby some decades ago, and are now on view in the National Maritime Museum, London, and in Hull.[9] Dating from 1500 BC, they are long, thin, flat-hulled vessels of oak planks lashed or sewn together with withies of yew, and were probably only suitable as ferries on inland waters. A more likely candidate for the kind of vessel that first plied the Firth is the hide boat. Those who made them left their image cut on rocks in parts of Scandinavia. In 1971, Professor Sverre Marstrander of Oslo University and Paul Johnstone of the BBC built a replica of a Scandinavian

Bronze Age boat, basing it on a rock drawing at Kalnes in Norway. The vessel was made from eight cow hides lashed over a frame of alder and lime; it proved to be seaworthy and strong in inshore waters, capable of carrying a cargo and six men.[10]

Accustomed to iron and wooden vessels, we need some convincing now of the seaworthiness of hide boats, but the archaeological evidence makes it plain that they were used throughout northern Europe. Tim Severin built a replica of one, the *Brendan*, and crossed the Atlantic in it in 1976. It was constructed from tanned oxhides stretched over a frame of ash and bound with leather thongs and flax thread. The hull was pliant and strong, and capable of taking on Atlantic gales. Paul Johnstone argued that only hide boats were strong enough to launch on the Firth.

Chronicles compiled by Irish monks provide us with some clues to events in the early Christian centuries. The Scots and Picts used fleets of hide boats, or currachs, to attack the Romans. Images of Pictish boats have been bequeathed to us at one or two places in Scotland, for example on St Orland's stone at Cossans near Glamis, and in a cave at East Wemyss, Fife; but these reveal little detail.[11] Descendants of the currachs are still in use in Ireland and, as coracles, in Wales. In the *Annals of Tigernach* and the *Annals of Ulster*, it is recorded that attacks took place on Orkney;[12] and during the spread of Christianity from Whithorn, Iona and other centres, missionaries reached Orkney. The Picts must have been fine seafarers in their time, but these hints and glimpses from the old chronicles are all that we have to fill in the story of the Firth until in the ninth century Norse longships sailed south from the fiords. With their arrival, the Picts all but disappear.

The Men of Mey - and the Bores

The *basic* tidal pattern in the Firth is fairly simple. During a neap tide, the stream from the Atlantic approaches at around three knots; it is slightly faster on the Hoy coast, where it touches four knots. It gains speed as it moves east until it reaches seven knots off Brims Ness. On the southern shore it passes St John's Point at six knots; and reaches six to eight off the ends of Swona. It rushes through the Outer Sound at nine knots, and through the Inner Sound at five. By the time the main stream has reached Duncansby Head, it is moving at eight knots, and the flow between the Skerries and Brough Ness is six. Off the Lother Rock at the tip of South Ronaldsay it makes eight knots, and reaches its maximum, of around ten and a half knots, just to the west of Little Skerry. The spring streams are stronger and surpass ten knots regularly. The ebb tide is weaker, reaching a top speed of around eight and a half knots in the Outer Sound.

Such currents were often more powerful than the momentum of a wind-powered sailing ship, but low-powered steamships, too, could be caught out; in his memoirs of a childhood at Duncansby in the early years of this century, John Banks recalls steamers unable to stem the tide and drifting backwards. In the 1930s, Sutherland Manson saw an eastward-bound German vessel, the *Triton*, forced off her course by the flood tide until she bumped on to Muckle Skerry; the iron hull survived the collision and the ship continued on her way, but the crew had their lifeboats ready for launching.

To describe the tide in simple terms is misleading. What ought to be a straightforward current is in the Firth distorted out of all recognition by reefs, islands, the seabed, the weather and differences in sea level and water density. In *Tidal Streams of the Waters Surrounding the British Isles*, the hydrographers of the Admiralty warn the seafarer of the great distances in direction and rate of stream over small differences: 'streams run very strongly, eddies of great extent and strength form, and there are races and overfalls of tremendous violence.' They add cautiously that no chart or description of the tidal streams can be correct under all circumstances, and that accurate measurements and observations are impossible. The variation in the rate of stream is greater than anywhere else in Britain.

The first variation in the easterly stream passing Dunnet Head is an eddy in Brough Bay, a stream flowing north along the coast throughout the tidal cycle, except for a brief half-hour before low water when it flows southward (Fig. 1 on p. 32). About half an hour after the first incursion of the incoming tide passes Dunnet Head, the companion easterly flow at Rora Head in Hoy is discernible.

In the centre of the Firth, however, the tide is still ebbing. Great masses of sea are surging in entirely opposite directions and rubbing against each other. It is not until some four hours after the flood passes Dunnet Head that the ebb in mid-channel surrenders and shuffles in an anti-clockwise direction until it too flows eastward (Fig. 2).

The eastward flood puts an end to the antics of the Men of Mey. At their maximum extent, the Men, or the 'Ould Ebbs' as they were called on Stroma, form a barrier running across the Firth from St John's Point to Tor Ness (Fig. 1). The *North Coast of Scotland Pilot* calls it the worst feature in the Firth, 'a natural breakwater'. The Men comprise a wall of water up to two miles wide, with breakers rearing 30-40 ft into the air, and are fully active three hours after the ebb has begun. In 1700, John Brand, an Edinburgh minister, saw the Men 'leaping and danceing, as it were ... tho Mirth and Danceing be far from the minds of Seamen and Passengers who shall be so unhappy as to fall in among them, especially when any Sea is going'. The 'lumps o' the ebb' is the local term for the rearing overfalls. Once, a television crew urged the coxswain of the Longhope lifeboat, their location for the day, to take them close to the Men for a dramatic shot, but a lump filled the lifeboat cockpit, drenching cameras and crew.[13] On Christmas Day 1806, a north-westerly gale struck the Firth unexpectedly. Fishing smacks were torn from their moorings in Thurso roads and one of them ran to Orkney to the shelter of Widewall Bay. This flight to safety was undertaken by one man, James Mackay of Mey, and his route must have taken him through the Men of Mey and within sight of his home. 29

He was not alone aboard the smack - a young boy was with him. Mackay locked the boy in his cabin and lashed himself to the tiller during the crossing. Mackay was in his twenties: James Calder records that the feat was probably too much for him, for he died soon after, 'quiet and reserved in manner'.[14]

The Admiralty cautions that especially with westerly or north-westerly gales the extreme violence of the Men 'can hardly be exaggerated'. HMS *Barham* passed eastward through them in 1906 with the tide against her but with a Force 8 westerly at her back: with praiseworthy under-statement, the navigating officer said that only personal experience could have made anybody realise 'what a seething cauldron' the sea was, and that a slower steamer or a sailing ship would never have been heard of again.[15]

The exact cause of the Men is unclear, but they begin their frenzied dance as a patch of turbulence extending outward from the rocks at St John's Point, just after high water. As the ebb proceeds, the Men grow livelier, moving outward into mid-channel (Fig. 5 on p. 33). They come in two bands, one north from St John's Point and the other south from Tor Ness. The engineer on the British coaster *Commodity* had this to say in 1984 about them: 'A westerly Force 8 gale was blowing and the tide was with us as we were going west. The Men of Mey [were] boiling and the forecastle head went right under the wall of water. We felt as if we were going down and water came up three quarters the length of the ship.'[16]

The high breaking waves produced when the tide is flowing against the prevailing wind and sea swell were of greater danger to sailing or oar-powered vessels than they are to modern craft with engines. Norman Smith of South Ronaldsay told me how he was surprised to learn, many years ago, from Captain Alfred Cromarty that conditions in the Firth were most dangerous for both ocean-going and coastal vessels when the tide, wind and swell were all acting together. At these times the large, solid waves move bodily forward at the speed of the current and can sweep the entire deck, potentially causing great damage. When tide and swell are opposed, a well-found vessel with engines can punch through the breaking waves in a spectacular though actually less dangerous manner. Norman Smith has borne this advice in mind during his work in the Firth and likes to take his boat with the tide against the wind rather than against both.

(Captain Alfred Cromarty OBE was a native of Herston and a notable character. He lost an eye early in his long sea-going career. When his ship was torpedoed in the Atlantic, he sailed his crew over a thousand miles in their lifeboat.)

In June 1937, the Peterhead drifter *Bydand* sprang a leak in the Men, about two miles from St John's Point. The Stroma Coastguard and Sutherland Manson watched the crew trying to seal the sprung plank with an old sail, and then saw the Banff drifter *Alert* rescue the men and some of their nets before the vessel sank, leaving only a small cloud of steam to mark where she had been.[17]

For up to eight hours the Men play away, until the flood creeping in along the coast from the Atlantic severs first their link to St John's Point and, an hour later, that to Tor Ness. As the eastward flood gains ascendancy, the Men lose their strength and gradually subside, a process more or less complete after one hour. The sea then remains quiet for a time until the next ebb tide rouses the dancers again (Figs 1 and 2).

When I first read Robert Louis Stevenson's short story 'The Merry Men', I recognised the Men of Mey, perhaps with a dash of the Corryvreckan, as the inspiration behind the fierce roost by the fictional island of Aros. Stevenson, whose grandfather, father and two uncles were all lighthouse builders, spent some months in Wick in 1868 in an attempt to learn engineering. He would certainly have heard of the Men of Mey; and he refers to the Firth in an essay as 'that grave of mariners'.[18]

The easterly incoming flood on the Orkney side becomes diffuse as it sweeps past Tor Ness and encounters Swona and the southern gate to Scapa Flow. At about this time, the Liddel Eddy forms off South Ronaldsay.

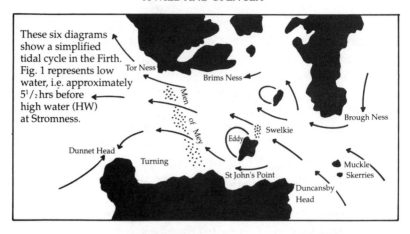

These six diagrams show a simplified tidal cycle in the Firth. Fig. 1 represents low water, i.e. approximately $5^1/_2$ hrs before high water (HW) at Stromness.

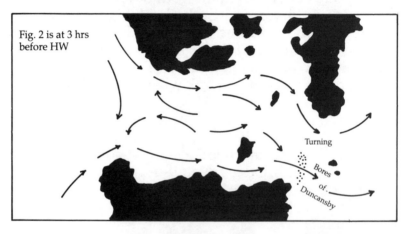

Fig. 2 is at 3 hrs before HW

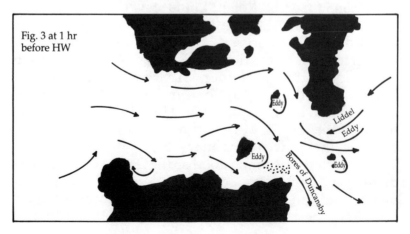

Fig. 3 at 1 hr before HW

32

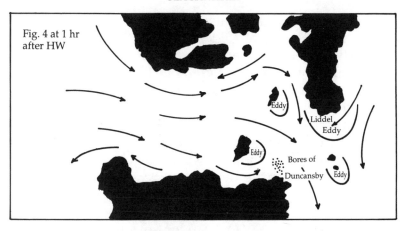

Fig. 4 at 1 hr after HW

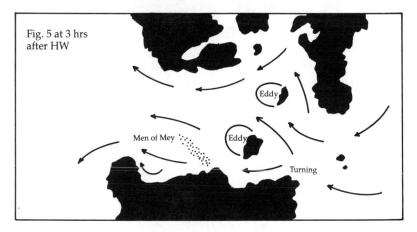

Fig. 5 at 3 hrs after HW

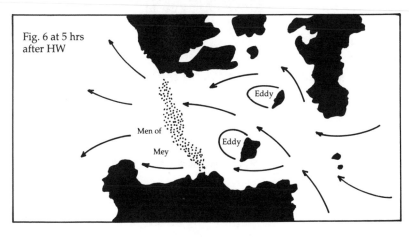

Fig. 6 at 5 hrs after HW

33

Along the east coast of this island, the tide flows south. At the rocky point of Old Head the two currents, the southerly and the easterly, meet. At first the union is gentle, but it quickly turns violent. The Eddy begins as a west-going current between the easterly flood and the South Ronaldsay coast, but it grows for a couple of hours as highwater approaches, until it occupies half the channel between Brough Ness and Muckle Skerry. In the southern half of the channel the tide is still flowing east, and the boundary between the two water masses is marked by a line of foaming breakers. The Eddy continues to seize territory until it possesses almost all the channel north of Muckle Skerry. Half an hour or so after it reaches its maximum extent, the true west-going ebb begins and the Eddy subsides for a few hours (Figs 3 and 4).

Where the west-plunging waters of the Liddel Eddy come clear of Brough Ness, they run slap up against the tide coming south-eastwards between Swona and South Ronaldsay. Off the Lother Rock, a reef visible except during times of extreme high water when its presence is marked by breakers, the encounter is fiercest and a race develops.

Six miles to the south, the Bores of Duncansby make their appearance at the same time as the Liddel Eddy begins. Five hours before high water at the Skerries, a race begins at the Ness of Duncansby and extends towards Muckle Skerry. It does not get far in this direction before it turns anti-clockwise until it is pointing north-westwards. As it wheels it runs over the shallow tongue of the seabed off the Ness, where it begins to break. Even on a calm day white water rages off the Ness when the Bores strike this shallow patch. As the flood tide continues, the Bores grow outwards. They begin to subside shortly after high water, and then cease altogether until about one hour before low water, when they reappear to reach once more for the Skerries. At low water they disappear again briefly (Figs 2 to 4).

The Bores are easier to understand than their companions, the Men of Mey, to the west, and are probably the result of a conflict between the ebb tide on the surface and the flood at depth. They are fiercest when the wind is from the east or south-east, contrary to the direction of the flood.

Other areas which can be fiercely turbulent lie off the Ness of Huna, and about a mile to the south-east of Little Skerry. The latter is due to a shoal, the Sandy Riddle, and here the sea breaks heavily during south-east gales. The strength of the tidal currents keeps the bed of the Firth scoured clean of sediment, and it is a curious fact that a shed-line extends roughly between Stroma and Swona, with sediment being carried from it to the west and the east. In the lee of the Skerries where the force of the tide begins to dissipate, deposits of sand, gravel and crushed shell have accumulated to form the Sandy Riddle, which rises to some 130 ft above the surrounding seabed.[19] The main channel of the Firth varies around a depth of 200 ft, but some shoal areas exist, for example the Triton Bank to the north of Swona, and some patches along the line of the Men of Mey. Some parts of the Firth have been incompletely surveyed and there may yet be uncharted shoals or rocks waiting to be pinpointed.[20]

That Fatal Euripus

The Norse invasions and settlement that began over a thousand years ago made north-east Caithness what it is, a place closer in culture and spirit to Orkney, Shetland and the Scandinavian communities of the north Atlantic than to the Gaelic world to the south-west. The Norse named our places and all the everyday things; my mother tongue carries a Viking lexicon.

I felt a kind of kinship with the Vikings: they were my ancestors, and they walked, talked and handled their boats as my relatives did. It was all very fanciful, simplistic and likely mistaken, but I could have chosen less worthy role models - and the whole thing probably did me little lasting harm.

For all the daydreaming, I had little factual information to rely on about the Norse until one day in the library of McGill University in Montreal I laid hands for the first time on a copy of *Orkneyinga Saga*.[21]

The grey, calm cold of the Canadian winter was rubbing at the windows. Inside, the efficient central heating was sending me to sleep. On impulse, and to shunt some blood from my legs back to my brain, I began to check through the library catalogue for this book I'd heard of occasionally but never seen. There it was. I borrowed a copy, edited and introduced by Joseph Anderson, published in 1873. It was the first important work on Caithness that I was to read, apart from a battered copy of James Calder's history that I had managed to borrow from an uncle some ten years before.

In the late 800s AD, Harald Fairhair became king of Norway and led an expedition west to rid the sea of the pirates who haunted Orkney and Shetland.[22] He drove out the sea-rovers (did they come to Caithness?) and established his sovereignty over the islands, declared Orkney and Shetland to be an earldom of Norway and gave it to a powerful chieftain, Rognvald, whose son, Hrolf, later conquered Normandy and founded the dynasty that would give rise to the Norman kings of England. Rognvald gave the earldom of Orkney to his brother Sigurd, who promptly enlarged it by annexing Caithness and Sutherland. At least, this is the story as given in the Norse sagas; the real course of events may have been more complex, but the upshot was that the Norse came to stay.

The Norsemen were the first to call the Pentland Firth by something like its present name. In the sagas it is *Pettlandsfjörðr* - the firth of the land of the Picts. They also gave us almost all the place-names we use today, eclipsing for ever the Pictish names they must have had before. Stroma is from *straumr*, a tidal stream, and *ey*, island. Swona is *svíney*, swine island; Hoy is *háey*, high island; Walls is *vágar*, inlets; and South Ronaldsay is *Rognvaldsey*, Rognvald's island. Our names for Duncansby and the Bores are Norse, the latter from *bára* - a wave.

From *svelgr*, which means a whirlpool, comes the name for the Swelkie which spins off the north tip of Stroma where the currents racing along the coast meet the main ebb or flood through the Outer Sound and form a giant wheel of water circling in the ocean. According to local fishermen, any object set free in the east of the Firth would end up in its whirling maw. The thirteenth-century *Historia Norvegiae* calls it 'the greatest of all whirlpools which draws in and swallows down in the ebb the strongest ships and vomits and casts up their fragments in the flood.'[23] The *North Coast of Scotland Pilot* says prosaically that it can be dangerous and 'should be avoided even in fine weather'. It spins most fiercely when the prevailing wind opposes the tide, and its force can be enough to stop a vessel in her tracks (Fig 1 on p. 32).

A Norse legend accounts for its existence thus. Once, there was a king called Fróði who owned a magic quern, Grotti by name, that could grind out anything he wanted. At first it ground out gold and peace and happiness but, when he overworked the two giant bondmaidens who turned it, they ground out instead an army to challenge Fróði, and that night the sea-king Mysingr slew him and took the quern. While sailing with it through the Firth, Mysingr asked Grotti for some salt and the obedient quern at once obliged. Unfortunately, in the haste of his actions, Mysingr had neglected to learn how to stop Grotti. The quern went on grinding out salt until it filled Mysingr's ship and sent her to the bottom, where Grotti lies to this day. As the stones turn the sea is sucked down through the quern in a swirling, rumbling fury.[24] John Brand referred in 1700 to its 'dreadful noise, heard at some distance'.

The belief that an oar or a barrel could be thrown to the Swelkie, as it were to divert its attention and let the unlucky mariner escape unharmed, was widespread. William Lithgow wrote of it in 1628: 'If ever ship or boat shall happen to encroach, they must quickly either throw over something into it, as a barrel, a piece of timber, and such like, or that fatal Euripus shall then suddenly become their swallowing sepulchre.'

It seems that small boats were indeed drawn into the Swelkie and sunk. Murdoch Mackenzie, on every score a sober man, wrote in the 1740s that some had been 'swallowed up'.[25] There are other vortices and eddies in the Firth. Mackenzie described them as inverted bells and noted that the larger ones could turn 'any Vessel quite round'. There are many records of this happening: in 1824 the Arctic explorer *Griper* was spun twice in an eddy[26], and in 1842 the fishery brig *Skylark*, on a fine August morning, was suddenly wheeled about so that she had to put out two boats to tow her back on course.[27] A merchant vessel, the *Euphemia*, eastward bound from Ballachulish to Dundee in 1843, lost her main boom and split her mainsail and gaff topsail when she was caught in the Swelkie; she won clear and stayed in Freswick Bay for three days to carry out repairs.[29] With the ebb tide, whirlpools also form off the two southern points of Stroma, at Mell Head and Scartan.

A skipper well acquainted with the Firth's tricks could make use of the eddies around Stroma. Coming west against the flood tide, such a skipper would steer directly for Stroma, as it were between the two main streams pouring round the north and south of the island and gaining some way from the counter-current of the eddy. This ploy was called 'shunning the tide' by the islanders. Near the island the skipper then had the choice of tackling the flood at Swelkie Point, or the Tails as it was also called, or off Mell Head, at the Beacon. Much skill was required, however, as the vessel's bow had to be kept at the correct angle to the flood, otherwise the pressure of the tide would force her round. Sutherland Manson told me he saw a steamer with a deck cargo of timber list over when the flood struck her until her gunwale was awash; on that occasion the skipper gave up, allowed his ship to swing round and waited off Duncansby Head for the tide to ease.[29]

A particular nasty series of eddies forms to the west of Swona during the ebb tide and are known as the Wells (Figs 5 and 6 on p. 33). Another legend accounts for their being there. Once, a witch fell in love with a young man who happened to be already betrothed, and persuaded the couple to come with her in a boat to Swona. Near the island, the witch capsized the vessel and seized the young man's hand. However, he also grabbed his beloved and all three sank. The foiled witch was unable to pull free from the grasp of the dead lovers and her frantic struggles stir up the Wells of Swona to this day. John Brand says that about twenty years before he visited the area, two fishing boats had been sucked into them. Brand thought the swirling of the water was caused by underground caverns down into which the sea was being sucked to emerge at some other place. As to why seamen did not stay away from them, he wrote that fish were bigger in their vicinity - 'so the Fishes draw the Man, and the Wells draw both'.

Underground caverns of the sort Brand imagined probably do not exist, but he was right in that violent upwellings of the sea happen in the Firth. These look as if a giant pump down below is hurling water upwards to break on the surface and spread in all directions. James Wilson observed some of these from the deck of the cutter *Princess Royal* in 1842: 'The boiling, and streaming, and bulging up, with here and there a comparatively smooth expanse, and then a rush as of a raging river, exemplified the power of waters.'

To the Norsemen the Firth was less a barrier than a highway - a road they took to trade, fish and fight. In about 1060 two fleets met in conflict off *Rauðabjorg*[30] to decide a dispute for the earldom between Rognvald Brusason and his uncle, Thorfinn Sigurðarson. The sagas have less to say about ordinary shipping, probably because it was just that - ordinary. We can be sure that the sea's tricks claimed a share of the trading and fishing vessels, but it is only in the context of some larger political adventure that they are noticed. A longship under the command of Earl Hákon of Lade was lost with all hands, perhaps in the Swelkie, in an autumn storm in 1029.[31] In 1263, a ship in the fleet of King Hákon of Norway, who had just been defeated at the Battle of Largs, went down with all hands, probably in the Wells of Swona, and another was caught in the tidal stream and borne out of control through the Firth.[32]

The sagas were written down mostly in the early decades of the thirteenth century. Thereafter, for almost 300 years, hardly anyone bothered to record events in and around the Firth; or, if someone did, their work is now lost to us.

Overgrown Cowrie Shells

Norse vessels are familiar to us. Slender, clinker-built and with a single square sail, they were seaworthy and strong.[33] They embodied several important technical advances: the use of a T-shaped keel and sails to maintain a course into the wind; the development of the steering board; and a hull shape that could slice through the waves at 10 knots. The oak planking flexed, enabling the hull to absorb the shocks of striking waves, a property for which anyone crossing the Firth is grateful. A number of replicas of Norse ships have been constructed and have revealed their sailing qualities.

The lines of the Norse ships are echoed to this day in the fishing boats characteristic of Shetland, Orkney and the north of Scotland. Although the exact pattern of descent is not clear, for want of written records from before the early 1800s, they show their Norse ancestry in their clinkered planking and their stems and sterns. The predominant model around the Firth was the yawl, or yole. Its most distant ancestor is probably best considered to be not the Norse longship but the small boats of Norse times. With the Gokstad ship, excavated from a mound at Sandar in Norway in 1880, were found two small boats; the smaller of the two was 21 ft long, had two pairs of oars, a pointed stem and stern and clinkered strokes, as strakes or planks are called in Caithness.[34]

The earliest reference to boatbuilding in Caithness is found in the Norse *Laxdaela Saga* where it is mentioned that

a ship was built secretly in a forest, an intriguing idea in view of the county's absence of standing timber. Has the saga writer simply made a mistake or is he applying the name Caithness to parts of what we now call Sutherland? Certainly, in later centuries, there were no indigenous sources of wood of a quality suitable for boat building in Caithness or Orkney. Wood is high on the list of imports to Thurso in the 1790s.[35] For the sixteenth and seventeenth centuries, there are records of a regular export of timber and boats from Norway to Shetland and Orkney - some timber and perhaps also some boats may have found their way to Caithness.[36] The Norwegian boats were often exported in kit form, their timbers and strokes shaped and numbered for easy assembly. The Napoleonic Wars cut off the trade with Norway for a while after 1800 but by this time Norwegian boatbuilding techniques had been firmly implanted in the northern islands, where, reinforcing the older traditions, they influenced the development of the Shetland sixerns.[37]

Shetland also had two types of yole - the Fair Isle and the Ness - mainly used for inshore fishing. In Orkney there was the North Isles or Westray type and the South Isles type.[38] They all represented variations on a masterful theme, differing in details, but details which were considered crucial by the makers and users of each. Until very recently fishermen had a conservative view of boatbuilding, with good reason - their lives depended on the seaworthiness of the structure under their feet and an experiment was a dice-throw.

The South Isles yole is the type that mainly concerns us here. Prominent among their builders was the Duncan family of Burray, a business that still operates, and there is a tradition that one of the Duncans taught the Stroma yole builders their craft in the early nineteenth century.[39]

A Duncansby man, Walter Green, learned his boatbuilding skills in Stromness and became the first man to build new herring boats, adapting the yole design, in Wick in the early 1800s.[40] Before that, in the 1730s, the Orkney yole had spawned other offspring when Joseph Isbister of Stromness, one of the many Orcadians who

41

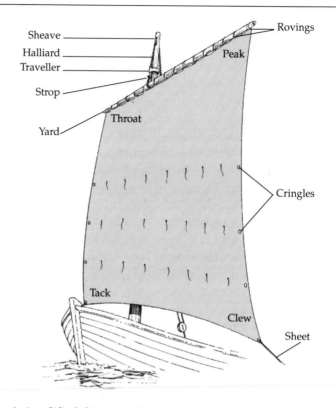

Sheave
Halliard
Traveller
Strop
Yard
Throat
Tack
Rovings
Peak
Cringles
Clew
Sheet

A simplified diagram showing the main features of a yole's rig. The yard hangs on a strop from the traveller, a metal ring which is hauled up the mast by the halliard. The halliard passes through a sheave at the end of the mast, and acts as a stay when the sail is under the wind's pressure. The tack, or forefoot of the sail, has a cringle attaching it to the stemhead. The main sheet, up to 5 fathoms long, runs from the clew to the person controlling the sail. A series of four or more rows of cringles and reefing points allow the sail to be shortened by rolling it up from the bottom.

For short tacks in bad weather, the sail was reefed down and the tack was fixed to the mast rather than to the stemhead. A mast 15 ft high would carry a sail 10 ft wide at the top and 12 ft at the foot. It was customary to bark the sails in tannin to make resistant to rot and salt. In 1900, such a sail would cost £3 to £4 new.

(from information supplied by the author's father and Sutherland Manson) worked for the Hudson's Bay Company, produced the York boat to replace native canoes on the inland waterways of Rupert's Land.[41]

The Firth yoles built on Stroma were characterised by broad beams, as the carrying of varied cargoes - cattle, sheep, peats, fish and grain included - was one of their vital functions.[42] On some the wide beam made them appear almost round in shape, and nowhere else were yoles with such a beam to keel ratio - perhaps 9 ft 6 in. to 24 ft - built. Brian Sinclair, of whom more below, has likened them to overgrown cowrie shells. This feature gave them great stability and the deep keel took a good grip of the sea. They were not built for looks, although they are handsome, but for safety and for seaworthiness. Like all yoles, they had to be hauled frequently and lightness was a consideration in their construction: 2 in. by 2 in. wood was used for the frame and ribs, and the inside fittings could be removed from the hull.

An oak frame was favoured by the yole builders, with larch or pine for the strokes. First the keel was laid and the stern and stemposts fixed to it by half-tenon joints with a knee and an apron. A difference between the Orkney and Stroma yoles lay in the manner in which the stem was scarfed to the keel: in the former, the stem continued to the lower side of the keel, whereas in the Stroma yole the stem, the keel and a piece called the knee or deadwood inside the hull formed a three-cornered joint, with a section of the knee showing outside the hull. The hull was built up by adding the strokes or planks on either side of the keel. The first plank, the garboard stroke, was fitted to the keel and slotted into grooves on the stem and stern. On a Stroma yole some of the upper strokes were in three sections: a stem and a stern piece called headings and an intermediate section called a slot or a steeler. Single lengths of larch were preferred for the lower strokes and would probably have been used throughout, if the material had been available. The joints of the three sections were staggered from stroke to stroke, and all the strokes were clenched with 'Swedish steel' (galvanised iron) nails to make the   43 characteristic overlapping clinker form. Copper nails are preferred now.

After some strokes (usually four or five but occasionally up to seven) were steamed, bent and fixed in place, the frame and the flooring timbers were added - this method of building the skin before the ribs may surprise those unacquainted with yoles. Sometimes the centre part of the ribs of the frame were cut as single pieces, like giant wishbones, masterpieces of the carpenter's art. The extensions to the ribs were scarf jointed. Another difference emerged here between Stroma and Orkney yoles: in the former, the frames were inset always at right angles to the keel, but the Orkney yoles had frames at right angles to the gunwale. Finally the gunwales were added and the thafts, or seats, inserted. A mixture of oakum and tar, called blair, was used to seal the strokes and make the timber waterproof.

Stroma yoles came in three sizes, with capacities of one, two or three tons. The smaller ones were more common.

Larger yoles had two masts, stepped midships and in the bow, to carry two spritsails and a small jib, or two lugsails. Smaller yoles had one mast. The lugsail rig, a modification of the lateen rig common in the Mediterranean, appears to have spread rapidly throughout the North Sea area in the latter half of the eighteenth century. Earlier rigs were simple square sails with spritsails and fore staysails on smaller boats. The use of a spar or sprit to hold the sail spread in the wind is a very old practice dating back to Norse times.

Our grandfather's boat at Keiss was a yole: called the *Pansy*, her keel was 15 ft 6 in. and until 1915 she was powered by oars and a sail. The mast was without braces or stays, and carried a lugsail 12 ft wide at the foot and narrowing to 10 ft at the yard, which ran up and down the mast on a metal ring called a traveller. A cringle held the tack, the forward corner of the sail, to the stemhead, the gunwale or even the foot of the mast. Four rows of reefing points allowed canvas to be shortened. In light winds the tension on the main sheet could regulate the yole's speed, and among her crew the man on the main sheet was all-important; he often had more experience and skill than his companion at the tiller and would give the orders during manoeuvres. Crews numbered up to five, with three men forward to handle the yard when going about. Going about meant dipping the lugsail, passing it to the other side of the mast and rehoisting it on the new tack, a cumbersome action by today's standards. The dipping lug developed into a standing lug where going about did not need the lowering of the yard.

Yoles were built at many places around the coast but Stroma had a notable number of craftsmen; Wildy Sinclair, who emigrated from Stroma to Keiss and whom I knew as a boy, has left us an account of the boatbuilding craft on his native island.[43] Stroma boats, he says, were regarded as the safest a man could buy and the last to be built there, the *Barbara*, was made by George Simpson in 1913. In the early decades of this century, John Banks built yoles at John o'Groats and sold them at the cost of £1 per foot of keel, the standard method of assessing costs.

The *Pansy* was powered by sail and oar in 1911 when our father went to sea. In 1915, a Kelvin petrol engine was installed at the cost of £75. This engine was nicknamed the 'fisherman's friend'. It is difficult now to appreciate fully how hard a life at sea was - the blisters from pulling oars and wet rope, the cuts and stings from the handling of tar, the numbing cold and the continuous exposure. Our father recalled passing out from the cold and being hauled aft beside the Kelvin where at least there was some prospect of a little warmth, some respite from the wind. During the four to five hours the inshore fishermen spent at sea each day, hot drinks were out of the question until the advent of the Thermos flask. Food was a 'piece', a bannock thickly clarted with butter and crowdie, or oatcakes. The toughness of the men who made long passages in yoles almost defies comprehension.

The introduction after 1908 of the Kelvin engine, of 6 hp giving 8 hp at the screw, brought about modifications   45 in yole design. The number of strokes in the hull was raised from twelve to thirteen, and half-decking became common. Such a vessel was owned by our family in the 1940s: we called her the *Lupin* but she had been built as the *Diligent* on Stroma by George Simpson in 1912 for a cost of little over £18. She sailed back into prominence a few years ago when Brian and Ronnie Sinclair completed a restoration begun by their cousin Peter Sinclair, the great-grandson of the *Diligent*'s original owner, Patty Sinclair.

The *Diligent* has a keel of 18 ft 6 in., an overall length of 24 ft and a beam of 9 ft. Her stem is high, at 6 ft 1 in., and she also has a rounded, cruiser stern, called an elliptic stern on Stroma, an unusual feature that may have been put in on a whim of Patty Sinclair under the influence of yachting design at the time of her building. Big and beamy, the *Diligent* has proved herself under sail; Brian Sinclair has reached nine knots in her running on an open reach in a Force 7, and has found he can take her out in dirtier seas than other sailing boats can manage. Her best sailing is just a few points off the wind, and a good breeze will push her at up to six knots on an easy ride.

Yoles, sadly, are less popular now. In his boatyard at Scarfskerry, the only yard now on the Firth itself, Peter Matheson told me that of the forty or so boats he has built in the last fifteen years only five have been yoles. Square-sterned boats are easier for creel fishing and are preferred by today's inshore fishermen. But respect, even love, for the yole remains strong. Some are famous around the Firth - and the *Diligent*, a pioneer in her early days, may prove to be a pioneer again, of a new generation of sailing vessels.[44]

Expeditionary Forces

On a slab of rock in Massachusetts is punchmarked the figure of a knight holding a sword and a shield with a design remarkably like the crest of the Clan Gunn of Caithness. The origin of the image is a mystery but it is accepted by some as proof that northern seamen made a voyage of exploration to the New World in 1398.[45]

The story is that the leader of this expedition was Henry Sinclair, Earl of Orkney. In 1390 he met Nicolo Zeno, a Venetian, when the latter was shipwrecked on Fair Isle, and later, with Nicolo and his brother Antonio, sailed west to Greenland and eventually to what are now Nova Scotia and New England. The evidence is derived mainly from a letter written by Zeno and a chart, although both present maddeningly obscure information and the interpretation of them is fraught with uncertainty. We are left with the question of whether seamen from Caithness and Orkney really followed Leif Ericsson's wake a century before Columbus. One can imagine news of Columbus's discoveries reaching Orkney, only to evince from an old man, 'Oh aye, I mind my great-grandfather speaking about it - bad place for fog.' It is a pleasing idea and an entirely possible event, new evidence in support of which has recently been provided by Andrew Sinclair.[46]

Another tradition ties Robert Bruce to the Firth.[47] The story claims that he was on South Ronaldsay, enjoying refuge with the laird of Halcro, when he saw the spider that inspired him to fight on to rid Scotland of English domination. Sober historians balk at this, but the Halcro family tradition maintains that they fought under their royal guest's banner at Bannockburn.

Among the oldest reliable documents to give a seaman's eye-view of the Firth is Alexander Lindsay's *Rutter of the Scottish Seas*, compiled in or about 1540.[48] A rutter was the name commonly given to pilot books in the sixteenth century. Navigation was still crude but discoveries were being made, and new techniques were emerging from the great voyages of the Portuguese, Spanish, Dutch and English explorers. Ships, too, had advanced: the rudder had replaced the steering oar, and three-masted vessels had become commonplace.[49] Coastal shipping still depended largely on following a course from one headland to the next, bearing in mind what was known about local tides, rocks and shoals. Navigators used the compass, the sand-glass, the lead and line, and a traverse board on which to record their progress.

We know little about Alexander Lindsay except that he was 'an excellent Pilot and Hydrographer' in the service of James V. His rutter, perhaps the only written guide to the northern seas, was in some demand: it was translated into French and English and widely copied. It seems likely that Lindsay put it together at the king's command, for James had a special purpose in mind.

The king's fleet left Leith in the summer of 1540 - twelve ships equipped with artillery and led by the royal flagship *Salamander* under the captaincy of John Ker. James wanted to visit 'the north and south isles for the ordouring of thame in justice and gude policy' and, because they expected bad weather, he had a new coat made for the trip. He took with him Cardinal Beaton and the Earls of Huntly and Arran, and his favourite, Oliver Sinclair, whom he appointed Sheriff of Orkney. According to Leslie's *Historie*, along 'the coast of ffife, Angus, Aberdone, Moray, Rosse, Sutherland, and Caitnes, they sayled with a sober and safte wind, [and] at last in the Ile of Orknay' landed.[50] Unfortunately there seems to be no evidence to back the old Caithness story that the king stayed for a night in Wick. The royal anchorage in Orkney was probably Scapa Flow, where the king was pleased by what he saw. While he was there, Johne Grote was paid twenty pounds from the Treasury 'for fraucht of his schip' from St Andrews to bring the king letters from his queen.[51] The main purpose of the voyage was political - Orkney, with Shetland, had been part of James's realm for less than one hundred years - and later in the voyage, in the Outer Isles, the king exercised his full might to break the power of the Lord of the Isles. Our main interest, however, is in what Lindsay had to say about the Firth.

Of the tides, the pilot recorded that 'betwixt Dungisbe Head and Quhyniknap [Dunnet] Head it flowethe south southeast and north northwest'. Under the heading 'Hauins, sounds and dangers', he advised ships to avoid 'the Boir' of Duncansby by making their course north-west from Duncansby Head 'till you come north to est from Stroma', and warned of the great danger at the north end of that island 'called the Swelle which is the meeting of iiij or v contray tydes with great circulationne of watter causing a deip hurlepoole in the middes dangerous for all shippis both great and small'.

The rutter mentioned other hazards: 'betwixt Swinna and Ronaldsa are great dangerous poplynis of watter called Hoppers'; and 'a halff a myle from the May Head lyeth dangerous rockis called the Men of May'. The rutter also described good anchorages in Scapa Flow and a 'good rod callit Skarbster'.

There are other records and stories that shed light on the shipping in the Firth around this time. About fifty years before, the now legendary Dutchman Jan de Groot is supposed to have started his ferry from Duncansby to South Ronaldsay; he deserves lengthy treatment and we will return to him later. The accounts of the Lord High Treasurer of Scotland also give clues to the commerce of the time. Falconers came regularly to Orkney to trap birds[52], and in 1526 four shillings' worth of Orkney butter was bought to grease the wheels of Mons Meg at Edinburgh Castle.[53] Thirty-four shillings were paid to Duncan Riche in 1531 'to pas and charge Johne Gibsoun skipper of ane bote callit *Balmalkin* to mete the schippis in Pentland firth'.[54] William Forestare was recompensed for buying spars, timber and 'other small necessaries' for two ships sent to Orkney in 1550[55]; and Gavin Hume's son received £10 in September 1552 after being 'schipe brokin in Orknay'.[56]

Most surprisingly of all in this search for references to shipping, I found by chance the text of a letter from Henry VIII of England to officials in York in September 1542 ordering them to equip a fleet to attack Orkney 'to devast and destroye all the corne and catall of the same'. Henry's officials replied that this was not a good idea, explaining: 49

There is one passaige that they must go through called
Pentley Frythe, wiche is rekened the most daungerouse
place of all Christendom, and such that scarce any
Scottisshe man, or any other that knoweth it best,
dar adventure to passe it at this season of the year...'[57]

They added that, anyway, there was little except oats to pillage. An English fleet did indeed attack Orkney several years later in 1557. Led by Sir John Clere, thirteen ships sailed north, ostensibly to protect the English fishing fleet on its way home from Iceland; the real purpose was to irritate the Scottish government. The invaders landed artillery, and burned part of Kirkwall on 11 and 12 August. On the third day, Friday the 13th, the local people fought back, killing ninety-seven English, including Sir John Clere; it is also recorded that bad weather forced the fleet to retire before they could rescue their comrades.[59]

It is tempting to imagine that a copy of Lindsay's rutter may have been aboard some of the ships of the great fleet that left Lisbon in May 1588 to conquer England. The Armada, 130 ships in all, with over 25,000 men, failed in its objective and had to flee north about Scotland to return to Spain. The majority of the fleet headed north-north-east from the English Channel and did not turn west until they reached a latitude that took them between Shetland and the Faroes. The Spaniards kidnapped some Scottish fishermen to act as pilots. In September that year *El Gran Grifon* was wrecked on Fair Isle, and some believe another Spanish vessel came to grief on Westray. A few of the Armada ships remain unaccounted for.[59] Did one of the captains, armed with Lindsay's rutter and seeking to shorten the long, cold voyage home, try a short-cut through the Firth? It is unlikely.

Thirty-seven years after the fleet of James V dropped anchor in Orkney, another group of explorers arrived, in three ships called the *Aide*, the *Gabriel* and the *Michael*, under the command of Captain Martin Frobisher. Orkney for them was only a way station: their destination was the iceberg-ridden waters of the Arctic; their hope was to find a north-west passage to the gold and silks of China. One of Frobisher's men, Dionyse Settle, kept a journal. This is how he described their stopover:

> *With a merry winde ... we arrived at the Islands called Orchades, or vulgarly Orkney, being in number 30 ... where we made provision of freshwater: in the going whereof, our Generall [Frobisher] licenced the Gentlemen and Soldiers, for their recreation, to go on shoare. At our landing, the people fled from their poor cottages, with shrikes and alarums, to warne their neighbors of enimies: but by gentle persuasions we reclaimed them to their houses. It seemeth they are often frighted with pirates, or some other enimies, that moveth them to such souden feare. Their houses are very simplie builded with pibble stone, without any chimneys, the fire being made in the middell thereof. The good man, wife, children and other of the familie eate and sleepe on the one side of the house, and their cattell on the other, very beastly and rudely in respect of civilitie.*

We do not know which island Settle visited; he may be scornful but his comments seem to give a precise picture of life for ordinary people at the time, and probably could stand for both sides of the Firth.[60] Travellers who described what they found 200 years later make it plain that not a great deal had changed by their time; and it may be safe to assume that neither had things moved much in the preceding 200.

Other explorers followed Frobisher.[61] John Knight left Gravesend in April 1606 in a 40-ton barque *Hopewell* in another attempt to find the north-west passage. After eight days they sailed into 'a sound called Pentlefrith', where a north-westerly gale storm-bound them for another fortnight. Knight brought two men aboard, 'both lustie fellowes at Sea and Land ... well acquainted with all the Harbours of these North parts of Scotland', who showed him the safe anchorage at St Margaret's Hope. Orkney hospitality won over Knight and his men and, though he

51

found the houses low and dirty outside, he described them as 'homely within'.

Another seaman glad to come upon Orkney was William Baffin. In 1612, Baffin joined an expedition to the Arctic led by James Hall, who was making his fourth attempt to find that elusive channel through the ice to the Pacific. There were two ships on this occasion - the *Patience* and the *Heartsease*. Disaster struck them in July in Greenland when Hall was speared and killed by an Eskimo. His companions set course homeward but, on the night of 4 September, the ships lost contact with each other in a gale. Four days later, the battered *Patience* reached Orkney. 'Toward three of the clocke,' wrote Baffin, 'we came to an Anchor in a Channell running betweene the Ilands; where the people came to us, and brought us Hennes, Geese and Sheepe, and sold them to us for old clothes and shooes, desiring them rather than money.'

Hard and primitive the life of the northern folk must have seemed to outsiders - and in many ways it was.

These Islands Afford Much Corn

Sea charts were first drawn in the thirteenth century, after the invention of the compass, and were concerned mainly with the Mediterranean and southern European coasts. On so-called portolan charts[62], drawn on parchment, Scotland is portrayed very crudely. In 1569 Diogo Homem and Paolo Fornani produced the first chart by the new method of copperplate engraving: the name 'dungesbi' appears on it.[63] 'Orcades' appears on earlier globes such as Mercator's in 1541.[64]

During the Renaissance, the early map of Britain in the works of Ptolemy, a Greek geographer who lived in Alexandria about a century after the time of Christ, was rediscovered and published. On the northern Scottish coast, Ptolemy named three headlands: Tarvedrum quod [est] Orcas, Viruedrum and Veruvium. It is difficult to say more than that the names seem to correspond to the headlands we now call Dunnet Head, Duncansby Head and Noss Head. Past interpretations of the names do not agree with this conclusion but it seems logical to use the reference Orcas or Orkney to mark the headland nearest the islands.[65]

Maps of the Pentland Firth remained crude representations of the land for another two centuries. A map, supposed to have been made during James V's voyage in 1540, was published in Paris in 1583 by Nicolas de Nicolay, chief cosmographer to the French king, and in Edinburgh in 1688 by John Adair as a frontispiece to a collection of charts 'for the Use of Seamen'.[66]

Timothy Pont is the first northern mapmaker of whom we know something.[67] The elder son of the Revd Robert Pont and the grandson of John Pont, a Venetian Protestant who had emigrated to Scotland, Timothy lived from about 1560 to about 1630. He was a graduate of St Andrews and minister of the parish of Dunnet from 1601. The last record of him there is dated December 1610 and by 1614, after a three-year gap in the evidence, he had gone. This was our mother's parish and on the wall of the kirk where I sat through many sermons is a plaque to Pont's memory.

What led Pont to compile an atlas of Scotland remains a mystery but this is what he started, probably doing most of the work between 1583 and 1596. He was commissioned by the Scottish Kirk in about 1592 to survey Orkney and Shetland for minerals, and Jeffrey Stone of the University of Aberdeen suggests in his recent book on Pont that perhaps all his maps were commissioned by the newly reformed Protestant authorities. Pont died before he could complete his task, leaving Robert Gordon of Straloch to finish the various maps for publication in Volume 5 of William Blaeu's *Atlas*, issued in Amsterdam in 1654.[68] The chart of the Orkney islands shows the Pichtland Fyrth, the Boers of Dungysby, Dungysbyhead, Men of Mey and Wenliknap head (Dunnet Head). There is a note to show 'Contrarie tydes', Stroma is shown but not named, 'Souna' is indicated, and various features such as 'the Welles', 'The

Heppers', 'Tarfness' and 'The Leuther' are marked. A note on Hoy tells us of 'The Stour [The Old Man], wher buildet that excellent Foul, called the Lyer [shearwater]'. Another map by Robert Gordon and labelled *Extima Scotia* shows a similar range of place-names. Curiously, on both, the names for Ham and Brough appear to be interchanged.

To what extent seamen relied on these charts is a matter of wonder; most probably they never used them at all. Because of the primitive survey techniques, inaccuracies abound. An atlas by Johannes van Keulen of Amsterdam in 1714 shows the Men of Mey as an island one mile or so west of Holborn Head: Dunnet Head is missing altogether, and the coast between Duncansby and Holborn Head is a nicely sculpted scallop edge, as if the mapmaker had given in to his imagination.[69] The result was no doubt aesthetically pleasing but, equally without doubt, would fail to impress any navigator seeking verification of what his eyes were telling him.

Even a work purporting to deal especially with the north could be inaccurate when it came to cartography. Such is the map in the book, *Description of the Islands of Orkney and Zetland*, by Robert Monteith, the laird of Egilsay and Gairsay, published in Edinburgh in 1711. This was later reissued by an enterprising Edinburgh publisher in 1845 to capitalise on the interest generated by Scott's novel *The Pirate*.

As well as maps, navigators had other publications to help them. One of the most popular handbooks was John Tapp's *The Sea-mans Kalendar*, which first appeared in 1602 and was regularly revised and reissued to the end of the century. Essentially an almanac of tidal information, it contained a table showing which moon caused high water in various places:

St Magnes Sound SE by E
At Fair Isles SE
In the Frith SSE
Fair Isle Roads S by E
At Orkney SE.

Tapp's baseline for longitude ran through the 'Westernmost parts of S. Michaels, another Isle of the Azores'; hence the Orcades are given as lying 22° 11' east. The Greenwich meridian was not adopted until 1880. Another handbook was *The Safegarde of Saylers* by Robert Norman. This was first published as early as 1584 and was originally a translation of a Dutch work of the 1560s, though it continued in use to the middle of the seventeenth century.

In 1693 Captain Greenville Collins published his *Great Britain's Coasting Pilot*.[70] Collins held the post of Hydrographer in Ordinary to the Royal Household, and his charts went through a series of editions, the last appearing in 1792 long after they had been surpassed by a new generation of cartographers. Although they incorporated a number of helpful features, such as depths in fathoms at high and low water, arrows indicating the direction of the flood tide, and symbols for reefs and shoals, Collins's maps were not very accurate. Distances were often widely out, in spite of the subtitle promising 'a New and Exact Survey' of the coasts.

Collins included some navigational information: 'From Tarbet-Point to Dungesby-head, the course is north east and by north and north north east fourteen Leagues. Between which Head and the islands of Orkney is a Channel, called Pentland Frith, where is the strongest Tyde in all the Coast of Great Britain.'

Non-local shipping avoided the Firth and went north between Orkney and Shetland to the Atlantic. Conveniently situated on the east coast of mainland Orkney, Deer Sound had become well known to English seamen. Collins gave detailed directions for finding this anchorage, adding: 'The English convoy and Fishermen for Iceland make use of this Harbour most commonly to fill freshwater, and take in Turff for Firing. Provisions are here good and Plenty, all these Islands afford much Corn. Fish of all sorts is very plenty and cheap.' Collins's book also contains a large-scale map of Stromness, called Cairston, the name

Stromness being reserved for the headland at the north side of Hoy Sound.

One Scotsman who produced maps of the north coast was John Adair. In 1686 the Scottish Parliament voted to grant him for the making of charts a fund raised by levying a shipping tax. Adair laboured over his maps for many years and, as he ran short of funds, had to have his work supported by two further Parliamentary acts. He is said by some to have died in 1718 and by others in 1722[71], and his widow sold his charts, including the one of the Firth, which is considered to have been drawn in 1715. It has the faults common to others of the period. Better maps had to await another century and the science of the Enlightenment.

Roost

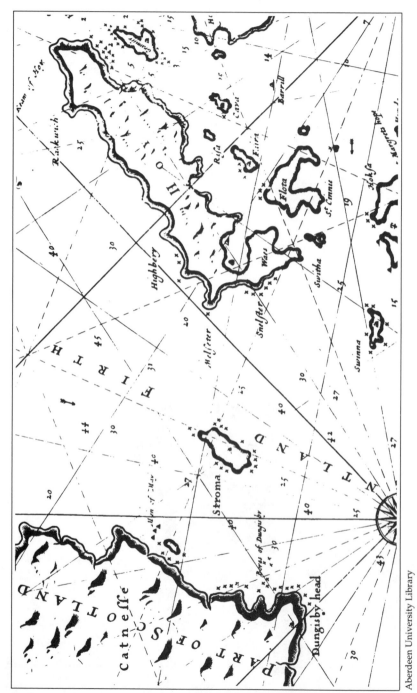

The Pentland Firth by Greenville Collins (from the 1744 edition of Collins's charts)

Life in our house was bound to the clock of the tide. Our father went to work and came home at different times every day. Occasionally this meant him rising at four in the morning and going to bed when we were up and about; and we had to go quietly or suffer parental wrath. Our grandfather used to sit down in winter and work out with a pencil the times of high tide for the following summer. Our father got a handy pocket almanac gratis from an oil company.

The flooding and ebbing of the sea was a wondrous thing. A spring flood brought green water to curl over the edges of the lower quays of the harbour, but the partnering ebb left the basin almost dry, and on the bared shingle banks the men beached their boats to clean and paint the hulls. A low ebb also gave us, the land-bound, a chance to sorn in rock pools and even set a creel or two after a lobster. The regular swelling of the sea was to some once a symbol of life's fruitfulness; and on South Ronaldsay in the 1700s weddings were held when the tide was flowing.[1]

The fishermen spoke of the weather changing when the tide or the moon changed, a cosmological connection I have still to fathom. Perhaps they were using the sea as a timepiece to keep track of some obscure natural rhythm; or perhaps it was an unconscious realisation that the average speed of passing weather fronts came close to matching the six- and twelve-hour periods of the tide. Whatever lies behind this, the accumulated and shared knowledge of several lifetimes went into each fisherman's assessment of what the sky and the sea offered. The morning greeting was more likely to be a question about the wind than some landsman's bland formulaic utterance.

Was it always so? How much, I began to ask myself, did my ancestors know of the tides?

'A Southeast and North-West Moon causeth high Watter throughout all this Country,' wrote James Wallace, the minister of Kirkwall who died of a fever in 1688. The correlation between high water and the moon's phases   59 had been known for centuries: the Greeks speculated on the link, and the medieval philosopher Robert Grosseteste, Bishop of Lincoln, attributed tides to the attraction of the water by the moon's 'virtue'. It was not until the end of the sixteenth century that Johann Kepler concluded that the moon's virtue was in fact gravity, but this theory was not widely accepted until some decades later when Sir Isaac Newton published his theory of gravitation.

The northern seamen probably knew as much as anyone, perhaps more, for theirs was a harder school. Fishermen have their ways for calculating tides. A man on South Ronaldsay told me about a certain rock on the west side of Swona where observation of the rising tide towards noon on the third day after the full moon enabled one to work out a fortnight's tides. It was also possible to get six knots of way on a sailing yole, even with no wind, by using the tidal currents.[2]

Before his death, James Wallace had been a correspondent of Sir Robert Sibbald, geographer to Charles II, and had passed to him manuscripts on local life and a map of Orkney. These were published in Edinburgh in 1693 by Wallace's son. The minister had been a keen observer. He used a microscope to look at the liver flukes that plagued local sheep and recorded that once a rare bird - the hoopoe - was blown in. But he could also accept that sea eagles carried off children and that there was still alive a man who, as a child, had been plucked skyward by one. He took delight in what the ocean brought to the shore: mollucca beans, used to make snuff boxes; a tortoise found alive; pieces of rare timber; and hogsheads of wine and brandy. (This sort of thing still happens: a six-foot leatherback turtle was captured near Bettyhill, on the north coast of Sutherland, in October 1989, having presumably come with the North Atlantic Drift from warmer latitudes[3], and one day a few years ago a tree canoe from the West Indies found its way into Rackwick Bay.[4]) Wallace wrote about the tides:

"Pightland Firth which divides this Countrey from

Caithness is in breadth from Duncansbay to the nearest point of South Ronaldsha ... about twelve Miles. In it are many Tides (to the number of twenty-four) which run with such an impetuous current, that a Ship under Sail, is no more able to make way against the Tide, then if it were hindered by a Remora; which I conceive is the cause, why some have said that they have found the Remora in these Seas."

Wallace was puzzled by the fact that the tide reached high water in different places at different times: why, for example, did it flood two hours sooner on the west coast of Sanday than on the east? If the reason was a mystery, the application of the knowledge was far from being an obstacle: 'Yet, notwithstanding of all this Rapidity of these Tides and Births, the Inhabitants dayly Travell from Isle to Isle, about their several Business, in their little Cockboats.'

The tides also exercised a considerable fascination for the Revd John Brand when he visited the north in 1700. Brand came as a member of a commission from the General Assembly to inspect the kirks but, however much time he gave to presbyterian affairs, he did not neglect more worldly matters.

The Orcadians were in his eyes astonishingly healthy: a woman of sixty-three claimed to have 'brought forth a child', and a man called William Muir on Westray was said to have reached the age of 140. The most common disease was scurvy. Oats and barley were grown, and the butter was 'good, yellow and sweet' and used to pay the rent. (Agriculture was obviously in a better state than arithmetic.) Brand also recorded local prices: a cow cost £5 Scots, a wedder lamb £1, a hen half a crown, a lobster at the most fourpence, and 1000 sellags (coalfish fingerlings) could be had for six shillings. He visited the Dwarfie Stane on Hoy, the standing stones at Brodgar and the ruined brochs studding the countryside. But of all the strange, new things he saw, the Pentland Firth impressed him most:

*The noise that Pightland Firth makes among many who
only have heard thereof as being noted and famous for
its Danger to Passengers, and the Causes which concur
to render it so, awakened us more particularly to enquire
concerning it ...*

The prospect of their own imminent crossing
sharpened this desire for understanding. Brand's account
shows that the topic could never have been far from his
mind: 'What is the number of these Tides cannot well be
condescended ... some say thirteen; others eighteen; and
others twenty-four.'

He attributed this complexity rightly to islands and
rocks affecting the flow of water, quoting the local saying
'Every craig-lugge makes a new Tide', and adding wist-
fully 'and many Craigs and Lugs are there here.'

He and his colleagues crossed from Burwick to
Duncansby. It was a fine day but they must have been
nervous, their heads full of stories of wrecks and drownings.
Half a mile from Burwick was a rock, from Brand's account
probably the Lother, visible only during the ebb and on
which, three years previously, an Aberdeen ship had come
to grief 'and all the Men in her ... lost'. Then there were the
Swelkie and the Wells of Swona waiting for them; a
minister in Shetland had told Brand how he had passed
their way on the day after two fishing boats had been
sucked into them.

Brand sought reassurance from his guides, and was
told that the Wells of Tistala off Burwick were only
dangerous during the flood tide and the Wells of Swona
during the ebb. Undersea caverns were to blame, concluded
Brand. During the crossing he saw the currents running
like 'the Torrents of some great Rivers, and in some places
we will see the Waters smooth, and rough ground about;
the Reason whereof I know not ...'

The modern traveller can share something of Brand's
experience by taking the summer ferry from Burwick to
John o'Groats. Even on a calm day the mixing of the
various tidal currents is plainly visible: smooth, glassy

patches of sea, yards across, give the impression of water bubbling up from the deep and are intermingled with choppy, fretted stretches, the whole heaving and rippling like a carpet with white ruffs and fringes of lace where the wavelets break. Occasionally the ferry bumps her head into a wave and throws a shimmering fall of spray from her shoulders.

Just over half-way across, Brand and his friends ran into the ebb tide sweeping northwest from Duncansby Head: 'For half an hour, we made not one foot of Way, tho there were four Men tugging at the Oars and no wind blowing; and in all probability we had been carried down upon Stroma, if an able man a Passenger: had not taken ane Oar. So that then there were 3 Oars upon our Star-Board Side.'

The crossing prompted Brand to record some local knowledge. It was best to set out when the ebb was starting at the shore, so that by the time a boat reached mid-channel the flood there would have died and the sailors would enjoy slack water. For the voyage from Burwick to Caithness, all winds except the south-west were suitable; for the return journey, the north-east wind was to be avoided. The seamen called the north-west wind the 'king of the Firth': when it blew, they could cross in either direction and stay clear of the Wells. The south-east wind caused the biggest seas: for then the tide was 'running in the Wind's Eye, the Roaring and Swelling Waves are very Terrible, and mount so high, that they could wash not only the Deck, but the Sails and Topmasts of the biggest Ships'.

Seamen passing through the Inner Sound used the chimneyheads of the House of Mey (now the Castle of Mey) as a meeze, or marker. If from the boat the heads could not be seen they knew they were too near the Caithness shore; but, if the whole house was visible, their course was too close to Stroma and the reefs of the island's southern tip.

Shaken and thankful, the ministers splashed ashore at Duncansby. Brand quickly recovered his poise and was delighted by the shells on the beach. The children made   63 beads and necklaces from them, and Brand filled his pockets with some specimens. Later, on his desk in Edinburgh, they would remind him of the day he crossed the Firth: and in the whorls of the buckies perhaps he could see the spinning of the Swelkie.

Taste and genius may spring up in the north

The first properly-conducted surveys of the Firth were made in the mid-eighteenth century, under the aegis of Colin Maclaurin, the professor of mathematics at Edinburgh University, a disciple of Newton and one of the foremost geometers of his day. One of his pupils, Alexander Bryce, obtained in 1740 an appointment as a tutor in the far north, and Maclaurin asked him to make a map while he was in the area. Bryce surveyed by triangulation the coast from Assynt to Wick. It was arduous work in remote, almost roadless country, but he proved conclusively that Cape Wrath was the north-western extremity of the mainland. Occasionally facing death threats from locals who feared that accurate maps would deprive them of the benefits of wrecks, he spent three years on the task. The results were published in Edinburgh in 1744.[5] Bryce returned to the Lowlands where he became a minister, kept up his interest in science, wrote some songs and succeeded in sorting out some of the chaos in Scottish weights and measures before he died in 1786.

One of the estate-owners in Orkney was the Earl of Morton, subsequently to hold the earldom. He was a keen amateur physicist and the first president of the newly formed Society for Improving Arts and Sciences, and in 1739 asked Maclaurin, his close friend, to carry out a survey of the islands.[6] Maclaurin was too busy and possibly ailing (he died in 1746) and suggested that Murdoch Mackenzie was the man for the job. Mackenzie, who was teaching at the time in Kirkwall Grammar School, was an expert in the use of triangulation and probably another of the professor's former students.

We know very little about Mackenzie's early life.[7] He may have been born in 1712 and was probably a grandson of Murdo Mackenzie, the Bishop of Orkney who died in 1688. The family originally came from Kintail. Maclaurin placed an advertisement in the *Caledonian Mercury* in April 1743 to announce Mackenzie's project. The schoolmaster began his survey in 1744 and six years later was able to present a paper on 'The State of the Tides in Orkney' to the Royal Society in London. His work was published as an atlas in 1750 and went through three editions, the last appearing in 1791. He went on to survey the west coast of Britain from Cape Wrath to Cardigan Bay and the whole Irish coast; and in 1771 he retired from the post of Admiralty Surveyor, to which he had been appointed in about 1752, to be suceeded by his nephew who bore the same name. For his contribution to cartography he was elected a Fellow of the Royal Society in May 1774, when he was described as being 'of Hampstead'. He died in 1797 and was buried at Minehead in Somerset.

His maps were highly valued and not only by the Admiralty. The first edition of the atlas was subscribed to by merchants in Edinburgh, Glasgow, Greenock, London and some continental ports, as well as by local men in Kirkwall and Stromness. Thirty copies were bought by the Hudson's Bay Company, who used Stromness as a stopping-place on their voyages to the Canadian Arctic.

Mackenzie was a careful, exact worker and was not averse to putting himself into danger to obtain the measurements he wanted. His account of his technique is matter-of-fact but, showing perhaps an anxiety over being taken seriously, begins:

The Method made choice of in taking this survey ...differs from the usual Way, of Sailing along the Land, taking the Bearings of the Headlands by a Sea Compass, and guessing at the Distances by the Eye, or Log-line; and also from a very common ... Method ... without viewing the Place themselves; but only from verbal Information, copied Journals, or superficial Sketches of Sailors casually passing along the Coast ...

Thus were the earlier mapmakers put in their place.

He spent some time exploring the islands before he began his triangulation. The technique depends on accurate cross-bearings being taken on all objects to be mapped, and on distances being measured precisely, starting from a baseline. To obtain a straight, level line, Mackenzie waited for a heavy winter frost and laid out a precise distance in chains on the ice on the Loch of Stenness. With this accurate baseline and with beacons and landmarks built on all the high points of the land, he proceeded to put together his maps.

He surveyed coasts and reefs, took soundings, recorded shoals, rocks and sandbanks, least depths, the nature of the sea bed, watering places, safe anchorages, the time of high water, eddies and currents. He sketched the land as seen from the sea, including notes on the colour of the soil as it appeared 'to the Eye at some Miles distant' and all 'remarkable' hills, houses and dykes, so that 'a Stranger, tho engaged with the Land in dark Weather' could compare what he saw with his chart and establish his route with safety.

To measure the velocity of tidal currents, Mackenzie let himself drift in a small boat in calm weather, using a stopwatch to time how long it took to pass known distances. He described how ships waiting in the Firth for a favourable tide could safely tack to and fro in the eddies downstream of Stroma, and he noticed that the turbulence from whirlpools did not extend far from them. He passed within twenty yards of one and 'was not sensible of any Attraction towards it', although he admitted it was near the end of the tide and its strength was 'considerably abated'. Fishermen told him how an oar or a barrel could be thrown into a pool to disrupt its structure. Mackenzie remained rational in his attitude to these swirling maws but was clearly impressed by them, called them inverted bells, and observed that those near Stroma or Swona could, during a spring tide, turn any vessel around. He saw that strings of whirlpools, growing and shrinking, followed each other like 'so many Pits in the Sea'.

His detailed comments on tide patterns show that he must have spent long hours discussing the sea with the local fishermen. What they thought of him, scrambling about the shore with notebook, theodolite and measuring chains, we do not know, but they probably appreciated what he was doing and helped him a great deal.

He warned against mistaking Noss Head for Duncansby Head, and reassured captains that should the wind fail when they were running with the tide, the stream would carry them past an island rather than on to it.

He read his treatise to the Royal Society in May 1749. 'No accounts of the flux and reflux of the sea were satisfactory, till Sir Isaac Newton's penetrating genius deduced their true cause from the laws of gravitation,' he began; and then went on, 'but as he, and all Philosophers since his time, have considered only, or principally, the influence of the moon in elevating or depressing the tides; their several directions, velocities, and other affections, resulting from the influence of land, shoals, and winds, remain still as inexplicable, and as little known as ever.' He could have added - thanks to me, no longer.

Mackenzie's work carried his name abroad. In his book published in Paris in 1757 for the guidance of the French king's ships, Jacques Bellin paid tribute to Mackenzie's charts which, he wrote, left nothing to be desired.[8] (They did not prevent Bellin from making the mistake of calling Duncansby Head the most northerly point on the Scottish mainland - an error often repeated in and since his time.) In 1805, George Barry, the minister of Shapinsay, claimed Mackenzie as proof that 'taste and genius may spring up in the north'; and a century after his work, Imray's *Sailing Directions for the East Coasts of England and Scotland* still contained Mackenzie's description of the Firth's tides.

Johno Grott's buckeys

Many a Caithness household had a jar of groatie buckies set away someplace. The shell beach at John o'Groats, where the sea throws up the remains of several deepwater molluscs, is supposed to be the best place to find this little member of the cowrie family. The scientific name is *Trivia monacha*. They are rare on most beaches but we searched for them, combing through the whelks and the limpets and the brown, yellow and red periwinkles left stranded by the tide's wash. Our granny had quite a collection of groatie buckies, a lifetime's luck in a sweetie jar.

Throughout the eighteenth century a succession of travellers left accounts of visits to the north, and many left with buckies in their pockets. The travellers came for many reasons: out of simple curiosity, to fulfil official duties or, most importantly towards the end of the century, for inspection with the aim of 'improvement', the word then in vogue for what we would call development.

First, the curious. Thomas Pennant from Downing in Flintshire had already published three volumes on the zoology of Britain and was a famous naturalist when he rode over the Warth Hill to Duncansby in August 1769. From the peat-hags on the braes he made his way down to the green pastures, little parks of oats and small houses by the shore of the Firth. He regretted not having come this far north in June, when the days are long and a man with normal sight can read a newspaper out of doors at midnight, but he found plenty still to catch his interest.

He observed the beach made up of broken shells and the dark rocks running out into the sea, where the tides and currents formed 'a most tremendous contest' and, beyond, the low silhouette of the Orkney islands. There were several small boats drawn up on the beach: Pennant noted that in these the locals 'passed with great safety' about their maritime affairs.

From John o'Groats he rode west to Canisbay where he had dinner with the minister. On his way back to Wick he passed close to the house of a 'gentleman' who had died not long before and who was reputed to be the last in the area with the gift of second sight. Whether or not this had been the topic of conversation at the minister's table we can only guess; but Pennant recorded how at first the gentleman had pretended only to believe in the second sight to impress others but had become 'a dupe to his own artifices', and had spent the last years of his life tormented by his clairvoyant faculties. The switch from pretence to firm belief, claimed Pennant, had arisen from an accident that happened to one of the man's boats. This vessel was at sea 'on a very tempestuous night' and the man, his mind filled with thoughts of what might befall her, 'suddenly started up, pronounced that his men would be drowned, for that he had seen them pass before him with wet garments and dropping locks'. Later the news came that the boat had been lost with all hands.

Perhaps the story gave Pennant an enjoyable frisson as he rode back over the Warth Hill, watching the gannets flying low and presaging bad weather.

George Low, a graduate of Aberdeen and St Andrews and a friend of Pennant, became a minister in Orkney in 1771. He, too, was a keen naturalist and made careful drawings of observations with his microscope, one of which he seems to have obtained from a wrecked ship. His accounts of travels in Orkney and Shetland are punctuated with comments on wildlife:

May 9th. Took boat in Waes [Walls] for Stroma. In the Pightland Firth saw vast numbers of Gannets ... also the first Scoutiaulin with several other more common birds ... Taisties, Lyres, Auks, Tommy Nodies, Scouts, Kittiwakes ...[9]

Low saw no other danger 'than one might expect' in crossing the Firth as long as the weather was reasonable. In bad weather, he admitted, 'there is no passing with safety', and wrote that the Men of Mey were 'impossible to stem with sails or oars, but the vessels will be hurried away by them like feathers before the wind'.

'All these evils and others', he continued, 'may be easily guarded against by choosing a proper tide, which is sometimes before slack water [when] the firth may be passed with great safety'.

He drew diagrams to explain how the origins of the Wells of Swona lay simply in the island's position in the tide, and dismissed the 'lugubrious stories' of accidents happening there. 'Vast quantities of Coalfish are caught around Swona, particularly near the Wells, which in this respect are no inconvenience but rather a happiness, as near them the fishermen find not only the best but the greatest number of fish.'

Travellers, then as now, can be lucky with the weather. I have crossed the Firth on days of almost tropical sunshine with hardly a whisper of wind, and been grateful for it; it makes up for the times when the vessel has done everything except stand on her head. Richard Pococke, an Anglican bishop, enjoyed a fine four-hour crossing in July 1760 from Thurso to Walls. The return trip, in two hours from South Ronaldsay to Duncansby, was on an equally fine evening when a great number of boats were out at the fishing. Pococke saw the ruins of John o'Groat's house and plenty of buckies.

Robert Forbes made two tours of the Highlands in his capacity as the Episcopalian bishop of the area - in 1762 and 1770.[10] At this time, although most folk adhered to the Presbyterian kirk, many of the landed gentry were Episcopalian. Forbes's progress from one wealthy host to another, preaching, praying and confirming as he went, has the air of an extended picnic, fond as he was of food, tea, punch and good company.

After carrying out a round of episcopal duties in Thurso, he arrived at the Castle of Mey on a fine evening in August 1762. On the following day, he made an early start, confirming Lady Sinclair, his host's wife, at eight o'clock and then, after Matins, climbing to the roof of the seven-storey castle to view the Firth. He saw the Men of Mey rocks, quiet at this time of low water, but learned that they raised 'a very hot and dangerous tide' when the ebb was running. A stroll around the garden revealed a fine crop of apples, strawberries and cherries; and at ten o'clock he set off with John Banks, his host's principal servant, to visit Duncansby.

The hooves of the horses sinking in the mire, they rode past Canisbay kirk to view the ruins of John o'Groat's house. There was little left to show where the famous ferryman had lived, but the stones indicated to Forbes that it had been a building of four to five rooms. There had once been a chapel and a burying place here, and the walls of a barn and a kiln were still standing. The bishop reflected on how the name of Groat had once been more common than that of Sinclair and how this situation was now reversed, and was reminded of the fickle fortunes of human life.

He and Banks dismounted at the beach to look for 'Johno Grott's buckeys' but found none. Just as they were about to leave, a small boy approached them shyly and offered some shells for sale. Banks told the bishop that a penny would make the boy happy, but Forbes was moved to proffer the boy sixpence. The boy 'stood on tiptoes, stared, trembled and reddened greatly, still reaching up the little Hand', recalled the bishop. When he had the coin, the boy ran home and promptly returned with his elder brother and his mother with a stocking full of buckies and a wooden cog containing about two thousand. Forbes did not record whether he bought any more.

Shipwrecks and Privateers

Early in December 1679, the *Crown*, bound from Leith to the American plantations and crowded with Covenanters, prisoners taken at the battle of Bothwell Bridge, went ashore in Deerness. The weather was bad, and the ship began to break up before all the hapless human cargo could be freed. Around 200 people drowned.

The *Crown*'s fate is fairly well recorded.[11] There have been many vessels lost in our home waters of which we know nothing and, often, only chance has preserved their names for us.

> *The Charm. Betty, Sword, bound from London for*
> *N. England is ashore on one of the Isles of Orkney.*[12]

Thus did the first notice of a north shipwreck appear in the closely printed columns of *Lloyd's List*, a bi-weekly newsheet of financial and shipping information that began publication in 1741.[13] The first line gives the name of the vessel, the *Charming Betty*, and her captain, Sword.

A small section of the two-sided broadsheet, headed 'Ship News', was tucked in among the port listings, stock prices and exchange rates, and gave brief mention of disasters at sea. It is easy to picture it being eagerly scanned by the City merchants and underwriters and to see them closing their eyes over a lost investment or turning to their coffee with relief that a vessel from the Indies had been sighted at last after weeks in the unknown.

Ships meeting in mid-ocean exchanged information and if the home-bound captain passed on his news to the *List* a paragraph such as this one on 8 August 1749 could appear.

> *The St Andrew, Capt. Blair, arrived in the Orkneys from*
> *Virginia, on the 2d of May, a little to the Westward of the*
> *Western Islands, spoke with the Neptune, of Aberdeen, from*
> *Bourdeaux for Virginia, who had lost her Main-mast, and*
> *sprung her Bowsprit and Fore-mast, but was other Ways*
> *well: She had got up Jury Masts and was proceeding her*
> *voyage.*[14]

News about shipping in the Firth is scarce in the earlier issues. Coastal vessels of little interest to the London financiers were the main users of this narrow route and, anyway, it was a long way from the City. News could take weeks to reach the editors, and when it did arrive it was frequently garbled and betrayed vague notions of northern geography. The *Merryfield*, Newfoundland to London, is recorded as 'lost at Duncarn-head' on 23 January 1747[15] - is this Duncansby? In June 1751, the paper recorded that the *Dalkeith*, driven ashore 'in the Orkneys' by a gale while en route from Dumfries to Norway, had been got off with the assistance of Harry Innes of Sandside.[16] This refers to the Innes family of Reay on the Caithness side of the Firth.

Reports of wrecks, groundings and other catastrophes from Orkney and the Firth became more frequent as the years went by. We cannot be certain whether this reflects an increase in the use of the Firth, perhaps by vessels armed with Mackenzie's new charts, or merely better correspondence with the islands.

On 5 November 1762, the *List* laconically noted that 'a Brig with Salmon, Name unknown, is wrecked in the Orkneys, and all the Crew perish'd'.[17] Other reports make tragic reading:

> *Stronsay, 10 Feb 1830 ... a number of small flitches of bacon have been cast on shore at different parts of the Island: a barrel or two of flour have also been found, and fishermen report, that the sea is in some places covered with grain. On the 8th inst. part of the wreck of a small vessel, fir built, and very old, came on shore on the south side. It is feared more than one vessel must have suffered on the coast.[18]*

A single gale could account for several vessels in an age without weather forecasts, organised rescue craft and radio. In the autumn of the same year that grain and bacon drifted to the beach on Stronsay, a north-westerly gale savaged South Ronaldsay for two days and blew three ships ashore.[19] The Leith schooner *Edina* went ashore on the south-west corner of Stroma on 8 April 1830[20], and on the following day, in thick fog, two other vessels joined her - the *Aasceili and Anna* on the north end of the island and the *Thetis* on the south side; all three crews were saved 'with difficulty'.[21] It is hard, however, to surpass the poignancy of a message in a bottle washed ashore at Ackergill in December 1848: it read 'Dec 16 ... on board the schooner 73

Juno of Swinmundie, lat. 27, 30N, lon. 3: 30 East. Spent all canvass, and vessel in a sinking state; two hands washed overboard in late gale; and to all appearances we must soon follow, unless Divine Providence intersedes for us - Wm. Maries, master.'[22]

But there were rescues too. An unelaborated 'Crew saved' ends many a wreck report in the *List* although occasionally, as in the case of the *Prudent Sarah*, smashed to pieces in November 1753[23], and the *Mary*, demolished at Scrabster by a northerly gale in January 1830[24], the rescues were performed 'with difficulty'.

Lloyd's List makes it clear that the seaways around the Firth could be busy, cosmopolitan places. A list of shipping in the area on 20 August 1747, a typical date, includes the *Three Friends* arrived from Carolina; the *Young William* from Montserrat; the *Humber* and the *William* both en route to Boston; the *Bazel, Gilben* and *Duke* all for Whitehaven; the *Sally* and the *Golden Star* for Hamburg; the *Britannia* for London; the *Edward and Mary* for Bergen; the *Betty* for Newcastle; the *St Patrick* for Rotterdam; and the *Phenix* for Colrain.[25]

Bad weather and roistering tides were not the only hazards the merchantmen had to contend with. Piracy seems to have been a frequent crime at some periods. Patrick Stewart, Earl of Orkney, owned a warship called the *Dunkirk* which attacked shipping off the Norwegian coast in 1612; the reason for the assault is unknown but piracy cannot be ruled out, though some connection with the mercenary expedition from Caithness to Sweden via Norway at this time is also possible.[26] In June 1690, a ship belonging to Patrick Fea was chased ashore at Deerness by a ship thought to have been French.[27]

Of genuine pirates, if I can use the phrase, we know some detail only about John Gow. Sir Walter Scott later changed his name to Captain Cleveland and made him the eponymous central figure in his novel *The Pirate*; a century earlier, Daniel Defoe also made Gow the subject of a book.[28] John Gow was born in Wick, the son of a merchant who moved to Stromness when the boy was very young. John went to sea and in 1724 found himself caught up in a mutiny aboard the merchant vessel *Caroline*. After the murder of the captain and other officers, Gow was the only man on board who knew how to navigate; he was elected leader. Renaming the ship the *Revenge*, the mutineers embarked on a course of piracy, seizing a number of ships in Iberian waters before Gow took the *Revenge* to his home port of Stromness early in 1725. Here, despite further change of name to the *George*, the true nature of the ship and her crew was discovered. Gow set sail but went ashore on the Calf of Eday. The pirates were captured and taken to London for trial. Gow refused to plead before the Admiralty Court until he was tortured and faced with a further ordeal; with some of his companions he was hanged in June 1725 in Execution Dock, Wapping. His body was hung tarred in chains as a warning to others.

Privateers, who were in effect pirates licensed by governments to harass the commerce of their enemies, operated widely in northern waters; the practice was finally outlawed at the Convention of Paris in 1856.[29] The earliest reference to them comes in a letter from Edinburgh in June 1694 to Sir James Sinclair of Mey, advising him that 'the coast is so throng with [French] privateers that they alleadge its not hardly possible it [cargoes of grain bound for Norway] can winn through.'[30] The *Susanna Snow*, a French ship operating from Calais under the command of William Dennis, took at least seven victims in the vicinity of Shetland in 1744. She carried a crew of 100, and was armed with ten carriage and ten swivel guns. One prize was the *Helen and Margaret*, captured en route from Norway to Inverness.[31]

Normal practice on seizing a ship was to strip the crew of anything of value and then take the ship and her cargo to a friendly port to await delivery of ransom money.

Another privateer, the *Roniame* from Dunkirk, had twenty guns and took the *Benjamin Johnson*, outward bound from Newcastle to New York, in June 1760, about twenty miles off Duncansby Head.[32] The victim was taken into 75

Bergen, a neutral port highly favoured by the privateers for parking their victims.

Some ships changed hands twice, as a privateer from one country could lose a prize to another. In May 1761, the *Wolf* was recaptured, probably from a Frenchman, and brought to Orkney.[33] The hapless *Anne*, a Waterford ship, was taken in August 1747 east of Orkney and ransomed for £360, only to be boarded twice afterwards by two different privateers.[34] A British sloop of war retook the *Increase* in January 1757 and escorted her safely to Orkney.[35]

Ransoms for captured vessels varied from £50 for a small ship up to £1,000 for a merchantman of the first rank. In July 1757, two ships, taken while southward bound from Thurso, were ransomed in Dunkirk for 200 and 300 guineas respectively.[36]

There was a flurry of naval activity in and around the Firth at the time of the last Jacobite rising. On 25 March 1746, HMS *Sheerness* chased the sloop, *Le Prince Charles*, carrying guineas to pay the rebel army then nearing Culloden, west through the Firth, catching her at the mouth of the Kyle of Tongue. Naval frigates used Stromness as a base at times, and in the summer of 1746 French ships, hoping to find and transport the fleeing Prince Charles, passed through the Firth, although their knowledge of the area was severely limited and they preferred the longer, safer route between Orkney and Shetland.[37]

A fresh outbreak of war - and there were plenty of these in the 1700s - could unleash a new swarm of privateers. During the conflict between Britain and the emerging United States of America and her ally France, a fleet of six privateers cruised around the Shetland coast.[38] The fleet was reported to comprise three 32-gun frigates and three 18-gun sloops during the war, and their avowed aim was to disrupt trade to Greenland and Scandinavia. Indeed, privateering served as a training school for the fledgling United States Navy. Coastal vessels were not immune to attack: the *Speedwell*, bound from Gardenstown to the West Highlands, probably with a cargo of grain, was taken in August 1780 by the aptly named *Fearnought* and later ransomed for 400 guineas.[39] Ships of the Royal Navy also took every opportunity that came their way to seize French and Americans, and British privateers also pursued the riches their profession offered: in August 1758, the London-based *Defiance* brought into Deer Sound a Dutch ship from the Indies, laden with sugar, coffee and indigo.[40]

The brig *Daphne*, bound from the Easdale quarries to Leith with a cargo of slate, was taken by an American privateer just west of Cape Wrath in June 1813. The *Daphne*'s skipper, Garrioch by name, wrote to say that his captor had lightened his ship (by dumping the slate?) and sent her to the United States under a prize crew, taken his charts and both his quadrants, transferred him and his men to another captured vessel, the *Six Sisters* of Inverkeithing, and 'sent us about our business'.[41]

The privateers also risked the sea itself: in September 1747, a French privateer was wrecked on the Scottish coast (the exact location is unrecorded) and all but three of her crew of seventy lost.[42]

The Royal Navy's answer to the threat from the privateers was twofold: they sent ships to patrol the north, supported by signalling stations on, for example, Fair Isle; and they organised and escorted merchantmen in convoys. The commander in charge of Scottish waters in 1807 was Rear-Admiral James Vashon. He was based in Leith, from where he corresponded with the Admiralty and tried to keep track of all that happened within his far-flung, stormy jurisdiction.[43]

Vashon had trouble with convoys, but more from crabbed owners and skippers than from the enemy he guarded them against. The Baltic convoy was a vital link in Britain's overseas trade. Its assembly point for the outward voyage was Longhope. Naval escort captains followed a code of Instructions, the original of which was deposited with the minister of Walls. A convoy should sail every fourteen days and, after escorting the merchant vessels to Denmark, the defence ships should stay at Elsinore for six days before returning to Longhope with such vessels as needed their protection. As well as British ships, Prussian and Swedish vessels were allowed to join the convoys, these three countries being allied against Napoleon's France.

Will Richan, the captain of the *Norfolk*, a hired defence ship, wrote to Vashon to report that in May 1807 he had arrived off the Pentland Skerries but was becalmed for a day and then forced to sail to Inganess Bay instead of Longhope. A month later, after escorting the homeward Baltic convoy to British waters, fog and wind once again forced him into Inganess. Here he waited for the appointed day of departure for the next outward convoy, but no vessels appeared. A few days later, three Liverpool merchantmen arrived; two more followed next day. They told Richan that a large fleet was on its way to join the convoy. Richan said that should twelve ships be ready at Longhope by 7 July he would sail and meet them off the Skerries.

The merchant skippers were impatient to be off. On 6 July they wrote to their London owners, complaining about the *Norfolk* being at Inganess and not ready to sail, and this with a north-westerly gale in the offing. The skippers sought out Richan at a farm near Kirkwall and had 'a strong dispute'. Richan argued that he was following the Code of Instructions, which stated that if he had waited for fourteen days and no ships had come he was duty-bound to wait another fourteen before sailing. It appears that the convoy did sail the next day.

Another armed naval vessel, HMS *Hebe*, served on escort duty from Longhope to the Baltic in 1808, and HMS *Nightingale* escorted America-bound convoys until they were '100 leagues to the Westward' of Orkney, after which time presumably they sailed on alone. At this time Vashon found out that a privateer had taken two ships off Caithness, and detailed a hired cutter, the *Queen Charlotte*, to join HM sloop *Childers* to deal with the threat. It seems that the *Queen Charlotte* failed to perform this duty, as two weeks later Vashon was annoyed to find her going into dock at Burntisland. In June, a Danish privateer captured three ships between Orkney and Shetland. HM sloop *Clio* captured a Danish brig near the Faroes but released her as she was carrying a cargo of grain and, at the time, the Faroese were described as 'starving'.

In July 1808, Vashon was promoted and at the end of the year resigned his northern command to Vice-Admiral Sir Edmund Nagle.

Captain Elliott of the *Hebe* wrote to Leith from Longhope to remind his superiors of what convoy duty in the north could mean:

> *[13 October 1809, Longhope] I beg leave to state that from the 12th of August, the day of my arrival at this anchorage, to the 16th ultimo on which I sailed with a Fleet for Gottenburgh; the wind was not to the northward of NE nor to the westward of SW excepting on the 16th, 25th and 30th of August and the 12th of Sept. On these days, the wind for a few hours only each day was from the NNW but so very light and uncertain that no officer, in his senses, acquainted with the Pentland Firth would have attempted to take a Fleet thro' it.*[44]

Nagle wrote to Elliott in March 1810 to ask if the *Hebe* was ready for sea to resume convoy duty on the same basis as before. The Admiralty correspondence at this time describes the *Hebe* as having sixteen guns and a crew of forty-six and as being 'very fit for the service on which she is employed'.

In May 1811, a naval brig called the *Fancy*, under the captaincy of Alexander Sinclair, won a brisk action against the privateers. Disguising herself as a merchantman and cruising between Buchan Ness and Duncansby, the *Fancy* lured a Danish privateer into chasing her. Once the enemy came within range, the *Fancy* opened fire and the Dane, presumably overcome by surprise, struck her colours. The prize was the *Kemplaa*. Immediately after this, the *Fancy* spotted two vessels to the east, gave chase and, after five hours, had taken another Danish privateer, the cutter *Prince Christian*. The *Prince Christian*'s companion was a 79 prize she had herself just captured, the sloop *Jean*, bound from Montrose to Stornoway with a cargo of meal. The *Fancy's* success was due in part to her enemies being lightly armed - the *Kemplaa* had only two guns, and the *Prince Christian* three - but it was a notable piece of seamanship and boldness on Sinclair's part.

I have no details of the *Fancy's* appearance but, as a brig, she would have had two masts, either fully square-rigged or with a fore-and-aft sail on the mainmast. She could have been up to 100 ft long, with a crew of up to 100 men. Her fate may have been a sad one for, at the end of October after her victory, she was caught in a severe easterly gale, and a fortnight later a letter from Orkney to the commander in Leith was expressing concern for her safety. The *Fancy* was listed in the Admiralty's books under 'Ships totally lost'.

The importance of Longhope as a rendezvous for merchant convoys led the British government to construct two Martello towers, at Crockness and Hackness, to guard the entrance to the inlet.[45] The Hackness tower was supplemented by a gun battery. The building began in July 1813 and they were partly completed when Walter Scott and his companions went to see them.[46] They found eight 24-pounder guns glowering at the sea but Scott was not overly impressed: all the weapons were pointing seaward and it would not have been difficult, he thought, for an attacker to avoid them completely. The towers look ludicrously small for their task, sitting as they do like robust, squat thimbles overlooking Flotta and the Sound between, but Scott was perhaps not fully aware of their ingenious structure.

Built from yellow sandstone shipped from the north of Hoy, each tower has thick walls, accommodation for nine men and an NCO, a magazine for the guns and a clever system for collecting and storing rainwater. They are designed to withstand attack and maintain fire on the enemy, and it is ironic but perhaps fortunate that peace with the United States was signed just as their construction finished in December 1814. In the following year Napoleon was brought to heel. The Longhope guns never fired a shot in anger.

The towers were refurbished in the 1860s, when new mountings were placed on the top to allow the guns to traverse through 360 degrees. But once again the threat of war in Europe receded and the towers were left in peace. After a brief period of use in the Second World War as signal stations, they were abandoned to moulder away. The woodwork rotted, the windows and the doors fell to pieces - all until the early 1980s when restoration began. Now these two handsome structures are back in their pristine state, with the addition of electric light for the benefit of their visitors.

The Royal Navy had further successes against the privateers during the last years of the Napoleonic period but the raiders could still strike and be gone, in the manner of maritime guerrillas. In April 1814, Christopher Nixon, the captain of the sloop *Nightingale*, hastily penned a letter to Leith as his ship was getting underway in Longhope.[47] He had just had word from an arriving Swedish vessel that, three days before, the aptly named *Scourge*, a well-armed American privateer, had taken and burned two merchant ships 12 miles west of Hoy. The wind was from the east and the weather thick - otherwise the capture may have been seen from the shore. Nixon gave a brief description of the enemy - her captain was a 'Scotchman' called Parry, and her hull had a small yellow streak - and set off in pursuit. The *Scourge*, perhaps the last privateer of the period, seems to have escaped.

Almost Every Farmer is a Fisher

In October 1786, a retired Edinburgh bookseller called John Knox walked along the north coast from Cape Wrath to Caithness. He was there on behalf of the British Society for Extending the Fisheries and Improving the Seacoasts of the Kingdom. This grandly titled body was collecting subscriptions to further its aim of developing - 'improving' - the fishing industry. Knox had made several previous trips: his first, in 1764, revealed to him a poverty and distress among the ordinary people that affected him deeply, and he was keen to promote the more organised exploitation of the sea's resources.

He had begun his 1786 journey at Oban and had spent some time on the west coast, the main subject of his report, but he had this to say about the Pentland Firth:

In the more imperfect state of navigation this passage was generally avoided by mariners, who chose to keep in the open sea, along the north side of the Orkneys; but, since the publication of Mr Mackenzie's excellent charts, the terrors of the Pentland Firth are become less formidable.

The habit of going north about, as it was called, was standard practice for deep-water ships. Daniel Defoe described how the Dutch East India merchantmen used to take the longer route, using Fair Isle as an assembly point for their convoys. Now, thanks to Murdoch Mackenzie, captains were emboldened sufficiently to save 150 sea-miles, even in winter, by passing through the Firth. 'It too often happens, however,' commented Knox, 'that by thus shortening the passage, they lose both ship and cargo, with their own lives, or the greatest part of them ...'

'There is always in some parts of the Pentland Firth,' he went on, 'a great swelling sea, with breakers during ebb-tide, in the calmest weather ... should a vessel be driven into the Firth by the violence of a tempest, in a fog, or in a dark night, her situation is dreadful beyond description.'

On the Caithness shore, he saw boulders that the wind and the waves had plucked up like counters and hurled into the fields, and learned that during the past summer no less than eleven ships had been wrecked, among them a Liverpool cargo ship of 800 tons, returning fully loaded from the Baltic. He wrote in his journal that beachcombing employed many people.

Knox was looking for suitable sites for harbours where fisheries could take root. He found no towns between Belfast and Cromarty; 'a coast of nearly five hundred miles could not ... furnish a sail, a cable or an anchor,' he warned, and there were no facilities for repairing large ships. He estimated that the losses of vessels and gear were costing shipowners some £40,000 every year.

Extra insurance premiums had to be paid on ships using the Firth. When a vessel was damaged or driven ashore, a message was sent south to the owners - to Liverpool, Leith, London, or wherever - to find out what they wanted to do. Sometimes they sent a repair ship north; more often, they cut their losses and asked that their ship be sold off to the highest bidder, which meant a return of some £40 to £50 for the hull for firewood, according to Knox, and about half the value of the equipment. Mackenzie's charts had opened the way through the Firth to many but it was proving an expensive short-cut.

If Knox had crossed the Firth to Orkney, he would have found a town that owed its existence to passing shipping.[48] Stromness, tucked into the north-western corner of Scapa Flow, was a favourite stopping place for the ships of the Hudson's Bay Company and for whaling vessels on their way to and from the North-West. The approach today is as dramatic as it was then. A vessel slipping in from the west, under the wall of the Hoy cliffs towards the island of Graemsay, rounds the Point of Ness and there suddenly are the houses. Piling up the brae in angular blocks of stone, they seem to grow from the sea itself; several have their foundations in the water, and instead of driveways there are piers. The oldest dated house in the town dates from 1716. Inns and shops catered to the visiting seamen; and Login's Well provided fresh water. With its long, meandering main street not greatly changed throughout its history, Stromness was home to merchants, agents and mariners. As an international maritime crossroads, the town crops up in some surprising contexts.

James Cook's fleet, returning from the Pacific in 1780 with the news of the great navigator's death, made its first

British landfall here. Among the crew was William Brown, a native of the town; and an officer called William Bligh. Bligh dined with the Stewart family of the Whitehouse and there met George Stewart who later served as a midshipman under Bligh aboard the *Bounty*. Stewart was put ashore by the *Bounty* mutineers on Tahiti where he lived for two years until HMS *Pandora* found him. He was drowned when the *Pandora* struck a reef and sank.[49]

The Hudson's Bay Company ships began calling regularly at Stromness from at least 1702. There were usually three each year: they arrived in June, stayed for a couple of weeks before setting their course for the north of Canada, and called again on the homeward voyage in November. As well as taking on water and supplies, they recruited men - so much so that by the end of the eighteenth century Orcadians comprised as many as three-quarters of the Company staff, and the wages from Hudson's Bay made a substantial contribution to the Orkney economy.[50] The Company liked the Orcadians for their toughness, skill and reliability; and their agents in Stromness acted as recruiting masters from their premises, the first of these being the house 'The Haven' and the home of the local manager of the Northern Lighthouse Board. In the 1790s, between sixty and 100 men went to the Bay every year, usually on a five-year contract.[51] As a labourer in the Arctic, a man could earn up to £18 in a year, three times the local wage for a farm servant; tradesmen received more - carpenters up to £36, boatbuilders up to £30, and so on. There were complaints back home in Orkney about the shortage of manpower during the harvests.

Company recruitment fell away gradually in the early decades of the nineteenth century, partly because the expanding Scottish herring fishery provided employment at home and also because, after the Hudson's Bay Company amalgamated with its rival, the North-West Company, in 1821, a policy of recruiting Canadians gained ground. But in 1841 the Stromness minister could still note 35-40 men going out to the Bay each summer[52]; and indeed men from Caithness and Orkney, as well as from other parts of northern Scotland, continued to find work with the Hudson's Bay Company right into this century, although the use of Stromness by their ships ceased in the early 1890s.

The Hudson's Bay connection had some beneficial consequences in Orkney. For example, William Tomison of South Ronaldsay rose to become the head of the Company operation in western Canada between 1760 and 1811; and he founded the first Fort Edmonton trading post before retiring to his native island where he had endowed a school. At a more humble but more typical level, several Orcadians could give as their birthplace when completing the government census the words 'Hudson's Bay' or 'Fort Churchill'.[53]

English fishing vessels bound for Iceland and beyond used Orkney as a stopping place from the early 1400s[54] - Deer Sound was the favoured anchorage in the early years - and they may have begun the custom of recruiting some spirited, willing hands from among the young Orcadians for their dangerous business. The visits by fishing fleets fell away towards the end of the eighteenth century, but was gradually supplanted by a grander, more dangerous fishery. The Arctic whalers started to use Stromness as a last place before the Davis Straits and the Greenland ice to stock up on supplies and men. This began in the 1760s[55] and hundreds of young men chanced a season or two after the whales, both for the adventure of it and for the wages, before Arctic whaling began to decline in the 1860s, although the last whaler to call at Stromness, the *Scotia*, did so as recently as 1910.[56]

Richard Ayton wrote in 1813 that it was not unusual to see in Stromness in the spring fifty whalers outward bound, and noted their 'heaving anchor with a fair wind, amidst cheering shouts of hope and enterprise, passing swiftly in succession under the frowning cliffs of Hoy Head, and in a short while disappearing on the verge of the horizon amidst the white curls of the ocean'.[57]

The minister on South Ronaldsay commented in the 1790s on the 'passion of the young men for a seafaring life'.[58] The wages on a whaler at this time were £2 a month or about £12 for a season, but it was not easily earned. The man digging ditches and swatting mosquitoes at Hudson's Bay had chosen a safer and more lucrative, if less exciting, option; and he probably felt more certain of returning home than his fellow out after a whale with a hand-held harpoon among the fogs and floes of Greenland. Whaling had a very high casualty rate. When the *Dee* of Aberdeen returned from the Arctic to Stromness at the end of April 1837 after being trapped in the ice, thirty of the crew were dead, and the surviving dozen, starving and racked with scurvy, were too weak to work the sails; two other whaling ships came back with her.[59] The *Swan* of Hull lost twenty-five of her crew that same winter.[60] After experiences of this sort, it was easy to disregard the moaning ministers who lamented the spending on drink and idle pursuits of those lately home from 'the Nor' Wast'.

Away to the east of Scapa Flow, at the head of a sheltered bay at the north end of South Ronaldsay, lies the village of St Margaret's Hope. In its architecture - the way the houses crowd together around lanes and closes and stagger up a steep brae from the shore - it is a miniature version of Stromness; and if it had been located on the Orkney Mainland instead of one of the South Isles it may have grown larger with trade. As it was, it became a busy place in the late eighteenth and early nineteenth centuries. Ships in the Baltic trade used it, twenty-four in one week in December 1831, for example[61]; and in 1841 the village numbered a doctor, two publicans, six merchants, eight tailors and seven shoemakers among its inhabitants.[62]

In the years following John Knox's visit, far-reaching changes in the social and economic conditions of the people living around the Firth came in a flurry one after another until, within the span of a couple of generations, they altered a way of life that had persisted since the Middle Ages.

The *Statistical Account of Scotland* gives a detailed picture of a society standing on the threshold of change. The brainchild of Sir John Sinclair of Ulbster, the *Account* is a series of portraits of the country's parishes, most written by the resident minister. Some are long and leave the reader with a sense of completeness; others hint that the minister could not be bothered with such worldly matters as a statistical survey and wrote maddeningly little. But, combined, they reveal the nation as it had never been seen before.

Five parishes bound the Firth: Dunnet and Canisbay on the Caithness shore, along with Hoy, Walls and Flotta, and South Ronaldsay on the Orkney side. The greater number of the inhabitants of all five in the 1790s, when the ministers set to work, were crofter-fishermen - a people 'apparently very simple, but in fact abundantly shrewd' in the opinion of the Revd James Bremner of Flotta. James Watson said of his South Ronaldsay flock that 'almost every farmer is a fisher'. When Thomas Jolly found one of his Dunnet parishioners wanting in knowledge of his Catechism and told him he had a thick head, he was told nonchalantly: 'Muckle need o' that, Mr Jolly, steeran aff t'e wast seas til catch codlanes.'

The typical dwelling was a stone and turf cottage, with the fire in the centre of the floor and the livestock under the same roof. Things had hardly changed since Settle's visit in 1577. Wages were low: a man servant earned around £3 in a year, a woman half as much. Prices were low too - beef fetched $2^1/_2$d per pound and eggs were $1^1/_2$d a dozen in Canisbay in 1793 - but not so low as to win folk away from being as self-sufficient as possible. In this, the sea played a vital part.

'Pentland Firth abounds with excellent cod and ling,' wrote Thomas Jolly, 'not of a very large size, but remarkably thick and of good quality.' The tidal streams precluded the use of nets, and fishermen used lines: 50-60 fathoms' worth to reach the marbled cod lurking in the deeper holes, and short lines, with maybe thirty or forty hooks, to take haddock, flounders, skate and turbot in shallower stretches. Dogfish were also taken for the oil in their livers and for their flesh, which was dried for the winter.

A cod fishery operated from Walls and Flotta in the 1790s. Described as 'extremely precarious', the work sometimes yielded nothing, but at other times the catch loaded the boats to the gunwales; and a good year saw between 50,000 and 70,000 fish being cured. About a dozen boats, with six men in each, worked at the cod. William Clouston, the minister of Stromness, described the financing of line fishing: the outlay - for a great line of 1000 fathoms with 400 hooks (£4), a small line with 300 hooks (£1) and a boat (£7) - totalled £12; and in a good year the profit, after paying for salt, maintenance and so on, was £21 10s, to be divided among the fishermen and owner of the boat as agreed.[63]

By 1800 George Barry was complaining about 'some neglect' of the Walls cod fishery, adding that the fishermen went to sea only in their spare time. 'The inhabitants [need to] acquire more enterprise and more skill', he said, in tones echoed today in many a report from the Third World, 'or proper fishermen be brought from another place to animate and instruct them.' He also noted that better boats, decked to provide some protection, were needed.

Line fishing continues sporadically to this day around the Firth. Baskets of lines were around in my early childhood, the neat vortex of brown twine in each giving off a musty, salty scent of hemp with the rank of hooks set in a cork around the rim of the basket. The fishermen used to bring home in the winter months fish as long as they themselves were tall, and on occasion a hook would catch a truly astonishing giant such as a halibut over 200 lb. Billy Mowat, who used to fish from Rackwick out around the cliffs of Hoy, recalled for me the calm, frosty days of January when the boats were beached and the cod and ling thrown on to the snow. Sea anglers have landed record fish in recent decades from the Firth, but the large fish are rare now, the stocks depleted.

George Low noted in 1774 that Swona was a centre for catching cuddanes and dogfish. Here the fishermen dried their catch in stone huts built to allow the wind to blow through them. The oil from fish livers sold at 6d per Scots pint. The cuddanes were caught 'particularly in the Wells,' wrote Low, 'which in this respect are no inconvenience but rather a happiness, as near them the fishermen find not only the best but the greatest number of fish'. John Brand had noted the importance of the Wells in 1700, adding morbidly, 'the Fishes draw the Men, and the Wells draw both,' but Low thought 'their power of swallowing ships, boats, etc has been a good deal magnified'.

The cuddane or cuithe, depending on whether you favour the Caithness or the Orcadian name for the coalfish, is the most abundant fish of all. These swarm in such numbers that they have acquired an entire vocabulary to distinguish their ages.[64] A 1719 rental for Nethertown on Stroma records that each of the tenants paid part of their rent in thousands of year-old dried cuddanes.[65] The fingerlings - sellags - crowd the geos and creeks in the autumn and were caught in dip nets, called sellag pocks, by the bushel. John Morison, the Canisbay minister, found them 'tender and delicious in the highest degree'.[66] In Birsay and Harray they were sold at 6d per 1000 [67], and in Wick at 1d per 100.[68] Sometimes their oil, extracted from the liver, was used in lamps or even to pay the rent. So many sellags could be landed that the rotting fish were ploughed into the earth as fertiliser. In times of want, they saved many a family from hunger. Sellag fishing was a favourite boyhood pastime for us, with limpets for bait - most effective if chewed before being put on the hook. I don't recall ever eating the sellags we caught, and the local cats were the main benefactors of our efforts.

Larger fish were split and cleaned and hung to dry in the sun, or smoked to preserve them for the winter. The hardening, yellowing triangles were a common sight hanging from the eaves of the houses. Our father treated cod in this way; and poached and smeared with melted butter this fish remains for me a favourite meal.

Line fishermen from other airts, for example Fife and Buchan, frequented Orkney waters in the sixteenth century, paying dues to the local authorities in ling, cod and salt.[69]   89

At the same time, Dutch herring busses ventured into northern waters, but Shetland rather than Orkney was the focus of their fishery. By the end of the eighteenth century, Orcadian and Caithness fishermen were exploiting some local stocks on a commercial basis, as in the case of cod described above. The most valuable species was the lobster. In earlier centuries, these were trapped in circular nets, baited with dead fish and lowered to lie flat on the seabed among the rocks and kelp where the lobsters lived. This technique was probably a very old one: in Canisbay in April 1665 a man was charged by the Kirk Session with taking lobsters and hauling dulse on the Sabbath and, though his gear is not described, it may well have been a circular net.[70]

About sixty boats, each with two men, fished for lobsters in Orkney in the 1790s. James Bremner, the minister of Walls and Flotta, estimated that the annual catch amounted to 120,000 lobsters and thought that it may have been reaching its natural limit.[71] Lobster fishing also took place along the Canisbay shore. The season was in two parts - from March until June, and again from October until December; and the catch was sold, at slightly under 2d per lobster, to Selby & Co. of London and to the Northumberland Fishing Society, who sent smacks with specially made holds for shipping them south live.[72]

The creel, now familiar at every northern harbour, came into widespread use only around 100 years ago to catch lobsters and increasingly crabs.[73] Lobster creels were normally deployed singly, but crab creels were attached at intervals to a standing rope whose ends were buoyed to float at the surface. A typical standing rope was 125 fathoms long and held forty creels. The fathom was a convenient measure, being roughly 6 ft but in reality the length of rope between a man's outstretched arms. A boat inspected the creels daily, moving with the tide along the rope, hauling each creel in turn. In 1935 a new system was introduced, where the creels were put out in groups of 18-25 on shorter standing ropes. A boat would have four to five such flights, or 'flychers' as they are called in

90

Caithness, and the advantage was that when a particular area seemed fished out a flycher could be easily hauled and shifted to a new spot.

Creels were made and repaired in the winter, often by the fireside or in small workshops by each boat's crew. Our house smelled of twine and resin and scorched wood; a red-hot poker plucked from the fire was used to drill holes in the creel frame for the woven net cover. Creel dimensions were more or less standard: 2 ft 3 in. long, 18 in. wide and 15 in. deep, a rectangular trap with a flat stone wired to the base as a sinker. Two funnels, one woven into each side, allowed crabs and lobsters to clamber in but not to leave readily. These entrances are called monkeys, a word I once fancifully thought was a corruption of 'monk's eye' but is more likely to be a long-forgotten borrowing from a Fife word for a type of bait basket. An arrangement of twine in the centre of the creel allowed bait, dead fish - the favourite being skate - to be easily inserted and held.

Many modern creels are made from steel or moulded plastic. Creels in wood and twine had to be dipped in hot tar to prepare them for the sea. The orange buoys and floats marking the position of creels can be spotted on the surface of the sea all around the coast, and along the west side of Hoy the St Ola makes a wide sweep to avoid them.

One fish whose name was once synonymous with wealth and security plays only a small part in the early accounts of the Firth. The herring, 'numerous as the sand on the sea shore,' in the words of James Watson on South Ronaldsay,[74] swam in millions along the north-east of Scotland in August and September, turning the sea oily in their passing and driving the birds into a frenzy of feeding. The standard method of catching them was by the drift net, set like a long curtain in the sea across the path of the shoals when they rose to feed on plankton at night. This technique was not suited to the powerful ebb and flow of the tides in the Firth and no herring fishery developed in its immediate vicinity.[75] Thomas Telford surveyed the Caithness coast on behalf of the British Fisheries Society in 1790.[76] He ignored the Firth, considering it out of the question from   91 the start, and concentrated on the east coast. He settled on Wick as the best place for the Society to invest their money, and that was that. Fishing harbours were to spring up along the east coast at such spots as Whaligoe, a more improbable haven than many on the Firth, but here the sea was kinder.

Stroma herring fishermen operated from Keiss, and the South Ronaldsay boats focused their efforts to the east and north of the island. The village of Herston sprouted from nothing within the space of six years in the 1820s, on the south-western shore of Widewall Bay, a sheltered anchorage customarily used by Baltic trading vessels, to form a complete herring fishing base, with bothies, a cooperage, a pub and slated houses. By the late 1830s, South Ronaldsay was home to almost 250 herring boats.

The Walls and Flotta men landed herring at whatever station was convenient. Burray had five curing stations before the First World War.[77] Stromness was also an important curing centre, but the main Orkney herring fishery developed on Stronsay in the North Isles.[78] In the Firth itself, however, drift nets were occasionally set in the calmer areas such as in Brough Bay; and a few crans of winter herring were landed sometimes at the little haven called the Bocht, tucked into the east side of St John's Point.

At the end of the eighteenth century, Wick was gathering its breath for the increased activity that would drive it in the next sixty years to become the greatest herring port in the world. In the Firth, neither Duncansby nor Gills Bay were 'to be regarded as eligible stations in rough weather', in John Morison's opinion.[79] Thomas Jolly noted that John Knox had been delighted by Brough, where a high stack and a bar of boulders created a natural haven sheltered from all winds except the north-west. Hoping to persuade the improvers to invest in his parish to relieve what he called the 'pernicious servitude' of his flock, Jolly pointed out that vessels would find three clear fathoms in which to anchor at low tide in the eastern part of the bay. He said that the little inlet of Ham, a mile to the east, could also be developed 'at little expense'.[80] Cargo boats of 100 tons used Ham to take on grain, 'even lying there for weeks in the summer season', he argued, although he had to admit that a ridge of gravel across the entrance allowed larger boats to enter or leave only during a spring tide. Ham was developed in the early 1800s but it was never very successful as a port, and today it is utterly ruined. The flagstone piers are shattered, the basin is filled with sediment and one or two wooden posts, white and crumbling with age, stick up to remind the visitor of where hawsers were once tied.

The Firth havens are sited where a natural creek offered a chance to beach and haul a boat. In a few places, the flat flagstone made natural piers, and a few of these 'peels' or pools are still used in their natural state in summer. Most, however, were developed to some extent in the nineteenth century and still show some fascinating relics of their past. Common features are sheds, storehouses and rusting winches. A few have ice-houses set deep into the brae, and at Summerbank at Auckengill you can see the niche on the braehead where a barometer was set last century for the benefit of the fishermen. In most of the harbours the slipway or stone pier has been kept in repair or enlarged and strengthened with concrete, and a yole or two are usually bobbing at their moorings in the summer. In winter boats were hauled and lashed securely when they were not required in noosts, boat-shaped depressions cut into the braes.

Scarfskerry pier, where a Firth ferry used to operate, had for many years a man-made stack at its entrance. On the morning of 10 November 1930, a northerly gale tore the steamer *Linkmoor* from her anchor cable and drove her ashore at the mouth of the little harbour. The crew were promptly rescued by the local rocket company, but attempts to salvage the ship were abandoned and she remained, blocking the entrance for some time, shifting a little with each successive bout of bad weather. Only a 10 foot gap remained at the end of the pier. The wreck was at last blasted apart and removed in pieces in 1935, but the boilers stayed where they were and, until they fell over in the winter of 1993-94, stuck up to the west of the haven, from a distance easily taken for an eroded sandstone stack.

Birds, Whales, Kelp and Grain

The cliffs around the Firth are home to many thousands of seabirds.[81] These avian tenements, cackling with life, have also been a resource exploited by the local people. The shearwater, called locally the lyre, was a favourite food: 'the old ones are little esteemed,' wrote Thomas Jolly, 'but the young ones are reckoned extremely delicate'.[82] Daniel Defoe thought the shearwater an 'extraordinarily fat fowl', the size of a duck and delicious with vinegar and pepper. In 1774, George Low commented on the 'tolerable eating' afforded by young kittiwakes. Patrick Neill hired a man on Hoy in 1804 to catch some for him: two young ones were taken and tasted. 'Very fat, and much relished by the natives,' opined Neill ambiguously. In Orkney, particularly on the cliffs of Hoy, the harvesting of the shearwater seems to have continued for many years after the custom had died out on the Caithness side. Despite the flavour, no one had taken any from the cliffs of Dunnet Head for several years, said Jolly in 1791.[83] On the other hand, Richard Ayton described in 1813 how young men on Hoy lowered themselves on ropes made of twisted hogs' bristles down the rockface to take the nestlings. Ayton also observed that fishermen were partial to a 'marrot', or guillemot. Nestlings were sometimes taken from the Caithness cliffs by lowering lines with fish-hooks for them to swallow.[84]

The Revd John Morison in Canisbay noted that in his parish birds were shot or trapped mainly for sport, a practice he thought 'cruel and unprofitable'.[85] Perhaps this indicates that life on Caithness shore was slightly easier than on the Orkney side, and what had once been done out of necessity had been relegated to the status of recreation. The harvesting of guillemot eggs on Copinsay continued until 1914 but now, in our time, with the exception of a few young braves who tackle the cliffs for gulls' eggs, the seabirds are exploited only by birdwatchers.

Whales played an important, if sporadic, role in the local economy. Large schools passed through Orkney in the late summer and autumn months: 'a regular visitation always exploited by the locals,' noted the *John o'Groat Journal* in 1845.[86] Sometimes a school took itself ashore, as they still do occasionally, but more often they were hunted. A bottle-nosed whale, 27 ft long, was captured and killed at Longhope by men in two small boats in November 1843, the only weapon used being an old sword.[87]

Schools were frequently chased in Scapa Flow. Forty-one whales were taken in Sandwick Bay in South Ronaldsay in the first week of August 1846.[88] When a large school of about 600 was spotted in Scapa Bay early one morning in the same month, the cry of 'Whales! Whales!' went from house to house until a fleet of boats set off in pursuit; after a long chase, the whales 'made off towards Flotta, and were lost sight of'. On the Caithness side, the hunting of whales seems to have been less common; occasionally, as at Thurso in June 1899, a school would be driven ashore and killed,[89] and a dozen boats chased a solitary wretched whale in Wick Bay in July 1848.[90]

But this source of meat and oil was, like everything else won from the sea, not to be exploited with impunity. In 1845, thirty boats chased a group of whales in Scapa Flow and, although several were harpooned, strong winds impeded the hunters. One lanced whale, probably by diving and rising, caused three boats to collide. The crews were thrown into the sea: the harpoon rope caught around the leg of John Spence, the son of a watchmaker, and dragged him down to his death.[91] These large sea mammals are no longer hunted locally. In 1986, a school of pilot whales came ashore on the island of Sanday, and the people put in a considerable effort to save them from dying on the beach.[92]

Little is known in detail about the biology of sea mammals in northern waters, but a total of seventeen

95

species have been recorded.[93] Only six of these are in any degree common, the most frequently seen being the porpoise (*Phocaena phocaena*). Leaping dolphins are most likely to be either *Lagenorhynchus albirostris* or *L. acutus*. Risso's dolphin (*Grampus griseus*), the killer whale (*Orcinus orca*) and the pilot whale or caaing whale, the one that was hunted (*Globicephala melaena*) make up the half-dozen. Dolphins, in particular, seem to show some fondness for rough water.[94]

Both grey and common seals are found in the vicinity of the Firth. The grey seal (*Halichoerus grypus*) is abundant: surveys in the late 1980s by the Sea Mammal Research Unit, Cambridge, discovered that the population in Orkney was increasing and had surpassed 70,000.[95] The common seal (*Phoca vitulina*) is rarer, its numbers in the same area being about 7000. Both species are now protected, although in the past they were exploited for fur, meat and oil.[96]

Another marine resource formed for a time the raw material for a substantial rural industry. Kelp, or what we in Caithness would call waar, is rich in iodine, soda and potash, extracted from the ash left after burning the raw weed. This activity began in Stronsay as early as 1722, but it was not until the Napoleonic wars denied British industry access to continental sources for important chemicals that the harvesting of kelp boomed.

George Barry described how it was done. At low tide the living weed was cut from the rocks with sickles and allowed to dry in the sun before being burnt. The kilns were rough circles of stone four or five feet in diameter, and up to six hundredweight of kelp could be burned at one time. The cold ashes formed a dark-blue or white, rock-hard mass.

July saw the height of the season, when nearly 3000 young people were employed, earning from 30 shillings to £3 for each ton produced. The best kelp had an acrid taste and gave off a strong smell of sulphur. At first, the burning was not liked. Barry said:

[The people] were certain that the suffocating smoke ... would sicken or kill every species of fish on the coast, or drive them into the ocean far beyond the reach of the fishermen; blast the corn and the grass on their farms; introduce diseases of various kinds; and smite with barrenness their sheep, horses and cattle, and even their own families.

The amounts of ash produced were low in the early years but, as the demand grew and the price rose to over £2 per ton, production reached a value of £2000 per year. From 1770 to 1778, when the price was over £5 per ton, production topped £10,000 per year. The price was still rising in 1800 when Barry was writing. More seems to have been produced in Orkney than in Caithness. Canisbay was yielding about 100 tons a year in the 1790s, Dunnet only about twenty.[97]

Smoky, smelly and dirty the burning of kelp may have been but it needed little skill and brought in ready money while the boom lasted. Patrick Neill, the secretary of the Edinburgh Natural History Society, noted on his tour of Orkney in 1806 that 'every consideration is sacrificed to kelp' to the neglect of agriculture. Many Orkney lairds and merchants grew very rich on the profits of kelp and enjoyed for a time lives of conspicuous consumption in their Kirkwall townhouses, epitomised by Esther Richan who won an argument over who could eat the most expensive breakfast by swallowing a £50 note placed between two slices of bread and butter.[98] The first kelp boom ended in the 1830s, but the growing popularity of iodine as an antiseptic after the 1840s gave a boost to the harvesting of the weed and, although it never again reached the economic heights of the early years, production lingered on into this century.

Lairds on the Caithness shore of the Firth also indulged in an extravagant mode of life in the eighteenth century; but in their case the furnishings, fine wines, books and expensive clothes were paid for from the profits of trade in grain. Victual, as it was called, was shipped from the small   97 harbours on a variety of coastal traders; Staxigoe was for a long time the main port.[99]

Before the present road and rail network developed across the country in the late Victorian period, the bulk of heavy goods was carried by sea; and in Orkney of course, all the islands of the archipelago still depend on seaborne commerce. In the days of sail, the coastal traders forested the harbours with their masts and spars. They came in a variety of sizes, from smacks which could carry up to 30 tons of cargo to three-masted barques of 500 tons; and in between were ketches, sloops, schooners, brigs and brigantines. A smack cost less than £300 in the 1870s, and a fifie could be converted from herring fishing to cargo carrying for less than £100.[100]

The cargoes were as varied as the vessels. Holds were filled with all manner of goods in barrels, bales and boxes. The harbours exported kelp and grain as mentioned above, and from the early 1800s barrels of salt herring and flagstones were carried to all the ports of Europe. In the middle of the century cattle were prominent on the Orkney export list. The home-based trading fleets grew in size, competing with vessels from other ports, and also provided a training ground for the seafaring life that many Orcadians and Caithnessians were to follow to win distinction around the world.

Among the earliest records of island trading vessels is the boat built at Kirkwall for two Stronsay men in 1662: her keel was 30 ft and she carried perhaps seven tons of cargo, and she was typical of the 'great boats' that traded to Shetland and Norway.[101] Thurso had sixteen trading vessels in 1798,[102] and two brigs and four sloops operated from Stromness in 1794.[103] The size of the home fleets peaked in the mid-1800s: seventy-eight ships, most of them schooners, were registered in Wick in 1878,[104] and twenty-two were registered at Kirkwall in 1857.[105]

Evading the Press Gang

In February 1805, John Bews, the son of a farmer in Stenness, met a man called George Davidson near the Brig o' Waithe, a few miles from Stromness where the fresh waters of the Loch of Stenness meet the sea. Davidson said he was the mate of the *Leviathan*, a whaler bound for the Davis Straits, and asked if Bews wanted to sign on. The farmer's son, who later swore he had never been to sea in his life, said he didn't know.[106]

James Anderson overheard this. He had a carpentry business in Stromness and, although no seaman, he had been on a ship for a month or so five years before. He asked Davidson what were the wages.

'Two pound a month and a shilling for each of you,' was the reply.

Anderson said that he and Bews would think about it and would let Davidson know later. In the evening, the three men met again in Stromness. But this time Davidson was not alone. He ordered Bews and Anderson to be seized and taken aboard the naval tender *Mary*. Davidson served on no whaling ship; his duty was more sinister - he was the leader of a press gang.

Press gang stories abound in Orkney. W.R. Mackintosh collected many for his book *Around the Orkney Peat-Fires* nearly a century after the events they recall, an indication of how deeply burned into the folk-consciousness was this threat to freedom. The press gang seems to have been less active on the Caithness shore, although Neil Gunn used the taking of fishermen for his opening in *The Silver Darlings* (1941), his epic novel of the herring boom.

Many of the stories are preserved only in folklore. In contrast, the case of John Bews is given in Admiralty correspondence, where I came across it one day in the Public Record Office.

During the Napoleonic Wars, the Royal Navy expanded considerably to meet the threat from the combined French and Spanish fleets.[107] The ships of the line carried very large crews to man the guns and work the sails during battle: the *Victory*, Nelson's flagship, had 850 men on board, and at Trafalgar there were two other ships of her size, each with 100 guns, and another twenty-seven ships with seventy-four guns apiece. There were two Caithness men and two Orkney men in the crew of the *Victory* in 1805.[108] Interestingly, but for unknown reasons, the two Caithness men were volunteers, the two Orcadians pressed men.

Life in the Royal Navy was harsh, with strict discipline.[109] The living space allowed to ordinary seamen barely gave each enough room to hang a hammock. The pay - £1 3s 6d a month, if and when paid - was poor in comparison with opportunities elsewhere. Disease accounted for more deaths than battle. Mutinies broke out when the men were driven beyond what they could thole: in the most notorious of these, the crew of the frigate HMS *Hermione*, which included William Moncrieff from Orkney, murdered their captain and several officers in 1797.[110] Sailors preferred to go to sea in the merchant service or to the Greenland fishing, and volunteers never came forward in sufficient numbers to fill the Navy's muster rolls. The press gang resorted occasionally to desperate measures and were known to stop and seize men from vessels at sea. In June 1814, two apprentices, released after capture by an American privateer, landed in Orkney; they had little time to enjoy the air of freedom, as they were promptly taken by the press gang.[111]

Among Rear-Admiral Vashon's duties at Leith was recruitment. The Quota Acts of 1795 had tried to put some order into the unjust chaos of impressment; under the Acts, public officials in each county and parish were required to provide a certain number of men for the Fleet. Vashon wrote to Sheriff Robert Nicolson in Kirkwall in April 1805 to remind him that Orkney's quota had not been filled.

Only a few weeks before, Nicolson had investigated the cases of John Bews, James Anderson and three others whom Davidson had dragged into the Navy. Lieutenant

Laurence Smith, the captain of the recruiting tender *Mary*, had been forced to bring the five men before Nicolson, after they had attracted the Sheriff's attention with a written petition.

Bews told the Sheriff about the fateful meeting near the Brig o' Waithe and swore 'as he shall answer to God' that his account was true. Anderson and the other three men also testified. One of the three was John Oman. He had never been to sea, he said, and was the sole support of his widowed mother, Isobel Thomson; also, he had a brother already serving in the Navy. William Chalmers likewise swore that he was the only son and only support of a bedridden widow and had two brothers already in the Navy. 'During last season,' he said, 'when almost famine raged in Orkney,' necessity had forced him to join the Greenland fishery to earn a few shillings - this had been the only time he had been to sea. The last man, George Loutit, had similarly been compelled to sail to Greenland to make a living. Nicolson ordered that all five men should be set at liberty.

Now Vashon was writing to the Sheriff with a guarded rebuke. Nicolson summoned what is called in the correspondence 'a meeting of gentlemen' to consider a reply. A Mr Fatheringham presented a list of ninety-seven men already furnished to the Navy and to whom bounties had been paid by the county, and added that several others had been rejected for service.

The gentlemen agreed to write to Admiral Vashon to say that no fixed quota of men had been given for Orkney but that they had been doing what they could to fulfil their duty. They had, for example, offered the largest bounties in Scotland, '5 guineas for the first 100 men who should volunteer', and had afterwards resolved to continue giving this sum to subsequent recruits. However, few had come forward in response to the official advertising. 'Anxious to raise the 100 at least', the gentlemen had surveyed Orkney parish by parish and, resorting to what was nothing other than a press gang of their own, had forcibly enlisted men. 'Many were got in this way,' they wrote, but they do not go into detail. The Admiralty correspondence, however, does - at least in some cases. For example, in 1804 Robert Tulloh was compelled by the bailies to enlist; he was discharged from the Navy almost at once when it was found he had a 'fatal disease' and 'imbecility of mind'. Orkney was not alone in seeing the quota as a convenient way of getting rid of undesirables. Vashon complained that the Orkney bailies were forwarding men for naval service after screening out the good seamen to be employed in their private interests, and at one stage wrote to the Lord Advocate asking if the bailies could be prosecuted for their duplicity.

In the wake of the Bews case, Vashon concluded that the authorities in Orkney were disposed to oppose Lieutenant Smith's press gang. In two months the *Mary* had come away with only eleven recruits. Vashon thought that James Anderson and George Loutit should not have been released, and informed the Admiralty in London of his opinion. The *Mary* was withdrawn from the Orkney station and by the following October was in Shetland trying to recruit men from the Greenland fishing fleet.

The northern islands were a great attraction to the press gang. The authorities knew of the inhabitants' great experience of the sea - it is often commented on. Stromness and Lerwick were favoured watering and provisioning ports for ships sailing to the Greenland fisheries and to Hudson's Bay, and Kirkwall and many smaller havens also had their complements of skilled seamen. However, virtually all of them preferred to sail in any ship but a naval one.

It was not unknown for vessels returning from Greenland to discharge their complement of Orkneymen along the north Sutherland coasts, even as far west as Cape Wrath, so that they could make their own way home with a better chance of evading the waiting Navy. The press gang officers were alive to this ruse, however, and on occasion Lieutenant Gourlay, a zealous recruiter who served in northern waters for some years, took his naval cutter west to intercept the Greenland ships. There are stories of seamen taking hastily to small boats and of skippers coming to blows with the Navy to protect their companies.

Once in Orkney, men eligible to be pressed had still to exercise extreme care and lie low, hiding in outhouses, cellars, hollowed-out peatstacks, anywhere to avoid detection while the press gang was locally active. Two men hid in a cave on Houton Head in 1803.[112] Evasion was all the more difficult if the searchers were local constables who knew whom they were looking for. Fights were frequent and on more than one occasion a bridegroom was hauled away from a wedding to serve His Majesty.

Women figure prominently in the war of wits with the press gang. For example, when George Firth of Finstown reached Stromness in a whaler, his mother met him on board, disguised him as an old woman with his head wrapped in a shawl supposedly for toothache, and led him safely home.[113] Quick-witted men could resort to pretence themselves: taken while in Flotta on some errand, Walter Rosie of Stroma began to act the fool and thwarted all attempts by his captors to get him to co-operate; when a shilling, the acceptance of which could have technically sealed his fate, was pressed into his hand and he was asked what he would do with it, he said it was a grand flat stone and threw it into the sea like a child to make it skip a few times before it sank. He was released as an imbecile.[114]

Vashon continued in his attempts to recruit them. In March 1806, he wrote to the Admiralty to suggest that, as it had been three years since a demand had been made on fishermen and those in other trades officially exempt from the attentions of the press gang, it was reasonable to ask for another quota of recruits. He complained about men 'skulking under the cloak of being Sea Fencibles'; these were locally recruited corps charged with defending the coast in case of invasion, a kind of Home Guard, and the Admiral obviously thought that many joined to acquire immunity from serving in the Navy. He also wanted a lugger so that recruits could be speedily taken south before they could change their minds about enlisting. Vashon 103 was told that it was impossible to estimate accurately how many fishermen there were in the north but that they could be asked to provide one-sixth of their number for naval service. The Admiralty replied to say that one in ten should be the quota for Scottish fishermen. Vashon stuck to his opinion that one in six was the right number.

In May 1806 Vashon ordered the *Mary* north again to Orkney to obtain 100 men but had to remind her new commander, Lieutenant Walter Scott, that fishermen were exempt. The Orkney and Shetland landlords who had extensive sea-fishing interests were pleased with this exemption, as it protected their labour force; but they had no scruples about the pressing of men from the Greenland fishery, whose better wages were drawing men from their own employ.

Lieutenant Scott waited in Shetland for the return of the Greenland boats and in August sailed back to Leith with 100 pressed men. Vashon decided, after this successful outing, to suspend the press for a while to let any fuss die down.

In October 1806, Lieutenant Gourlay wrote to Vashon from Thurso to complain that 'none of the men whom the county promised to give to the Navy on condition of its fishermen being exempt from impress' was ready, although young men 'fit for service' were available. Gourlay pressed 'two fine young fellows' despite their Fencible protection.

Tired of the foot-dragging local authorities, Vashon ordered Gourlay to take such 'fishermen as he may chance to fall in with' as their protections were bogus. But, in the corner of Vashon's letter copying his orders to Gourlay to the Admiralty, there is an anonymous note that says 'Direct him to discharge these men'. London thought Gourlay had no grounds to detain protected men. We do not know who the 'two fine young fellows' were or whether they were released. By the end of the summer, Gourlay had 'collected' forty-five men.

The correspondence between Leith and London charts the continual battle the Navy had with other seafarers over impressment. Vashon lamented the contemptuous and disrespectful attitudes of merchant skippers and argued against withdrawing the press gang because it upset local landlords.

One of Vashon's successors, Vice-Admiral Otway, had to contend with the same problems. In 1812 Otway had the Lord Advocate ask the Lords Lieutenant of the East Coast counties to put 'their utmost exertions' into recruitment and appealed to the Admiralty for more staff, to serve under Captain Gourlay's direction. Gourlay's zeal obviously had not stood in way of his promotion. His impressment drive, however, suffered for a time from the reluctance of the Treasury to provide funds to hire more boats but after a few months Otway could record that the brig *Bracken* had sailed for Wick to Gourlay's assistance.

Impressment virtually ceased at the end of the Napoleonic Wars in 1815. The Royal Navy shrank rapidly in size, and thousands of men were released from service. In the years that followed, a number of legal reforms led to the abandoning of the press gang as a means of recruitment, and gentler techniques of persuasion were in use by the mid-1800s, with naval officers touring the coast to speak at public meetings and call for volunteers. Some will argue that impressment was not forgotten but was renamed conscription.

Tiderip

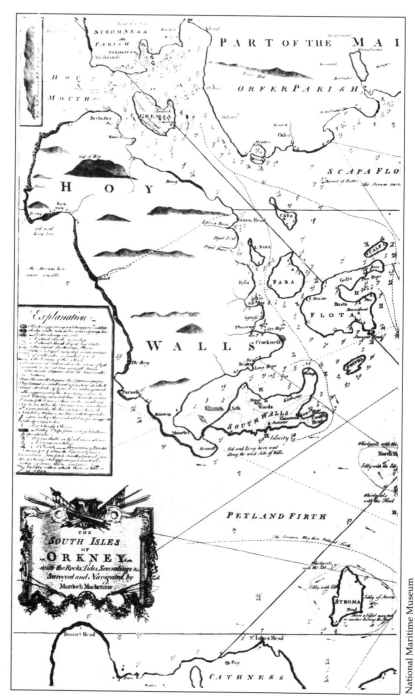

The Pentland Firth by Murdoch Mackenzie, 1749

A Man of Herculean Frame

A traveller crossing the Firth one day in 1825 may have been granted an astonishing sight. He would have seen a giant raft, 450 feet long, laboriously edging south at three miles an hour from Orkney to Caithness under seemingly tiny sails on sheer poles. A closer look would have revealed the crew working at hand-cranked paddles and among them a tall, well-built man, urging his crew to greater exertion. This would have been James Bremner, one of the great engineers of his day.[1]

The son of a soldier, Bremner was born in a cottage at Stain, a few hundred yards from my own birthplace. He would have been two years old when John Knox tramped to Duncansby and lamented on the lack of ship-repair facilities around the northern coast. Before he died, Bremner had altered the Caithness shore, salvaging ships by his own ingenious means and building many small harbours.

After some education in the village school at Keiss, he was apprenticed in 1798 to the shipbuilding firm of Robert Steele & Sons in Greenock where at one time he worked on the extensive improvements to Greenock harbour. Finally free of his indentures, he made two voyages to America and considered setting up business as a shipbuilder at Pictou. Fortunately for Caithness, some friends persuaded him to start at Wick instead.

This was at the time when the herring fishing was bringing hitherto unknown prosperity and opportunity to the area. Bremner opened his shipyard at the north-west corner of the new harbour at Wick. He was to build fifty-six vessels there; by 1841, he was employing sixty men and it has been estimated that he earned nearly £190,000 from this activity.

The wealthy, genial engineer is better remembered, however, for his harbour building and salvage operations. In 1806 he assisted George Burn to construct the pier of the North Harbour at Wick, and went on to build harbours at Keiss, Ham, Castlehill, Sarclet and Lossiemouth, to list a few; and in all these operations he devised unusual ways to defeat the erosive power of the tide on half-finished masonry. Blocks of dressed stone, sometimes weighing 40 tons, were carried to the sites by skilful flotation techniques - Bremner was an expert at using the sea to combat the sea.

He established the principle of laying the blocks in a vertical rather than a horizontal fashion so that the explosive effect of air compressed before a rushing wave was channelled harmlessly upward. Some of his walls stand to this day. The outer wall of the north quay at Keiss is a splendid example of his work; and the aesthetic appearance of the stonework cannot be matched by the grey, stolid concrete with which repairs have been done this century.

Bremner started the construction of Keiss harbour in 1818, but in 1821 work stopped when the owner of the estate, Kenneth Macleay, fell ill and also ran out of money. Work resumed in 1833 after the estate obtained some government assistance, and in December 1835 the trustees were pleased to write:

> We beg to state, that as Engineer and Contractor for the erection of the Harbour of Keiss, which was finished last year, you implemented your contract in a very perfect manner, and executed the whole work to our entire satisfaction ...
> Wm Horne
> Dond Horne.[2]

Bremner's greatest fame came from rescuing ships or their cargoes. His raft was his way of recovering the 40,000 feet of timber that comprised the cargo of the *Orion* which went ashore at Water Sound between Burray and South Ronaldsay. When the cargo was offered for sale, Bremner stuffed £1500 in his pockets and crossed the Firth in a yole to claim his purchase. The return crossing was not trouble-free: the ebb tide caught the ungainly raft north of

110

Duncansby Head and dragged it westward, but Bremner let it go until the flood tide pushed it back again on course - the crossing involved, he estimated, an actual distance of 100 miles.

In his *Treatise on the Planning and Construction of Harbours*, published in 1845, Bremner claimed to have salvaged 211 sailing vessels. His *Treatise* is written in an elaborate, classical style that seems untypical of the man. It has been said that he was sometimes slow and awkward in speech, although not when excited by some project, and it may have been an unpleasant labour for him to resort to inkpot and paper. However, he was not shy of listing his achievements, given , he says, 'to obviate the imputation of conceit and arrogance for thus intruding on public attention, the results of his application to subjects not precisely pertinent to his own profession', and, after his success with the *Great Britain*, he sent a copy of his book to Prince Albert.

Joseph Mitchell, the apprentice and protégé of Thomas Telford, met Bremner in June 1838. Mitchell was a lively and talented engineer - by the time he was twenty-five, he was earning £1000 a year in salaries and fees - and he recognised in the Wick shipbuilder a kindred spirit. They were both men of technology, of the new breed who were driving roads through wild country or thrusting out harbours on stormy coasts.

'Bremner was a man of herculean frame and undaunted courage,' recalled Mitchell in his chatty memoirs.[3] 'I do not think he comprehended what fear was, and he seemed to have the power of inspiring the same courage among the work people he employed.'

Bremner seems also to have been open-handed with his wealth. Mitchell reports that he used to accommodate 'for months' seamen who had lost their ships, and that he was 'very amusing, making friends with everyone he meets by his kindly and rattling manner and the liberality of his payments'.

Mitchell wrote to Bremner in 1834 from Inverness to encourage him to bid for the Sarclet harbour contract. 111

Twice - in 1829 and 1830 - attempts to finish a haven at this herring station had been thwarted by the sea's pounding. Bremner seems to have been reluctant to take it on but, once persuaded, he set to work with his customary panache. He invented a crane with an extending jib that could operate from beyond the reach of the sea; and he went along with the workmen on the barges transporting the building material through dangerous roosts. By the summer of 1836 the main breakwater of the new harbour was securely in place.

Grateful shipowners often wrote to Bremner congratulating him for his efforts in salvaging their vessels. In 1842, letters from Hull, Greenock, Newcastle, Aberdeen and Sunderland arrived at Lloyd's in London recommending Bremner for the post of Lloyd's Agent in Thurso. In one, William Sturrock, the manager of the Dundee Marine Insurance Co., described him as a 'man of strong nerve, great intrepidity and uncommon activity and perseverance'; Sturrock added that he was also 'possessed of means'.

Bremner's triumph came in 1846. During his lifetime great advances had taken place in marine technology: the paddle steamer had chugged into prominence and had then been superseded by propeller-driven ships; steel rigging had been patented; and the first iron ships had splashed like ugly ducklings from the builders' yards.

One of these, the *SS Great Britain*, the brainchild of Isambard Kingdom Brunel, was launched at Bristol on 19 July 1843.[4] Before a month had passed, she had made the first screw-driven crossing of the Atlantic - Liverpool to New York in a little over fourteen days. With her slim, dark hull and the thin smokestack poking up among her five elegant masts, she was a technological triumph. But on a damp evening in September 1846, she struck the beach in Dundrum Bay near Belfast and was gripped fast in sand and gravel.

Her owners, the Great Western Steamship Company, were appalled and began attempts to salvage her. James Bremner's eldest son, Alexander, was invited to assist. He built a breakwater around the stranded ship but a gale tore it away. A winter passed. Finally, in May 1847, Brunel recommended that his Board of Directors should ask Bremner senior to help.

Bremner hurried to Belfast. He devised elaborate systems of pulleys and weights to lift the ship and free the hull from the sand that held her. The lifting process was slow but, inch by inch, the *Great Britain* came clear of her bed. After six weeks, the bow had been raised 9 ft. Bremner decided to try to refloat her at the next spring tide. The 'holed saucepan' was patched and, by 29 July, the whole bottom had been repaired. Just before noon on 27 August, the *Great Britain* moved free from the beach and was towed to a berth in the Coburg Dock, Liverpool.[5] (The *Great Britain* has proved herself a survivor. In 1937 she was beached again at Sparrow Cove in the Falklands, where she lay, a rusty hulk, until 1970 when she was rescued and taken back to her home port of Bristol for a lengthy restoration and an uneventful retirement.)

The salvaging of the pride of Britain's mercantile fleet made Bremner a hero. Although he reached Wick at six o'clock on the morning of 11 September aboard the steamer *Queen*, the town was ready with flags and cannon to celebrate his triumph.

He died in August 1856, aged seventy-two, three months after the death of his wife. He went for his customary daily walk and retired to bed at 9.30 pm as usual. Later he complained of feeling unwell and at 11 pm he suffered his final, fatal stroke. A memorial to him stands above the harbour at Wick.

Freets

There is a belief in seafaring circles that a caul has the power to protect from drowning and, in the past, seamen would advertise to get one. For those unfamiliar with this infrequent biological extra, the caul is a shred of one of the membranes surrounding the foetus in the womb that attaches itself harmlessly to the head. I was born with a caul. The old neighbour woman who assisted at my birth was delighted, and our father carried a piece of my caul in the back of his pocket watch. I was never allowed to see it, as this would be unlucky, and for all I know this bit of me is still in his watch. For reasons I cannot be rational about, I don't want to see it now - just in case ....

To cope with the dangers of their profession, to try to make some sense of their chancy world, fishermen observed a gamut of superstitions - or freets.[6] These sets of beliefs and little rituals were often different from those of landsfolk. Certain words and subjects were taboo - hare, pig, salmon - and it was a foolhardy man who would utter them at sea. Whistling was forbidden, lest it summon up the wind; our father laughed at many of these superstitions, but even he disliked anyone whistling in the house.

Freet is a form of the word 'fruit', and originally the word meant the spirit or essence of something good that was stolen by witchcraft - a spell could take the freet from milk, for example, and curdle it. The word expanded in time to cover superstitions in general. Ministers and women were the subjects of several freets. Those about ministers and priests can be traced back to the Mediterranean and to Jonah, some claim. The freets about women probably have a very ancient ancestry. It was bad luck, for example, to meet on your way to the sea a woman with flat feet or a squint eye, or a married woman suspected of being barren. Cautious fishermen would go out of their way to avoid such a woman, or even command her to stay away from them; to be on the safe side, really superstitious fishermen avoided women entirely on the way to the sea. One man once asked my grandmother to leave the road so that he could make his way to his boat. A woman's behaviour while her husband was at sea was also important, e.g. blowing loose meal off her baking or allowing oatcakes to burn brought bad luck, and the tossing of fishbones into the fire would make fish scarce.[7]

Such freets were not confined to Caithness or Orkney fishermen. Some were very localised but others were kept religiously along the whole Scottish coast; a few, such as the belief that Friday, the day of the Crucifixion, is unlucky, are international. For instance, there is the curious case of the jinxed yole, the *Rival*, built in Stroma in 1918. This boat was sailed to its first owners in Keiss on a Friday, and ever after was looked on with such suspicion that it is reported she spent more time idle than at sea.[8]

Local variation in freets could lead the men of one village to scorn those of the next for being 'queer' and play tricks on them: the leaving of a pig's tail in a net could drive the target of the prank into trancelike anger. Whether by accident or design, a hare's foot once found its way into a herring net belonging to some Wick fishermen; the fishermen had just arrived in Stornoway when it was found, having sailed all the way from the East Coast, but they immediately packed their gear and returned home.[9]

I am told that the late James Rosie of Swona always turned his boat in an anti-clockwise direction, just to annoy fishermen who felt that only turning clockwise, or with the sun, was lucky. He was challenging an old belief; a 1798 guide to Orkney describes how seamen 'would reckon themselves in the most imminent danger were they, by accident, to turn their boat in opposition to the sun's course'.[10]

That some fishermen have always shown a cavalier attitude to the spirit world is exemplified also in the following extract from the Canisbay Kirk Session records for 23 May 1655: 'John Gills being at sea, the rest of the boat getting fishe and not he, Did throw over his hook, saying, "If thou slay not in God's name, slay in ye devill's name." ' This blasphemy earned Gills the wearing of sackcloth and a spell in the jougs.[11]

The hare features commonly in witch tales, and this points to sea freets having their origins in more   115 widespread beliefs in witchcraft and the occult. George Sutherland's collection of north folktales tells of Bell o' Brims, a witch who lived near Holborn Head, who habitually crossed the Firth to Orkney on the back of an obliging crab and could raise storms to discomfort an enemy.[12] Daniel Defoe dismissed the notion that Stroma was haunted by witches and spirits who drew ships to the rocks; it seems unlikely that many of the locals would have shared his derision. That the minister, the agent of the kirk, should be included in a gallery of the familiars of another power is not surprising; any boat with a clergyman aboard would form an ideal target for the devil. And thereby, as they say, hangs a little tale. Once, the Free Kirk minister in our village asked our father cautiously if he could go to sea with them on a fishing trip; our father was a religious man in his own way and readily assented, but no one caught a thing that evening, much to the minister's chagrin and everyone else's amusement.

Like so much else, freets are rare now and there are young fishermen who have never heard of them. Others, more canny, won't admit they know them but keep their own counsel. Religious feeling has also been very strong among many sections of the fishing community. There was an evangelical revival in 1860, when it was common to hear herring fishermen sing hymns and psalms as they tended the drift-nets, and another in 1921. Both began along the Buchan coast and spread across the Moray Firth to Caithness and Orkney. The Royal National Mission to Deep Sea Fishermen, founded in 1881 to bring both physical and spiritual comfort to crews, has always been highly respected.

The fishermen had an immense practical knowledge of sea-life; when I was studying marine biology, I was frequently surprised to learn what they knew. Once, when I was talking about plankton, a fisherman said 'Oh, you mean breed.' *Breed* is the Caithness form of *brit*, an obscure English word not in most dictionaries, although Herman Melville uses it in *Moby Dick*.[13]

116

Some fishermen divided the marine fauna into useful species and vermin, much as a farmer or gamekeeper might classify land creatures; and some sea creatures were credited with special powers. Stories about the selkie abound along the northern Atlantic seaboard. They have in common the belief that seals can shed their skins, adopt human form and walk freely on land, a belief that is not so surprising to anyone who has spent time secretly observing seals: they bark, cough and wail with the most eerie, human likeness. The present tourist empathy for seals seems a spiritless echo of old folk beliefs.[14]

Some birds embodied evil forces. John Horne recorded in the 1870s how John Sinclair of Stroma thought it was a waste of time to try for herring because, every night when he went to collect his net, on it sat 'the ould enemy' in the shape of a guillemot, and it was useless to fight such a curse.[16]

Tucked under the cliffs of Dwarwick Head at Dunnet is a cave where a mermaid is reputed to dwell. Our uncles often spoke of the place: one day, during an exceptionally low spring tide, we clambered along the foot of the rocks to the cave entrance and found a mute, dark opening disappearing into the sandstone. Mermaids have been around for a long time - they are carved on door columns at St Magnus Cathedral, Kirkwall. Eliza Mackay, the daughter of the minister of Reay, caused a stir in May 1809 when she claimed that with her cousin and others she had seen one on the shore. The 'forehead, nose and chin were white ... the hair thick and long, of a green and oily cast,' said Eliza, adding that the creature found its hair a nuisance, as the sea kept washing the long locks over its face. She got close enough to ascertain that the mermaid's fingers were unwebbed. Her claims were regarded as a hoax.[16]

At the head of the bay at Burwick on South Ronaldsay, above the curving shingle beach, stands Ladykirk. It is a long, low church with crowstepped gables and a stumpy bell-tower on the west gablehead, and in summer the fields behind it are bright with buttercups. This site has been for centuries a landing-place for travellers crossing to and from Orkney, and in the vestry of the church can be found a stone slab associated with miraculous journeys. The slab resembles a short surfboard, and bears the impression of two human feet. Many tales have arisen to explain its existence. One tells how an exiled Gaul escaped from his sinking ship by hitching a ride on the back of a sea monster; when they arrived safely at Burwick, the Gaul built a church and the monster became petrified in a new religious duty. Another story is that the stone helped St Magnus to speed news to Orkney of the victory of Bannockburn. The probable true purpose of the stone is equally fascinating - it was an inauguration or coronation stone for Pictish rulers.

The fact that the sea from time to time can throw into our ken such obscure, strange creatures as the sunfish or the giant squid probably lies behind the widespread belief in sea serpents. The really weird creatures that make science fiction creations look mundane generally are microscopic, but a few, such as the oarfish (*Regelecus*), or the 'king of the herring', as it is sometimes called, can reach very large sizes. A deep-water species that can grow to 20 ft or more in length, the elongated ribbonfish fits the popular image of the sea serpent very well and could be what some fishermen see and report as a sea serpent. In March 1895, the crew of the Banff fishing boat *Campbells* spotted what they took to be a derelict boat floating off Noss Head. When they came close, however, the mysterious object 'suddenly rose in wavy folds above the surface of the water, its head and tail... remaining below. It appeared to be fully half a mile long, eight enormous fins being seen, each about the size of a large boat's mizzen sail.' The fishermen did not stay to make a closer look.

Another account of the sighting of a monster, in 1910 in the vicinity of the Head of Work, was recorded by the late Bill Hutchison.[17]

The same man has described another monster washed ashore at Deepdale on the eastern side of Scapa Flow in

1942: he said that it looked like a similar or younger version of the 1910 animal and that it had a grey, seal-like body, some 20 feet overall, with a head like a 'Shetland pony without ears' and two large flippers on the tail. Mr Hutchison cut off a chunk of the tail to keep but it decayed to a jelly and, in his own words, was 'no use at all'.

The people along the shores of the Firth live with the constant presence of the sea: it shapes their consciousness and their world-view. The exile can grow homesick for the roaring of the Men of Mey, or long to see the black silhouette of Hoy as a summer sun slips redly into the western ocean. Like life itself, the sea brings good and bad fortune; like life, it cannot be escaped but has to be endured, to be made the best of.

In the past it provided food, oil for lamps, sealskins, feathers; the tide left strange treasures tangled in the ware, and the horizon threw up sails promising new things and unusual knowledge of faraway places. The *John o'Groat Journal* noted in September 1880 that no fewer than eleven pulpits in Caithness were said to be constructed from wooden wreckage and that sometimes no attempt was made to disguise this, the names of the wrecked vessels still being visible on the wood.[18] Robert Stevenson, the lighthouse engineer, noted an Orkney field fenced with salvaged cedar and mahogany, and learned of one island where the folk were having claret with their porridge.[19] Wrecks were regarded as godsends, and if God was tardy in sending one, then ministers such as the Revd John Gerard in the 1830s would remind Him with a prayer: 'No juist asking Thee to send a ship but if Thou art sending a ship be sure to send it to the puir island of Sanday.'[20]

In 1771 a Liverpool vessel, the *John*, was wrecked at Reay.[21] The local people helped themselves to the cargo but James Hogg, a farmer and an incomer, instigated a search for the plunder, an observance of the law that turned the people against him. A few tried hard to set fire to his home and finally he was forced to emigrate. There is, however, no evidence that folk ever indulged in luring ships deliberately to an untimely doom. John Knox referred in 1786 to a 'humanity and strict regard to justice' among the people of Caithness and Sutherland 'where shipwrecks are most frequent'. In the 1600s, the folk on South Ronaldsay held collections to assist shipwrecked mariners,[22] and the Canisbay Kirk Session collected two shillings sterling to aid twenty-four wrecked Dutchmen in Orkney 'and sixpence to one to guid them' in 1665.[23] When a westbound fishing boat was lost off Scarfskerry in September 1840 and two bodies were washed ashore, the sum of £4 found in the pocket of one of the drowned men, a Highlander, was forwarded to the minister in Lochbroom, the boat's destination, probably because the finders were well aware that the money had been intended to see a poor family through the winter.[24] Once lifeboats began to operate on the coast, the courage of their crews became legendary.

For all that, people took the utmost advantage of any wrecked vessel, and the pursuit of plunder could blind folk. Richard Ayton recorded with horror one story that shows this. In November 1815, the *Albion* of Blyth was driven ashore between Rackwick and the Old Man of Hoy. Two survivors were on board - one lying on the quarterdeck, the other tied to the rigging. The quarterdeck man was found by two fishermen from Rackwick who climbed down a geo to the ship; he had been stricken speechless by his ordeal and could not communicate with his rescuers. The fishermen searched the ship for all they could carry off her and, drunk on pilfered rum, they then dragged the survivor up the cliff after them, only to leave him on a shelf of rock while they continued their spree. It was a bitterly cold night, wild with wind. In the morning the fishermen recovered to find that the man they had rescued had perished during the darkness. Then, they noticed the man tied to the rigging: he too was dead but his body was still warm.

When an Aberdeen brig, aptly named the *Favourite*, was wrecked at Duncansby in May 1857, she was found to be outward bound to the Arabian Gulf with two years'

provisions aboard.[25] 'We regret to say,' reported the
Inverness Advertiser pompously, 'that considerable pecula-
tion of the stores has taken place ... wine, beef, tobacco
and even a living pig have suddenly disappeared.' *The
Scotsman* called for sharp punishment in 1880 when locals
pillaged the barque *Poolscar*, ashore in Orkney; on that occasion, wine bottles were said to have been hidden in peat
stacks.[26] Once a ship was doomed and once all that could
be done to save life had been done, it was not unknown
for the local men to use their seafaring knowledge to
ensure that a wreck took place in the most convenient spot
- thus, I learned how the *Anna Marie*, a schooner with a
useful 200 tons of coal on board, was almost towed ashore
on Swona in 1925. On another occasion, the date of which
I do not know, Swona men boarded a ship found drifting
crewless but with a cargo of salt and, discovering nothing
of interest on her, let her go.[27]

In 1956, the fishermen on Stroma were suspected of
having stripped everything movable from the *Dovrefjell*,
ashore on the Skerries, and the Chief Constable of
Caithness, John Georgeson, organised a well-equipped
party to scour the island for salvaged goods.[28] All the
houses were searched, potato patches and flower-beds
were overturned; the lighthouse, although the keepers
were above suspicion, was also visited. The police
left empty-handed. A few years later, when the last of
the islanders had left for a new life on the mainland, it
was revealed that the plunder from the *Dovrefjell* had
been safely hidden on a ledge of rock under the lip of the
Gloup.

Unofficial salvage brought some comfort into the lives
of a few crofters and fishermen, and occasionally furnished
the gentry too. George Low, a keen naturalist, was said to
have obtained his microscope from a wreck. Duty-free,
indeed totally free, liquor was a constant attraction. James
Wallace, a minister of Kirkwall in the late 1600s,
beachcombed for hogsheads of wine and brandy. I have
already mentioned how Alexander Bryce in his survey of
the Caithness coast in 1740 met with opposition from   121

people who thought his work would deprive them of the benefits of wrecks. According to one story, the masons working on the Stroma lighthouse stopped using their hammers when it was foggy and they heard a ship in the offing, so that their noise would not warn away a potential windfall.[29]

Up to the present day, the people have looked upon what the sea casts up, whether in a wreck or as flotsam, as free for the taking. We often beachcombed, particularly after an easterly gale, for wood and whatever else the sea might disgorge; and customarily any object 'laid up' above the shore was recognised as having already been found and claimed, and was left alone. There are stories well into this century of wrecks being defended by the first to board them, against the depredations of more tardy marauders.

Such behaviour is perfectly understandable. Poverty was widespread and deep and the people themselves were living in peril of death among the waves: the benefices of this whimsical neighbour were accepted when they were offered.

Dabbling in Salt Water

Of all those who lived with the Firth, the folk on Stroma and Swona had cause to know it best: it was all around them. 'They are dabbling in salt water from their childhood upwards,' wrote Revd John Morison of his Stroma parishioners in 1791.[30] Swona is the smaller of the two islands and belongs to the parish of South Ronaldsay. Stroma is part of the parish of Canisbay. A legend explains how this partitioning came about; there are several versions, but here is one. Snakes were brought to the islands to settle a dispute between the earls of Caithness and Orkney over who owned which island. On Stroma the snakes lived (though there are none there now); on Swona they died. As Orkney is free from adders, this was accepted as a sure sign that the smaller island was rightly part of that archipelago.[31]

Let us look at Swona, the island where snakes can't survive. The name, variously spelled in the past as Swinna, Svina or even Sownay, means in Norse 'swine island'. George Barry recorded in 1805 that it had twenty-one inhabitants who subsisted 'by means of a little grain which their industry raises, catching fish, when the weather permits, and particularly by their skill in piloting ships'. The population varied over the years, but the style of life remained unchanging. Swona is about a mile and a half long, from the isolated rock of West Windi Skerry to North Head, and reaches only half a mile in width. The dwelling houses were on the north-west side of the island and the rocky shore encloses a small haven near the north-east corner opposite South Ronaldsay. Swona dips in and out of history. The *Orkneyinga Saga* names the earliest known inhabitant - a Norseman called Grim. He had two sons, Asbrn and Margad, whose exploits as followers of Svein Asleifarson show them to have been Vikings of the first order.

In 1586 a chapel on Swona was dedicated to St Peter; another with the same dedication was built on Muckle Skerry. There were also two chapels on Stroma, and several scattered through the parishes bordering the Firth. After the Reformation the chapels fell into disuse although this did not happen quickly, as it took several generations of Presbyterian preaching and discipline to eradicate the older beliefs of the people.[32] The new ministers of the Reformed faith worked hard on their mission, but sometimes the sea was too much for them. On a February Sunday in 1661, the South Ronaldsay minister and one of the Orkney bailies 'took boate and went to the Isle of Sownay'. Their intention was to try a woman who had been cursing others after they had accused her of unchastity: the minister forced her to confess and 'before the night had past' she provided conclusive evidence of fornication by giving birth to twins. On the following Sunday on South Ronaldsay, however, the folk had to go without a sermon as the minister's visit to Swona had left him 'of paine of the seatiche'.[33]

George Low recorded in 1774 that there were nine families on Swona. Fishing was their livelihood, the main catch being cuddanes and dogfish. The fish were wind-cured by being hung in specially built stone huts. Oil from the livers was sold at sixpence per Scots pint. Swona had no ploughs, the cows were yoked to pull harrows, and peat had to be brought from Flotta. Low expressed his admiration for the skill with which the Swonamen dared the Wells in their hunt for fish.

James Watson described Swona some twenty years later in the *Statistical Account* as 'a barren inhospitable island, exposed on all sides to the utmost rage of the Pentland Firth'. By this time, a simple kind of iron blade was in use as a plough, and each family grew carefully-tended potatoes. Watson thought that only the possibility of high wages from pilotage induced the twenty-one inhabitants to live there. But live they did, and flourish, for many decades; in 1871 there were still nine households and a total of forty-seven souls.[34]

About four times the size of Swona, Stroma has nearly always attracted favourable notice from writers.[35] Life here was for many centuries similar to that on its neighbour: fishing, some farming, and the peats being imported, this time from Canisbay. The island figures briefly in the *Orkneyinga Saga*, but it may have been a more important centre than this scant record indicates. At the south-west corner, the ruins of a fortified building called Mestag lie on a wind-plucked clifftop. It is probably contemporary with twelfth-century castles in Caithness and Orkney, but no one knows for sure. At the other end of the island, near the lighthouse, is a chambered cairn of Neolithic age.

The island also won a modest notoriety in the eighteenth century for the strange activities of a family of Kennedys. John Kennedy of Kenmuck in Aberdeenshire was granted a wadset of part of Stroma in 1659. A doocot in the little cemetery on the south-east corner of the island also served as a family mausoleum. The salty sea-air preserved bodies for an unusually long time; the pickled corpses were regularly mentioned in travellers' tales, and visitors told with some horror of a young Kennedy who played on the belly of the dead father as if it were a tom-tom. (The Moodie family tomb at Kirkhope was also noted for preserved bodies at this time.[36]) 'A little isle, but Pleasant and Fruitful,' wrote James Wallace. George Low crossed from South Walls to Stroma in 1774 and found thirty families living there. There were no ploughs and the cultivated, eastern part of the island was dug by spade. The houses were grouped in two, loosely clustered townships - Nethertoon in the north and Uppertoon on the slope of Cairn Hill facing the Caithness shore. Low also observed that the 'women while young are tolerably well looked' but that they acquired 'a peculiar ghastliness in their countenances' with age. He was disappointed when the people refused to give him flint arrowheads they had found, as they thought these objects kept the fairies away from their cattle.

At the eastern end of the Firth, swept by wind and spray, sprawl the rocky islets of the Skerries, part of the parish of South Ronaldsay. In the past cattle and sheep were pastured on Muckle Skerry. The islet also has a number of unexcavated archaeological sites but in the main its only inhabitants were birds and seals - until 1794, when this green eye in the sea was chosen as the site for the Firth's first lighthouse.

There is a local tradition that braziers of peat were once used as primitive navigation lights on the Skerries; the only evidence for these is some peat ash to be found there. The Norse and probably the Picts before them were in the habit of using signal fires, usually to transmit emergency messages rather than to serve as permanent markers of hazards.

The story really begins in 1786 when an Act of Parliament created the Board of Commissioners of Northern Lights and authorised them to collect a levy of one penny per ton from British ships and two pence per ton from foreign vessels passing any or all of the Board's lights.[37] The revenue from the levy was to pay for the country's first modern lighthouses - on Kinnaird Head, the Mull of Kintyre, Eilean Glas on Scalpay, and North Ronaldsay. The amount of money brought in by the levy proved too small; a second Act in 1788 raised the dues and a third, in the following year, relaxed the rules to allow the Board to erect light-houses where and when the levy income would permit. Cargo vessels above a certain size are still required to pay light dues. The light-house on Kinnaird Head shone for the first time on 1 December 1787. The North Ronaldsay lighthouse was built in 1789 and the light shone first on 10 October that year. The dues collected by the Board in the same year amounted to only £290 14s 6d but after another four years the annual income had risen to about £3000 and it was decided to proceed with the construction of the Muckle Skerry light.

The Skerry was picked only after hot dispute for the best site. The varying opinions found their way into the *Statistical Account*. The Revd John Morison of Canisbay argued for the Skerry site, though he admitted that it could prove difficult to find personnel willing to live for long periods in such stormy isolation. Captain John Dunnet wrote to Sir John Sinclair to point out the advantages of Duncansby Head as a site.[38] Both Morison and Dunnet agreed on the need to allow seamen to distinguish the entrance to the Firth from Freswick Bay and Sinclair's Bay; mistakes, said Morison, with 'the most fatal consequences have ensued' from confusing these coastal features. Eventually the opinions of the Clyde and Liverpool shipowners decided the debate.

The engineer in charge of the Board's works was Thomas Smith. His stepson, appointed to supervise the building of the Skerry light, was Robert Stevenson. Robert had been born in Glasgow in 1772, the only son of a West Indies merchant who died on St Christopher in 1774. His mother, Jean Lillie, brought him up alone until in 1787 she married Thomas Smith. Robert learned engineering in his stepfather's firm and became Smith's partner in 1796; he also married Jean, Smith's daughter by a previous marriage. Robert went on to succeed his stepfather as engineer to the Board and remained in that post for nearly fifty years. When he died, in Edinburgh in 1850, he left twenty lighthouses, methods and procedures still to some extent followed today, and three sons who were all to carry on his work.[39]

On Muckle Skerry, he built two towers, 60 ft apart: the taller was 80 ft high and the shorter 60 ft. The towers were first lit on 1 October 1794. Two South Ronaldsay brothers, William and John Gray, who worked on the building, embarked on a lifelong association with lighthouses: John helped to build Bell Rock, and William stayed at home to become, as a boatman operating from Burwick, the Skerries' link with the outside world. Seafarers were misled into thinking the two lights were ship-mast lights, and in the 1820s the twin towers were heightened and moved further apart. The new arrangement continued, however, to cause confusion and finally in 1895 the lower light was permanently switched off. It was converted into a foghorn in 1909.[40]

His work finished on the Skerries, Robert Stevenson sailed back south on the sloop *Elizabeth* from Stromness. Close to Kinnaird Head the wind fell and, impatient at being becalmed, the young lighthouse builder went ashore to continue his journey to Edinburgh by land. It was a lucky decision. After he left the sloop, a fierce gale suddenly sprang up and drove the *Elizabeth* back to Orkney where she was wrecked with the loss of all hands.[41]

The Commissioners of the Northern Lights included the Lord Advocate and a number of advocates and sheriffs. One of the latter joined the Commissioners' yacht for a cruise around the north coast in 1814: Walter Scott, not then a baronet, was in high spirits from the success of his first novel *Waverley*, and he took a rifle and a fowling-piece with him to join the yacht at Leith. They sailed on Friday 29 July. To add an edge to the excitement they were accompanied by a naval sloop to protect them from American privateers. First stop was the Bell Rock light, perhaps Robert's greatest achievement, where Scott was

127

delighted by the elegant brass and woodwork. From there, they sailed to Shetland. The sea grew rough as they were passing Arbroath, and it is here that Scott recorded 'all sick, even Mr Stevenson'. The three Commissioners and Scott and his two pals played chess, piquet and backgammon to divert their thoughts from their tortured stomachs.[42]

In Lerwick the streets were full of men from the Arctic whalers. Scott gathered information on folklore which he was later to use in his novel *The Pirate*. By 14 August they were south again, in Scapa Flow. It was a bright, breezy day but the Firth was too rough to allow them to attempt a landing on Muckle Skerry. Instead, they decided to call at Thurso. Scott's journal reads: 'Enter the Pentland Firth, so celebrated for the strength and fury of its tides, which is boiling even in this pleasant weather; we see a large ship battling with this heavy current and, though with all her canvass set and a breeze, getting more and more involved.'

Between Stroma and Swona, the wind fell away and the yacht found herself at the mercy of the tide. Unable to make way against the flood, they turned into Longhope and anchored under the gun battery that was then in building. Scott had better luck the next day. Travelling in the lighthouse boat from South Ronaldsay, he sprang ashore on Muckle Skerry at 10 o'clock. He was delighted by the trip and by the boatmen, recalled Robert Stevenson. On the Skerry, he walked around the cliffs with his rifle, hoping for a shot at a seal but seeing none. There were 50 cattle pastured there, and Scott noted that the only source of fresh water was the rain.

They left the island at one o'clock with the ebb behind them and sailed at 14 knots back to Longhope and then Stromness. It was at Stromness that Scott met Bessy Millie, an old woman who lived in a 'wretched cabin' above the town and sold favourable winds to sea captains at sixpence a time. She also claimed to remember John Gow, the notorious pirate, and told Scott about him. We can imagine Bessy - a 'withered, sharp-featured woman,

The author's grandfather, James Miller, mending a seine net in Keiss in the 1930s.

Daniell's view of John o'Groats in 1813. On the skyline at left is South Ronaldsay and the Skerries can be seen on the right. Lapster kists, for keeping captured lobsters alive, lie beside the yoles drawn up on the shore.

A view of Scarfskerry in 1813 by William Daniell. The ferry house on the left has not changed a great deal. Note the yole being repaired in the foreground, and the silhouette of Dunnet Head on the skyline.

The Pentland Skerries lighthouse at some time in the late 19th century. Note the people on the shorter tower, and the donkey (*The Orkney Library*).

Four Swona men at the haven on the island. From left to right they are George Allan, his son Davie, Tom Allan and James Norquoy (*The Orkney Library*).

Goods from the wrecked steamer, *Croma*, laid out for sale on Stroma in 1899 (*The Orkney Library*).

Rackwick Bay, Hoy, around 1889 (*The Orkney Library*).

James 'Quebec' Mowat, one of the Freswick pilots (*John o'Groat Journal*).

The *Dickinson Edleston*, the first Longhope lifeboat (1874-1891), pictured in Stromness harbour (*The Orkney Library*).

The crew of the Huna lifeboat, *WMC*, equipped with cork lifejackets and ready for sea at about the turn of the century (*J. Dunnet and W. Rosie*).

The SS *Express* in Stromness harbour. The *Express* ran between Scrabster and Stromness from April 1869 to July 1877, and again for brief periods on charter from October 1890 to August 1891 and in March-April 1892 (*Stromness Museum*).

The first *St Ola* steams into Stromness (*Stromness Museum*).

A group of pilots and fishermen at Nybster, Auckengill, taken around 1900 (*John o'Groat Journal*).

Captain George Swanson on the bridge of the *St Ola* (*Stromness Museum*).

The *Pansy* (WK732) moored in Keiss harbour in the 1920s.

The steamer *Linkmoor* hard aground at low tide by Scarfskerry pier in 1930.

The *Pennsylvania* aground on Swona in 1931 (*The Orkney Library*).

The Stacks of Duncansby with the Thirl Door in the foreground.

The Swedish steamer, *Stellatus*, ashore at Freswick in March 1959. The fishing boat moored alongside is the *Sans Peur*, owned by Jock Sinclair (*J. Calder*).

The Belgian fishing vessel *Lans* lies wrecked at the foot of the Hoy cliffs in December 1974. The nine-man crew was rescued by a helicopter from 202 Squadron, RAF Lossiemouth, whose pilot showed superb skill and courage in manouevring his aircraft within yards of the cliff face (*Orkney Library*).

A breaker smashes over the quay at John o'Groats (*B. Johnstone*).

The BP oil production vessel, *Seillean*, transfers oil to the Finnish tanker, *Bonny*, in Scapa Flow (*Orkney Harbours Department*).

The late Peter Sinclair steers his yole *Kelvin Star* into John o'Groats.

The restored Stroma yole, *Diligent*, under sail, with Brian Sinclair at the tiller (*Brian Sinclair*).

The ferry *Pentland Venture*, southbound from Burwick, approaches John o'Groats harbour (*B. Johnstone*).

with two light-blue eyes gleaming weirdly in her corpse-like face', as Daniel Gorrie recalled her in 1869 - sitting down with the young, excited writer from Edinburgh. Scott, of course bought a favourable wind: later that day his sixpence proved well spent and they sailed for the West Coast.

A portrait of Robert Stevenson, by John Syme, hangs in the Scottish National Portrait Gallery in Edinburgh. He appears as a plump-cheeked, bald-headed individual in a high collar and white cravat; there is a hint of a smile about his mouth, and Syme has added, as background, a slender lighthouse tower beset by raging waves. His eldest son, Alan, succeeded him in 1843 as engineer to the Lighthouse Commissioners. Alan built ten lighthouses, the tower on Skerryvore being his crowning triumph. He was stricken with paralysis in 1852, and spent the last part of his life in Portobello until his death in 1865. Robert's two younger sons, David and Thomas, became in their turn engineers and invented many devices to improve illumination. Thomas was a moody, religious man but he was also a high-minded humanitarian and refused to take out patents for his many inventions, believing they should be free for the use of all. He fathered a weak son, who was destined to be the most famous Stevenson of them all - Robert Louis. One of David Stevenson's sons, David Alan (1854-1938) carried the family's engineering heritage and association with the Firth into the present century by building the Duncansby Head light in 1924.[43]

The lighthouse keepers and their families became the Skerries' first permanent residents. In 1841, James and Elizabeth Brown with their seven children, and John Morrison and a servant, Mary Bews, were staying there.[44] In 1851, when the population was thirteen, one of the keepers had a lodger.[45] The island acquired small fields and dykes and the keepers kept poultry, milking cows and, for transporting goods from the landing place, a donkey.[46] In time, a graveyard was created: it holds the remains of two children, who are said to have died from diptheria, and the crew members of the *Vicksburg* who lost their lives in a wreck in 1884.

There were two landing places: the main one, Scartan Bay, on the south-east side; and Hunigeo in the north-west corner where steps were cut into rocks and mooring rings were fixed. In the room under the south-tower lamp a visitors' book was kept. Thirty-one copper cisterns lined with tin stored the 2000 gallons of sperm oil which the lamps used each year. As there was no source of fresh water on the island, the roofs of the towers and the houses were designed to collect rainwater for storage in lead-lined tanks; in stormy weather, spray turned the water brackish. A cast-iron sundial presided in the garden over flourishing vegetables, but flowers were difficult to grow in the salty air.

The barque *Vicksburg* was outward bound in ballast from Leith to Quebec when shortly after midnight on 16 July she passed the Skerries. She made her way west with the ebb, but when she was abreast of Dunnet Head the wind changed to the north-west and began to push her back into the Firth. Rising to gale force, the wind and the flood tide now running prevented the ship working into Longhope. The captain, John Watson, said later that he could not find a pilot to help him; the local men said he did not signal for one. They also said that no sane man would try to beat a large ship in ballast to windward to round Cantick Head. Watson, in their opinion, should have run east before the wind and waited in the lee of Duncansby. As it was, the *Vicksburg* was pushed east past Stroma where Watson made another mistake. He tried to haul the barque to windward too soon, before passing the Skerries. The ship was driven on to Muckle Skerry. Most of the twenty-one-strong crew took to two boats; one won safely to land, but the other was swamped, and five men were drowned. Four men who remained aboard with Watson were swept away by the breaking swell. Watson himself was lucky to survive: hanging on to a piece of wood, the sea first pulled him away from the shore then back towards it. The lighthouse keepers threw a rope to him several times before he caught it. By the time he reached the rocks he was too chilled to tie the rope around himself and is said to have gripped it in his teeth.[47]

In 1831, a new lighthouse was built by John Smith of Inverness to mark the Firth's western entrance. Until then, shipmasters sometimes mistook Dunnet Head for Hoy and tried to pass to the south of it. On a dark night in November 1811 the *Fingal*, east bound with a cargo of timber, did this and drove ashore with the loss of all on board, on Dunnet sands.[49] The Dunnet Head light is a single tower with its lantern 346 ft above sea level; in clear weather it can be seen for 24 miles. In a sense, this was my first lighthouse. Although the winking eye of the Noss Head light struck my childhood bedroom, it was not until I was older and capable of cycling from my uncle's croft in Dunnet to Dunnet Head that I ascended the steps of a lighthouse. The approach to the Dunnet Head light is itself impressive: the road winds across a high moor to end at the windy, exposed clifftop, the most northerly point of the British mainland. Here the white, harled lighthouse with its yellow trim and the squat outbuildings and dwellings seem to hold grimly to the ground. The keeper was always a willing guide, and at the top of the tower he allowed us to turn the huge lamp, floating in its bath of mercury, with a gentle push. Far below the sea fretted and the white birds hovered, screamed and dived. The windows in the lighthouse, for all their height, have been broken by stones hurled up by the waves; and further illustration of the sea's power comes from the story of Dunnet Head's foghorns. The first fell into the sea as the cliff was undercut, and a second had to be abandoned in 1953 when its collapse was feared to be imminent; however, it was still there in 1981 when it had to be broken up and pushed over the edge.[49] The third foghorn tower was closed in 1989 when the lighthouse became an automatic station.[50]

Dunnet Head was the site of an impressive feat of endurance one night in April 1847. A gale drove the brig

131

Salima from her moorings in Scrabster roads to the cliffs of the Head. Of the five men on board, only one survived, the thirty-year-old mate William Kelland, who climbed the 300-foot cliff to safety. The bodies of some of his companions were later found and buried in Dunnet churchyard.[51]

Lighthouse keepers have always held a place of respect in the north, and with good reason. Seven of the Skerries keepers have been commended for their bravery in rescuing sailors from ships wrecked on their doorstep. In May 1910, when the Findochty fishing boat *Stratheyre* was broken up against the Skerries, James MacHardy, one of the assistant keepers, swam out with a line to the raft the crew had fashioned from spars so that they could be pulled to safety.[52]

As the years passed, more lights were erected on Noss Head in 1849, Cantick Head in 1856, Holborn Head in 1862, Stroma in 1890 and Duncansby Head in 1924. Minor lights in the Firth are Hoxa Head (1901), Swona (1906), Lother Rock (1910) and Torness (1937). Strathy lighthouse, filling the long gap between Holborn Head and Cape Wrath, was completed in 1958. The two lighthouses on Graemsay, called the Hoy Sound High and Low lights and signposting the western approach to Stromness and Scapa Flow, were built in 1850 and first lit in 1851. The sheer, wedge-shaped bulk of Copinsay acquired its lighthouse in 1915.

All the lighthouses in the area of the Firth are serviced from a depot in Stromness, where the tender vessel, the *Pole Star*, is based. Helicopters are also used now. In the last few decades, many island lighthouses have been redesignated 'rock' stations: the families of the keepers live in Stromness and the keepers themselves work on a month-on-duty, month-off basis. The Skerries became an unmanned station in March 1994, almost exactly two centuries after the light-house was built. By 1998, the remaining two manned lights in the Firth - Duncansby Head and Stroma - will be automated. There has been a steady spread of auto-

mation, beginning with Hoy Low (1966) and pro-
ceeding through Hoy High (1978), Noss Head (1987),
Holborn Head (1988), Dunnet Head (1989) and Cantick
Head (1991).

Commander Away Surveying

In October 1807, Alexander Dalrymple, the first officially appointed Hydrographer to the Admiralty, sat
down and wrote in a matter-of-fact, slightly peevish tone
to the Admiralty Secretary.[53] The substance of his letter
was a complete list of all the charts published in Britain,
and to make his catalogue manageable Dalrymple classi-
fied the charts geographically. Those of the North Sea,
including the Pentland Firth, were put into Class 6a: their
total value was £3 11s 6d. 'The Charts by Mr McKenzie
Senr. are represented to be very exact,' wrote Dalrymple,
underlining for emphasis. 'They were not made at the
Public Expense, and are *private property*, but I conceive the
single sheet chart of these Islands will be sufficient for
common use.'

The other charts in the list included 'The NE. Coast
of Great Britain' by John Chandler, 'Orkney Islands
with Directions' by George Eunson, and 'Orkney Islands
with the N Coast of Scotland' published by L. Whittle
in 1794. Eunson, a Kirkwall shipmaster, made his chart
in the late 1780s, drawing on both his own surveys
and Murdoch Mackenzie's earlier work; his aim was
to update Mackenzie's survey and produce for his fellow
mariners a convenient, one-sheet chart. It included
notes on fishing grounds and navigation marks,
although in stating that 'Johnny Groats house is situated
on a high rock and may be seen in fine weather 5 leagues
off' it was surely referring to Duncansby Head or the
Stacks. Eunson later served as a Customs officer and
then as a pilot with the Northern Lighthouse Commissioners; his chart was in use until the mid-nineteenth
century.[54]

Dalrymple drew up a separate list of the charts that had been made by serving naval officers and published privately: 'altho no such have been sent to the Admiralty,' he complained. This list included 'Sketch of Orkney, Shetland and Faroe Islands' by Ross Donnelly of HMS *Pegasus*, which is dated 1797 and includes insets showing the approaches to Stromness, Thorshaven and the Sound of Bressay.[55]

During the eighteenth century a number of private mapmakers had published several series of charts and guides to the British coast. Most of them are listed in L.S. Dawson's *Memoirs of Hydrography*, with biographical details of some surveyors.[56] Strangely, Dawson, a naval commander, thought Murdoch Mackenzie's work 'not ... remarkable for accuracy', an opinion seemingly at variance with those of others. Among the guides available to navigators was William Heather's *The Marine Atlas*. Heather had a shop in Leadenhall Street in London: his *Atlas* in 1808 was priced at nine guineas, a substantial sum. His representation of the Firth, which almost certainly owes a considerable debt to Mackenzie's work, shows the Men of Mey, the Liddel Eddy and whirlpools between Swona and Stroma; a course labelled 'Best Passage with the Flood Tide against you' is drawn going through Inner Sound, and the Outer Sound is described as 'Common Track through the Firth'. Murdo Downie, the master of HMS *Champion*, also compiled his own chart and sailing directions for the Scottish coast, including the Pentland Firth, in 1792.

Official Admiralty surveys of the Firth began in 1826, and during the ensuing decades the coasts were mapped and surveyed several times. It was a long, slow business. The survey vessels were based at Woolwich and came north each summer to work with leadline, compass and theodolite. The surveyors themselves, usually the commanders of the naval ships, became familiar local figures.

The first survey ship to work in Orkney was HMS
Investigator. She was built at Deptford in 1811, was 75 ft

long, and carried a crew of twenty. She worked as a survey ship until 1836 when she was handed over to the Thames River Police, and was broken up in 1857. Her commander was George Thomas, whose own career reads like a plot by Defoe. Born in 1782, Thomas sailed for the South Seas on a whaler in 1796, but was wrecked and marooned for four years. After being rescued by a chance passing ship, he was press-ganged on the way home.[57]

Extracts from the *Investigator's* log give a flavour of the work. Here is the ship's arrival in Orkney from Scalloway on 26 September 1834, with the wind in the north-east:

> *A.M. Light airs and fine. Trimmed as required.*
> *2 In all studding sails. Brailed up fore and aft*
> *mainsail. Up Square Mainsail. Altered course to*
> *WSW ... Running for Hoy Head. Noon ditto Weather.*
> *Hauled out Boom Mainsail. Set square Mainsail.*
> *Tacked Occas. Working into Stromness Harbour.*
> *1 Shortened Sail and Came to ... in the Harbour off the*
> *Town in 4 faths.*[58]

On that occasion the ship stayed at Stromness for almost a fortnight. The life was busy but not too arduous. On Sundays some of the crew were sent ashore to attend the kirk, and barrels of rum were opened regularly for grog. As the working of the ship in the tides necessitated continual adjustment of the sails, the log shows what seamanship involved before the advent of engines:

> *10 Up jolly boat. Weighed and made sail out of*
> *Stromness harbour. Set Lower and all Studding Sails.*
> *Trimd as Reqd. Running between the islands,*
> *intending to run through Holm Sd. Opened Rum.*
> *Eighteen ¹/₂ Galls. Noon. Light airs (SW) with heavy Rain.*
> *2 In all Studding Sails and braced up on Starboard tack.*
> *4 Light breezes and cloudy. Tack occasionally.*
> *Working into Longhope between the islands of Fara and*

Flota.
7 Short Sail & came to in 4 fathoms in Longhope.

Two days later, the *Investigator* continued her homeward voyage to Woolwich, the wind now from the north-west:

11.50 Weighed and Made Sail out of Longhope...
12.30 Set Square and Boom Mainsail. Hauled to
wind on the Starboard tack crossed the Pentland Firth.
2 Weathered Swona Isld. Set FTM and F Main TGallt
Studding Sails. Trimmed as Reqd running through the
Pentland Firth.
3 Fresh Breezes and Squally. In TGallt Studg Sails
3.20 Took in FTM Studding Sails.
4 Moderate and rainy. Duncansby Head NW 3 miles.

When surveying was taking place, the log assumes a relaxed, almost languid tone. For those of the crew left on board, put to work with the stores, repairing equipment or scrubbing hammocks, the day was probably less pleasant; but as life in the Navy went this could not have been so bad.

In 1836 a larger ship HMS *Mastiff* took over the northern surveys. Her crew numbered forty-four; she was 84 feet long and displaced 184 tons. George Thomas remained as commander. The tender *Woodlark* was attached to the survey at this time. From the *Mastiff's* log comes this extract that shows some of the dangers the Firth presented. The date is 29 June 1841:

AM Light winds and thick fog.
1 Made the High Land of S Ronaldsha ahead -
tacked ship. Sounded in 14 Fms. 20.25.33. 37 fms.
5 ditto
5.30 Taken aback filled on Lb Tack - Lt airs
6.30 Sounded in 38fms. S.Sh. Light airs and dense fog
9 In Courses and Top Gallt Sails and anchd in 40 fms
with Stream and hawser

11 found ship drifting. Two hawsers out
Noon Ship drifting - Strong tides. Weighed and
made sail. Light breezes NNE
1 Standing off...
1.30 fog clearing Made the Land, Copinsha Isld
NE by N - 8 miles.[59]

Alexander Becher assumed command of the *Mastiff* in 1847 and completed the survey of Orkney in the following year.[60]

Two of the naval officers who became well known around the Firth while engaged on survey work were Lieutenants Henry Otter and Michael Slater.[61] They worked together for almost ten years, after Otter was appointed Slater's assistant in 1832. The partnership was brought to an end one fateful afternoon in February 1842, when Slater fell to his death from Holborn Head. One account of the event says that the officer was working with his theodolite and stepped too near the edge of the cliff. The local version of the tragedy, however, is that Slater fell from his horse: a shepherd is said to have found the riderless animal, suspected something was wrong and followed its tracks back to the cliff, where it was obvious what had happened. However, in his biography of the self-taught geologist and Thurso baker Robert Dick, Samuel Smiles alleged that Slater was afterwards seen in Australia and that a jealous love affair lay behind the officer's staged disappearance. In a later book published in 1891, David Stephen thought this unlikely. Stephen tells how Slater believed a horoscope that predicted that 2 pm would be his fatal hour. This idea took such a hold on Slater's mind that Dr Laing, a Thurso physician, prevailed upon the town council to stop the town hall clock from striking two for weeks prior to the accident, if that was what it was, to avoid distressing the popular officer. As it turned out, it was about 2 pm that he fell to his death.

Lieutenant Otter took over Slater's work and in 1844 was appointed to the command of HMS *Sparrow*, a survey ketch. Otter went on to command HMS *Avon*, a

137

160 hp paddle-steamer, and achieved the rank of post captain before retiring in 1863. As well as surveying all the northern coasts, he piloted the Baltic Fleet during the Crimean War. His ship was by now another paddle-steamer, HMS *Porcupine*. Otter and the *Porcupine* also played a key role in the laying of the first transatlantic cable in 1858 from Europe to Newfoundland.

In the early decades of the nineteenth century, Stromness became the last watering place for a special series of north-bound ships when the peaceful years after the end of the Napoleonic Wars allowed attention to focus once more on the search for the North-West Passage.[62] Several expeditions, starting with John Ross in the ships *Isabella* and *Alexander* in 1818, went out to find a feasible route through the Arctic ice to the Pacific. In the summer of 1845 the *Erebus* and the *Terror*, under the command of the veteran explorer Sir John Franklin and with some Caithness and Orkney men in their crews, passed through (a Pulteneytown pilot called James Mackay took them through the Firth[63]). Both vessels met a terrible fate: trapped to the west of King William Island off Canada's northern coast, their crews gradually succumbed to starvation and exposure. It was several years before the grisly details of the tragedy became known, and then largely through the work of the Orcadian explorer John Rae.[64]

Born at the Hall of Clestrain in 1813, Rae studied medicine at Edinburgh University and joined the Hudson's Bay Company as a surgeon in 1833 (his father was the Company agent in Stromness). He had a great scientific curiosity and, for example, experimented with solar-heated balloons before embarking in June 1846 on an amazing programme of exploration. With a few companions, he adopted the techniques of the Inuit and travelled some 23,000 miles in the Arctic by boat, sledge and snowshoe to make maps and collect specimens. In April 1854, almost by chance, he found out what had happened to Franklin, when an Inuit brought him items of clothing and equipment left by white men who had perished some years before. With his share of the reward for this discovery, Rae built a schooner for possible use in further expeditions. He later retired to London where he died from influenza in 1893. An impressive monument showing him resting on his explorer's furs stands in St Magnus Cathedral in Kirkwall.

Excellent Judges of the Weather

With lighthouses, new charts and better ships, the number of vessels passing through the Firth increased: in one year 'upwards of 4000 loaded vessels ... exclusive of ships of war and vessels in ballast,' wrote W.L. Bremner, in exile in Guildford and longing for a view of Stroma.[65] Other sources give estimates of the numbers of passing ships from 2000 up to a hardly believable 10,000. James Watson estimated an average of nine vessels passing per day in the 1790s.[66] North-westerly gales could result in 40-50 sail lying offshore between Duncansby and Noss Head waiting for a chance to attempt the westward passage.[67] The northern gate had become a busy thoroughfare.[68]

No charts and no end of lighthouses could better the knowledge in the heads of local fishermen, a knowledge gained through generations of struggle with the Bores, the Wells and the Men of Mey. The piloting of ships through the Firth grew into an important source of income. James Watson thought it the only reason for living on Swona.[69] Strangely, in view of their local fame, very little has been written of the Pentland pilots. Bremner's long poem 'The Pilot of the Pentland Firth', an uninspired tale based possibly on a true incident, was published in 1861. David Grant, a schoolmaster in Canisbay at one point in his life and later, from 1857 to 1861, the editor of the *Sheffield Post*, wrote a volume of verse in a similar vein, *Yarns of the Pentland Firth*.

Most of the information I have on the pilots has been gleaned from the columns of newspapers, particularly the 139

John o' Groat Journal which began publication in 1836, and, therefore, relates to the last decades of the era. We can take it, however, that what follows are the last verses of an old and honourable song.

When a ship was in need of a pilot, she signalled on approaching the Firth. The main picking-up places were off Noss Head and Freswick Bay on the east coast, and the area around Thurso on the west. The pilots lived at Sandside, Crosskirk, Staxigoe and Papigoe - where a street of council houses is still named Pilot Row - and Auckengill and Skirza. There is nothing left at Crosskirk to indicate that six families lived here in the 1840s except sprawling heaps of stone along the curve of the shore and one desolate, crowstepped house. Pilots also operated from Stroma and Swona, and in fewer numbers from the Orkney side of the Firth. Stromness had its own pilots for working ships in and around the port.

On sighting a potential client, pilots took to sea immediately, and rowed or sailed as fast as they could to reach her; the first pilot to arrive was normally assured of the job. After navigation of the Firth, the pilot was normally allowed to leave in his own boat, if it had been towed behind with his companions, or was put ashore and left to trudge home on foot.

I say 'normally', because occasionally an impatient or ungrateful captain did not stop to release the pilot but carried him along to a foreign port. For example, David Banks, a Stroma pilot, signed on as a member of the crew of the ship he could not get free from and, when he arrived in America, signed on another which he hoped was about to make the return voyage. However, this vessel set out on a long detour via many South American ports and was almost lost in the Roaring Forties. Banks finally won home long after he had been given up for lost by his relatives.[70]

Sometime in the 1840s or 1850s, James Miller of Nybster was taken to Ireland and landed at Limerick. Miller had another, more perilous, adventure in which he came off best. The date is unknown but it must have been later than 1851, when the lighthouses on Graemsay were built. Miller had taken a ship through the Firth but the captain was short of crew and refused to land him. According to the story, Miller went below. The ship fell into difficulties at night off the west of Hoy and, in imminent danger, the crew were preparing to abandon her when Miller decided to take charge. He took the wheel, gave the captain instructions and brought the vessel safely into Stromness, navigating with the aid of the lighthouses. The captain sent him home with an extra fee.[71] James Mowat, in 1869, won the race to the *Confidence*, outward bound from Newcastle, and next set foot on land in Quebec - still in his carpet slippers, as he had risen from his fireside in his eagerness to get the job. 'Savannah' and 'Jamaica' were the nicknames of another two pilots who unexpectedly visited the New World. A picture of James Mowat was published with his obituary in 1936.[72] He was a square-faced man, with a full white beard but no moustache; and on his head he was wearing the type of hat long favoured around the coast and known as a cheese-cutter. He lived at Skirza on the north side of Freswick Bay.

In November 1891, David Banks of Stroma - not the same man mentioned above - was piloting a Norwegian schooner, the *Cupido*, to Stornoway when the ship was caught in a severe storm west of Cape Wrath and stripped of her topgallant mast, deck cargo and boat. Banks and the Norwegian skipper decided to run before the wind to Shetland, but then the topsails were carried away and holding a course became impossible. At last the *Cupido* made land at Vestmanna in the Faroes. Catching a steamer from Torshavn to Granton, Banks finally returned to Caithness by train; he was probably the last of the Firth pilots to be carried off in this way.[73]

These men were local heroes and their adventures can still stir the blood. They were 'excellent judges of the weather', according to the minister of Walls and Flotta in 1845.[74] They had to be, for their work was dangerous in the extreme, and several lost their lives in tragic circumstances. The number of men who worked as pilots is hard to assess as it was, in the main, a casual activity undertaken if and when the opportunity presented. However, some evidence can be found in the various censuses of the nineteenth century. In 1841, five men on Stroma, seven at Freswick, one in Staxigoe and four in Papigoe, gave 'pilot' as their occupation. One man on Walls described himself as a 'farmer and pilot', but none of the eight households on Swona gave pilotage as an occupation, although pilots certainly operated from the island.[75]

The number of pilots on the Caithness side of the Firth peaked in 1851, with a total of forty-one. The majority lived on Stroma or at Freswick, more especially at Skirza on the north side of the bay with a commanding view of the southern approaches to the Firth. Competition for business led several men to move from Canisbay to Pilot Row beside Papigoe where they were better placed to intercept vessels; some Canisbay families moved to Crosskirk for the same reason. One of the Freswick pilots in 1851 was Andrew Bremner but, as he was seventy-seven years old, he could not have been very active; the majority of pilots were men in their prime. As well as piloting, all of the men held crofts or fished.[76]

Among the earliest mentions of the pilots in the Caithness papers is a possible death: The *Enterprize*, bound from Riga to Liverpool, took on a Freswick pilot on 24 February 1836 but was caught soon afterward in a gale; a week later, fears were being expressed for her safety.[77] The outcome is unknown in this instance but the situation was a common occurrence: two years later, some ships with Staxigoe pilots were caught in a gale and it was seven days before word came back to the waiting families that the men were safe in the west, although they had lost their own boats.[78] From the records it seems that only a lucky few, such as the Longhope pilots carried to Shields in 1843, had their return journey paid by the shipowner they had assisted.[79] Seven men from Freswick went missing for a fortnight in February 1856. They were last seen by their neighbours on the afternoon of the 13th boarding a west-

bound vessel. This ship - her name turned out to be
Sunshine - was caught later that day to the west of Stroma
by a gale and nothing more was heard about her in
Caithness until the 26th, when it was learned that she had
put in to Belfast. The seven Freswick men were safely
aboard her, their own boat having sunk.[80]

Many pilots lost their boats when bad weather snapped
the towing line. A yole belonging to William Manson of
Nybster drifted as far as Aberdeen in May 1838.[81] Two
years later, a Freswick boat and a Nybster boat were lost
in the same gale, and it seems probable that the latter also
belonged to William Manson.[82] For a crofter-fisherman
such a loss could cripple his livelihood. On another
occasion, pilots in Sinclair's Bay were saved, when their
boat sank, by the ship they had gone to solicit, and were
taken to Dundee.[83]

An otherwise straightforward passage of the Firth
could take some time. The barque *Prince Regent*,
outward bound to Quebec, took on a pilot at Noss Head
on 13 May 1845, but with the northerly wind was unable
to make Longhope until the 17th.[84] The length of time the
pilot was aboard could lead to strange consequences: there
is a story that a South Ronaldsay pilot was in the habit of
taking his daughter with him, and that she returned from
one such outing pregnant by the skipper.[85]

If the wind and the tide were judged favourable, some
captains did not bother to shorten sail to take a pilot. In
these cases, the men could only shrug off their
misfortune. Other incidents were less acceptable.
Incredible though it may seem, captains were not averse
to playing cruel tricks on the pilots. One possible
instance took place in March 1843 when the *Lord Gambier*
flew her signal jack for a pilot as she was passing
Longhope, and then refused to let either of the two pilot
boats that launched come alongside.[86] The *John o'Groat
Journal* attacked the captain's 'wanton conduct in taking
men off during a gale of wind for the purpose of laughing
at the poor fellows'. An Auckengill pilot called Steven
was shown an axe by the captain of a whaler and told that

if he grounded the ship he would lose his head.[87] A Russian captain in 1845 tried to cheat a Staxigoe pilot out of his £10 fee for the passage to Stromness by giving the man an unsigned note.[88]

Rarely, an act of salvage could bring the promise of extra money. In 1836, pilots from Brims boarded a dismasted Norwegian ship called the *Astree* and found no one on board and the cargo of dried fish intact. The pilots towed her to Scrabster where her own crew later turned up, having earlier abandoned her off Tongue.[89] The local men who helped the schooner *Swift* to refloat after she struck the south-west point of Stroma in fog in 1841 received £30 for their trouble.[90] When pilots helped another schooner, the *Earl of March*, refloat on Stroma and one of them offered to guide her to Stromness for £12, the master refused and proffered the men one sovereign to share between them; they indignantly turned down this derisory reward.[91] Occasionally they must have felt vindicated, although it was not in their nature to gloat. In September 1843, the skipper of the *Angeline* refused to accept a Freswick pilot's offer to take her through the Firth for 10 shillings; twenty minutes later, the ship was ashore at Duncansby Head.[92]

There are other less savoury instances of the breaking of some of the cardinal rules of the sea. The Freswick pilot boat *Traveller* was blown miles offshore in July 1843 and was refused a tow back to safety by a British schooner; a Dutch fishing boat later helped them.[93]

Much was done to relieve the hardships of the pilots and their families by Lieutenant Edward Medley, the commander of the Freswick Coastguard. After Naval service in Africa and the North Sea, Medley joined the Coastguard in 1834. He was posted to Caithness in 1840 at the age of forty-nine, and was not long in Freswick before he was campaigning to improve the pilots' lot.[94]

In a letter to the press, he revealed that pilots were being cheated by the ships' masters they served. They were being paid in spirits or sometimes not at all despite having been promised a fee and, if they complained, they were told either to take what was on offer or stay on board. In this way, several had been carried to foreign ports, leaving their families uncertain of their fate. One pilot had been put ashore in Hull and risked imprisonment for vagrancy as he tried to make his way home. At other times, and particularly if the pilot was illiterate, a captain gave him a promissory note instead of money, leaving Medley to try to contact the ship's owners to honour the payment. One fee - of £1, the normal charge by a pilot in the early 1840s - took Medley four years of effort to extract.

Medley was outraged by the way the pilots were being exploited, and to thwart the meanness of unscrupulous captains and owners proposed a systematic organisation to look after the pilots' interest. He suggested that pilots over the age of twenty-five and with three years' experience should be registered or 'enrolled'. These men would pay a 10-shilling fee in the first year and five shillings annually thereafter to keep their certificate, and would train apprentices who, after five years, would be examined to obtain a certificate. His scheme asked for these pilots to be given priority over others by ships' masters, who would be encouraged to co-operate by risking the loss of their insurance cover if they did not. The pilotage fee should be in proportion to the size of the ship.

He drew up and had printed blank forms for the pilots to use, hoping to instil in the men a sense of proper record keeping. A pilot could be fined for not responding to a call for assistance, and pilot boats were to carry flags. The Coastguard would inspect the pilot's boat and equipment. Medley presented his scheme in detail to the House of Commons in March 1843, but nothing appears to have been done in response by either Parliament or the Admiralty as, five years later, Medley was still trying to bring his plans to the notice of the authorities. The pilots on the whole warmed to at least some of the Coastguard officer's ideas. Those who used his blank forms escaped being cheated. A hint that the pilots saw themselves as a body of professionals comes from their complaint in April 1845 that fishermen were taking business away from them.

Medley also tried to obtain a cutter for the use of the pilots. He felt that their own rowboats and yoles were not up to the task although a pilot, Donald Gunn, did not consider there to be any need for a decked vessel. Did some pilots fear losing their independence through over-organisation of their profession? Not all that Medley did in the course of his duty gained approval; his condemnation of masters paying the pilots in goods and liquor, and thereby evading Customs, was not popular.

Fatalities among the pilots were all too frequent, and many showed tremendous courage before succumbing to the sea. A Duncansby man, Robertson by name, went aboard the barque *Belfast* at noon one day in March 1846 to take her west. The wind changed suddenly to the north-east and at midnight, having been unable to enter Longhope, the *Belfast* was driven ashore at Armadale. The crew gave up hope of being saved, but Robertson rallied them and led the watch during the night. One by one the masts broke away, each time taking some men to their deaths. At dawn and the ebbing of the tide, Robertson tried to stir the survivors to get ashore and led the way. As he was struggling over the rocks to safety, a wave caught him and tore him away.[95]

A Broadhaven pilot boat went down in a gale in October 1838 and her crew of five were lost.[96] Three Nybster men were drowned when returning from Longhope after guiding a ship through the Firth in April 1840: their boat shipped a heavy sea and capsized off Burwick.[97] In March 1842, five pilots were lost in Hoy Sound; a sixth survived, being the only one who could swim, and the *John o'Groat Journal* gloomily noted that in the last forty years no pilot had died a natural death.[98] Four pilots were drowned off Flotta in 1847.[99] In April 1848, five Duncansby men were lost when their boat was thrown against a ship's side.[100] Four Staxigoe men died in 1853 when their boat capsized in a heavy sea.[101]

When disasters such as these occurred, appeals were launched to raise money for the widows and children. The Elder Brethren of Trinity House in London sent £20 to the minister of Canisbay in 1842 for distribution among the families of the lost pilots.[102] Lieutenant Medley appealed to the pilots and fishermen to subscribe 2s 6d annually to join the Shipwrecked Fishermen & Mariners' Benevolent Society and acted as the Society's local agent; the dependants of lost men were able to get small but welcome sums, but there seems to have been some reluctance among the people to take out this simple kind of assurance - perhaps they thought it was tempting Providence. The Duncansby men lost in April 1848 had been members of the Society; their families received £12[103] and in all, that year, the Society had given out £170 in Caithness, the bulk of this to the widows of the many men lost when a sudden storm on 19 August had caught the Wick herring fleet and destroyed forty-one boats.[104] In December 1848, commenting on the Society's ninth annual report, Medley noted that still only a minority of the Caithness fishermen had joined.

Medley died in April 1849 after a short illness. A large number of people attended his funeral, in a snow-laden northerly, in Wick kirkyard, and men of the Coastguard escorted the coffin to its last rest.

The first steamship to appear in Thurso bay arrived in about 1829 and caused a great stir; a crowd of 1000 was reported to have gathered to see her.[105] In January 1838, the *John o'Groat Journal* recorded the passage through the Firth of a large steamship. The sea was rough and the unnamed ship 'laboured much, although at the same time her progress was pretty rapid'. Pilots, watching her progress from the Canisbay shore, admired the seamanship of her crew, and perhaps they sensed that they were seeing the future, when iron and steam would make their skills redundant.[106]

After 1851, the number of pilots recorded in the decennial censuses continually declines. By 1881, there were five men on Stroma, aged in their forties and fifties, who gave pilotage as their occupation; and three men at Papigoe, aged between seventy-two and eighty-three, who most likely were retired.[107] It is possible that James Rosie of Swona was the last man to pilot a vessel under sail through the Firth in about 1900.[108]

Among the last pilots on the Caithness mainland were George Manson in Auckengill and Simon and Donald Bremner in Freswick.[109] Manson and Donald Bremner, whose basic piloting kit was a Shipwrecked Fishermen & Mariners' Benevolent Society medal to get him home, a half-crown in case he needed to buy anything, and a handkerchief to wipe his nose on a cold quarterdeck, both died in about 1915. John Allan, who died in 1925, aged sixty-nine,[110] and George Banks, who died in 1933, may have been the last of the Stroma pilots. When James Mowat of Skirza - 'Quebec' - died at the age of ninety-seven in 1936, the newspaper described him as 'the last of the pilots'.

A new breed of pilot now operates on the northern side of the Firth, guiding tankers safely in and out of Scapa Flow and the oil terminal on Flotta.

On 11 January 1977, Dr Armand Hammer, president of Occidental Petroleum, and Tony Wedgwood Benn, the then Secretary of State for Energy, pulled a lever to start the flow of the first cargo of oil from Flotta into the waiting hold of the 70,000-ton Shell tanker, *Dolabella*. The oil had originally come from the Piper Field, 138 miles through a pipe worming its way over the floor of the North Sea to pass into the Flow along the northern shore of South Ronaldsay.[111]

From all over the Firth, one can see the dancing orange flame at the tip of Flotta flare-tower. It was lit on 28 December 1976 at 2 am and has flickered over the island since, a Christmas coming that added another beacon to guide the mariner.

The statistics of the shipping calling at the Flotta terminal, owned by Elf Enterprise since 1991, stretch the imagination. In its first year of operation, 121 tankers loaded almost nine million tonnes of crude oil; and the average annual figure hovered around 300 ships and 15 million tonnes of oil until the Piper Alpha tragedy in July 1988 reduced the flow of crude from the North Sea field. Now, around thirteen ships call each month, and ten pilots work full-time. The tankers are up to 800 ft long and 120 ft in beam.[112]

Although the Piper field is now back in production, through its new operating platform Piper Bravo, the throughput from it and its neighbouring North Sea fields will decline by the end of the century. Orkney, however, is already looking ahead to the potential of new fields out to the west of the islands, and the flowing of more oil to Orkney, either by direct pipeline or by shuttle tankers using the shelter of Scapa Flow for ship-to-ship transfer.

The control centre of the Orkney Islands Harbour Authority keeps a constant eye on the Firth. The upper floor of the building at Scapa is like the bridge of a ship, with wide windows overlooking the Flow, and an officer is continually on duty. On the radar screen, no larger than a small television set, slowly moving blobs track every vessel in the area. No longer do the pilots watch from a headland, ready to race in their yoles for business. The Scapa centre is alerted two or three days in advance of a ship's approach, and VHF contact with the vessel herself is established a few hours before she is due at the pilot station marked on the sea charts. The 'station' is in the area of sea between Swona and South Walls, although the pilot may board anywhere in the Firth if the conditions demand it. A fleet of three tugs is also on hand to help dock ships. The pilot launches are ready to go to sea in all weathers, although operations are generally suspended when the wind speed passes 45 knots.

A touch of the old sailing days remains: pilots board an incoming vessel while she maintains 7-8 knots, enough to keep steerage way. Whatever else has taken place to ease a pilot's task, the currents of the Firth run as they have always done.

Flood

The Pentland Firth by Murdoch Mackenzie, 1749

At the beginning of the nineteenth century, travellers from Caithness to Orkney had a choice of ferries - from Scarfskerry to Brims, or from Huna to Burwick. Neither offered a comfortable crossing. A fine morning, with the sea calm and inviting you to dip your hand to dimple its smoothness, had every chance of not staying that way: the Firth is a great leveller of stomachs. The earliest mention of Brims ferry is found in a letter dated October 1603: it was the property of the Moodies of Melsetter.[1] The old ferry house still stands above the pier at Scarfskerry, little changed from its appearance in the illustration by William Daniell who crossed to Brims in August 1813. He and Richard Ayton left at nine in the morning, at high tide. There was only a gentle breeze and the sea was 'smooth as glass', but as the ebb began from the east the mood of the Firth changed. The day before, the sea had been too rough to attempt a crossing, and now the ferry began to sink in troughs until all sight of land was lost. Despite this, Ayton found the passage pleasing. He noted that in the eight years the boat had been making the trip only one mishap had occurred, about three years before when the ferry had been run down by a ship.[2]

'An association of gentlemen,' wrote Ayton, 'have proposed the establishment of a decked vessel for ... mail and passengers.' This tells us that the ferry he used was open, and most probably a yole. That voyages in these waters were sometimes dreadful experiences comes across from an anonymous manuscript entitled *A Journey to the South in 1737*. The writer travelled in a yole from Sandside to Thurso; on reaching their destination, the seamen pulled the yole up the beach and it almost fell apart, moving the traveller to comment, 'Surely God was at ye helm.'[3] In November 1659 a ferry capsized in bad weather and the crew and their passengers were washed up on the Skerries, from where they were safely rescued.[4]

The bride of Alexander Graeme suffered grievously on a thirteen-hour crossing to her new Orkney home in 1828. Graeme described what happened in his diary:

We were taken in a little open boat to the larger vessel [a fishing smack]. Here the dear angel had to exercise her little strength and pull herself up on deck by means of a rope. The wind was in our favour for about 12 miles when it sank into a perfect calm. Dearest Mary was terribly sick.[5]

The first ferryman whose name we know was the famous, indeed legendary, John de Groat. According to the *Statistical Account* of Canisbay, written in 1791 and containing the oldest version of the story, John arrived in Duncansby during the reign of James IV (1488-1513) with his two brothers, Malcolm and Gavin, and a letter in Latin from the king, commanding the locals to respect and assist the incomers. The date is reasonable, considering that the king might want to improve communication with Orkney, now that it had become part of his realm through the dowry of the ill-fated Margaret of Denmark. John de Groat is often held to have been Dutch, his name more properly being Jan de Groot, although this does not sit too well with his brothers having Celtic names. The surname of Groat is also found in records from Fife, particularly Dysart where the first reference occurs in 1545; as the Fife ports traded with the Low Countries, perhaps the Groats entered Scotland by this route.[6] Some versions of the story behind the Caithness Groats are probably wildly inaccurate, and are most interesting simply for the way they illustrate how folk memory can work. There is no evidence, for example, for the often-repeated assertion that John got his name from his charging of a groat for the passage of the Firth; this first appeared in print in 1829 in Robert Mackay's *History of the House and Clan Mackay*, where it is said to be a tradition.

A footnote to the *Statistical Account* describes how the story of the letter was 'told to John Sutherland esq. of

Wester, above 50 years ago, by his father, who was then advanced in life, and who had seen the letter wrote by James IV in the possession of George Groat of Warse'.[7] The earliest existing mention of the name of Groat is in a charter, dated 14 March 1496, from the Earl of Caithness, giving rights in a land tenancy at Duncansby to John Grot, son of Hugh Grot. There is a possibility that the 'letter' referred to above was in fact a version of this charter.[8] An inscribed tombstone is preserved in Canisbay kirk and is dated in April 1568.[9] A Gilbert Grote lived in Edinburgh for many years and handled the legal affairs of the Earl of Caithness.[10] Johne Grote received £20 in 1540 for carrying letters across the Firth to King James V in Orkney.[11] The various land holdings of the Groat kin are detailed in many documents, but the earliest mention of the ferry and ferryhouse comes in a record dated November 1549. George Buchanan in 1582, describing Duncansby, wrote 'at the foot of the hill is a little bay which vessels coming from the Orkneys use as a harbour'.[12] In 1700 John Brand met a John Grot running the inn at Duncansby who maintained that his house had been in the possession of his family for 'some hundreds of years'.

John o'Groat's House became a tourist attraction during the eighteenth century, although little remained to be seen. I have already mentioned Bishop Pococke's and Bishop Forbes's visits. The fame of the house rested upon it having had an octagonal shape, each of the eight sides with its own door giving access directly to one side of an octagonal table. This was said to be the ferryman's answer to a dispute among his seven sons as to who had precedence and should sit at the head of the table. The site of the house is said to be the green knoll close to the present John o'Groats Hotel, and the octagonal shape is commemorated in that structure's design. Aeneas Bayne, writing in 1735, was a little sceptical about the whole business: he said that an old table was preserved in the Groat family house (he makes no mention of the shape) whereon travellers could carve their names but that every twelve years the table was planed bare to receive new impressions.[13] In some sources, it is clear that the Stacks of Duncansby were known to seafarers as John o'Groat's House,[14] but perhaps the application of the name to the Stacks was a later development.

In 1680, Sir Robert Sibbald wrote that 'Burwick ... is the usuall Ferrie to Duncansbie'.[15] An Orkney Act of Bailiary, dated 6 August 1644, states that the ferry charges for freight over the Firth were to be no more than 48 shillings 'in ane great boat' and 30 shillings 'in ane small boat'.[16] Presumably these sums are in Scots currency; the equivalents in sterling were approximately 4 shillings and 3 shillings. In the 1720s, the fare is recorded as having been 40 pence (3s 4d) between Duncansby and 'Barwick' (the Scots currency was officially abolished in 1707, and amounts were henceforward sterling).[17] Daniell and Ayton paid 15 shillings for the crossing from Scarfskerry in 1813. John Henderson gave details of the fare structure in 1812.[18] A passage from Scarfskerry to any part of the Orkney mainland cost 21 shillings, whereas a crossing to Walls or South Ronaldsay was 10s 6d. From Huna the crossing cost nine shillings, if the work required only four hands, and 10s 6d when more were needed. Cattle cost up to 21 shillings to ferry across, according to numbers and circumstances. It seems that once the cost of the trip was covered, the ferryman would let a latecomer join the passage for one shilling. The Post Office paid an annual allowance of £40 for the maintenance of the boat.

Sadly we do not know a great deal about the ferrymen, but the Canisbay minister, John Morison, thought them 'perfect masters of their business, and acquainted from their infancy with every circumstance, respecting the variation of the tides they have to go through'.[19] The boats were powered by men working four oars until the wind allowed hoisting a sail. One ferryman is quoted as having boasted that 'his boat was made to cheat the tide on the one side, and to defy it on the other'.[20]

During the summer months, there was a continual traffic across the Firth in horses.[21] Orkney farmers were in the habit of buying young horses from Caithness and

Sutherland and returning the same animals to their native braes when they were old and done. This was such a common practice that in some parts of Orkney a dead horse was said to be a curiosity. How skittish colts coped with the Firth has not been recorded, but they were transported in specially-built yoles at the cost of one shilling per colt or 1s 8d for a grown horse. John Henderson records that about 300 went to Orkney in 1798; and Thomas Jolly, the minister of Dunnet, confirms this, adding that about half that number returned. Numbers of cattle were ferried from Orkney to join southbound trade in cattle, and James Moodie obtained injunctions against rival ferries operating from Houton and Holm.[22]

At some point, probably early in the eighteenth century, Huna took over from Duncansby as the southern terminus of the eastern ferry. After more than another century had elapsed, the ferry between Scarfskerry and Brims fell into disuse.

For many years, mail was carried across the Firth independently of passengers and freight. Kirkwall opened its first post office in about 1747,[23] and Bishop Pococke mentions a mail-boat crossing from South Ronaldsay to Rattar (Scarfskerry) every Tuesday in the 1760s; he must have been in confusion over the route, as Huna was the usual destination for boats from South Ronaldsay. The mail-boat and her crew was lost in 1815 and again in 1817.[24] Dissatisfaction with the efficiency of the service was frequently expressed. It was claimed that a letter from Kirkwall to Edinburgh had to follow this route: it was taken on foot from Kirkwall to Holm Ferry, by four-oared boat to Burray, by foot across the island to Water Sound, by boat again to St Margaret's Hope, by foot down the length of South Ronaldsay to Burwick, by boat to Huna and then by foot to Wick where, at last, the epistle could be placed on the daily coach south; this circuitous routing of the mail was later denied.[25] The cost of sending a letter south from Kirkwall was 1s 2d.[26]

A correspondent to the *John o'Groat Journal* in December 1837 pleaded for a gig to be put on the Huna/   157

Wick section, as a runner took five hours to cover the 28 miles.[27] The runners, by the way, had an annual salary of £28. Bad weather often interrupted the Firth crossing, to the annoyance of the Orkney business community. The Huna/Wick gig began service at last in October 1839; it is described as a strong, handsome four-wheeled vehicle with ample room for three passengers.[28]

The Burwick/Huna mailboat sailed daily, weather allowing, but was not allowed to take passengers southward; returning to Burwick without mail, it could carry passengers. The fare was one shilling in 1839; it was still one shilling in 1845, when the charge for freight was 10 shillings.[29] Anyone wishing to go south, however, had to hire another boat, and this cost 10s 6d. The result, noted one man, was a 'locust-like' flood of 'vagrants, riff-raff and tatterdemalions' into Orkney.[30] There were also complaints about the habit of boats setting out from both sides of the Firth to meet in the middle to pass the mailbags to each other, an arrangement that eliminated the possibility of the ferryman having to remain overnight on the 'wrong' side.

The ferrymen complained, too - of low pay and poor support from the postal contractors. The Huna ferry skipper threatened to resign in December 1840. The press was unsympathetic and practically accused the ferrymen of laziness.[31]

But progress was catching up with the ferries; steamers were plying the Firth. The paddle-steamer *Helensburgh* chuffed her way from the Clyde to Kirkwall in 1832, arriving just before Christmas with a cargo of poll books for the forthcoming General Election. The voyage had been so hard on her, however, that she was unable to proceed to Shetland and the vital poll books were transferred to a sailing vessel.[32] The *Velocity* began the first steamer service in 1833, sailing fortnightly between Kirkwall, Wick, Aberdeen and Leith; and the *Sovereign*, a paddle-steamer of 378 tons, began to operate between Kirkwall and Newhaven in July 1836, also calling at Wick and Aberdeen on the way.[33] She was owned by the

Aberdeen, Leith, Clyde & Tay Shipping Company which, in 1875, changed its name to the slightly more manageable North of Scotland, Orkney & Shetland Steam Navigation Company. The *Sovereign* added Shetland to her route and began to make the Kirkwall/Wick passage in four hours, startlingly quicker than the old ferries.[34]

The paddle-steamer restricted her operation to the summer months. When she left Lerwick at 6 pm on 17 June 1839, one of her passengers was the Danish Governor of the Faroes, Christian Pløyen, who was visiting the north to see how he might develop the Faroese fisheries, and who later published an account of his trip. Their first port of call was Kirkwall where they loaded 150 small cattle. Pløyen was unimpressed by the flat, agricultural landscape of Orkney; only Copinsay with its high cliffs caught his attention, and he reflected that their seabird colonies would not remain long undisturbed if Faroese fowlers could get at them. 'We are now approaching the Pentland Firth,' he wrote:

> *renowned for its violent currents and heavy sea; on some small holms in the firth called Skerries, two lofty lighthouses have been erected, which must be dismal places of abode. There was a strong breeze from the east, and the tide ... was running against the wind, so I had an opportunity of experiencing a rather heavy sea - the whole bowsprit of our large steamer was often underwater, and we shipped great seas, to the consternation of the poor cattle that stood bound on the deck. I am used to a rough sea, and enjoy contemplating it, especially when this can be done from the deck of a large and excellent steamer. I was, however, the only passenger on board who was not sick ...*

With his sailor's stomach, Pløyen was also the only passenger able to join 'honest' Captain Phillips for dinner. Pløyen was delighted to see Duncansby Head, although he thought it 'of no great height'.

The Surveyor of the Post Office visited Caithness in 1842 and concluded that the best postal route to Orkney would be a steamer running from Thurso.[35] The annual cost of £1000 was justified. This came as good news to all the inhabitants of the northern islands. Some Shetlanders had to rely on the chance passing ship to send a letter; and ten years before, Stromness Town Council had petitioned the government to open a steamer service. A public meeting in Kirkwall in 1843 called for the same facility and further support came from shipowners in Aberdeen and elsewhere along the mainland coast.[36] Nothing happened for a long time, despite a lively correspondence in the press pointing out, among other things, the absurdity of a letter from St Margaret's Hope to Kirkwall having to go via Wick, thus crossing the Firth twice; this was later denied.[37]

In April 1845 one of the Kirkwall/Burwick post runners died - he was sixty and his name was Robert Groat.[38] At more or less the same time, a meeting in Kirkwall raised money to start a steamer service; the proposed route was Thurso/Houton.[39] Debate focused on the best kind of steamer and especially on the horsepower needed in the Firth. The *John o'Groat Journal* considered a 20-hp steamer with sails to be sufficient, and that any traveller would prefer a tumble in such a vessel to 'the horrors of the portmanteau-carrying, boatmen-hoaxing and whisky-bribing pilgrimage' of the Huna ferry. After barely two months, all the shares in the new venture had been subscribed.[40]

Again there was a delay, local politics being the cause, according to some. In January 1846 the Orkney mails were almost lost when the boat was caught in a squall.[41] With talk now of railways, the public was growing impatient with old technology; using fishing yoles to deliver mails was 'not in keeping with the spirit of the age', said the *John o'Groat Journal*.[42] A proposal was made to build a new harbour at Scrabster, capable of berthing a steamer. Time went by, and it was cynically observed in May 1848 that the mail-boat had lost only two trips that month - was this

160

a record?[43] Finally, in 1852, the new harbour at Scrabster opened for business.

John Stanger, a Stromness shipbuilder, obtained the first contract to carry mail by steam from Stromness to Scrabster. In 1855 he built in his yard at Ness a wooden paddle-steamer and christened her, appropriately enough, the *Royal Mail*. Stanger took his new ship to the Tyne to have her paddle-wheels and engines fitted, and began daily crossings of the Firth in April 1856. The *Royal Mail* was 82 feet long and 103 gross tons. She ran for twelve years, until 1868, when the contract was won by another Orcadian, Captain George Robertson. The *Royal Mail* was converted into a sailing vessel but, as if discontented with her new and lesser status, she was wrecked in the Forth barely three months after leaving the mail run.

George Robertson was a South Ronaldsay man who had been brought up on Stronsay. After a career in the merchant service in the Mediterranean, he returned to Orkney and bought a wooden screw steamer in 1863 - the *Quarry Maid*, which he renamed *Orcadia*. With this vessel he ran a service between Kirkwall and the North Isles, before he tackled the Firth route with his new steamer, the *Express*, in 1869.

In 1874 the railway reached Thurso, and three years later George Robertson's *Express* lost the mail contract to the railway company. Their boat, the *John o'Groat*, a steamer of 384 tons built in Dundee, came into service in July 1877. She did the run for five years and then passed through various owners until she was wrecked in the Adriatic in 1892.

In November 1861 the *Queen*, a screw steamer of 448 tons, began the first regular winter service between Kirkwall and Scotland. By 1883 there were three ships a week on this route. The railway steamer was replaced on the Scrabster/Stromness run in 1882 by the *St Olaf*, owned by the same company that had the Kirkwall/Leith run, the North of Scotland, Orkney & Shetland Shipping Company. In 1890, the *St Olaf* was sold and for

161

the succeeding two years the *Express* and the *John o'Groat* ran the service once more.

The first *St Ola* made her debut in 1892 and served for fifty-nine years.[44] Built by Hall Russell & Co. in Aberdeen, the *Ola*, as she and her successors were known, became a familiar sight, with her single, tall, stovepipe funnel; folk told the time by her regular appearance, and her failure to sail on any particular occasion became a barometer. With a length of 135 feet and a 22-foot beam, she was a slim, bonny ship, but she rolled too much for the comfort of all her passengers and I have been told that in bad weather she did everything except turn upside down. Ronald Miller described her as 'hideously uncomfortable' because, at 231 tons, she was too small for the job of taking on the Firth each day.[45] However, when she steamed into Wick for the first time on Saturday 16 April 1892, in good time for the 2.45 train south, she was described as handsome, and her top speed of 13 knots obviously impressed the audience waiting to see her.[46]

Her daily route took her from Stromness to Scapa in the morning and thence to Hoxa and on to Scrabster - the trip to Wick took place twice a month. Once, in February 1895 when snow blocked the railway line to Thurso, she took the mails to Helmsdale. After taking on the Orkney mails, the *St Ola* sailed from Scrabster for Scapa in the early evening. The fare at first was seven shillings for a first-class cabin and four shillings for second-class. Her first two skippers were Robert Robertson (until 1903) and Robert Swanney (1903-11), but the third was to become the most famous, inseparable from his ship.

George Swanson joined the *St Ola* in February 1906 as an ordinary seaman and progressed through the ranks, until on Captain Swanney's retirement in October 1911 he took the commander's stance on the bridge. All the crew of the *St Ola* were looked up to in Stromness, but Swanson became a celebrity in his own right. He looked bluff and tough - with a face like a pound of mince, I was told - and liked to play the role of the stern, competent seafarer, welcoming important passengers to the bridge. Underneath he was, however, a kind man and very good to his crew - he tried to win increased wages for them during the Second World War - and he took his ship across the Firth, keeping Orkney regularly supplied in all weathers until his retirement at the end of 1942, by which time he had been awarded the MBE.

It was during Captain Swanson's long service that a rival to the steamer as a means of transport across the Firth appeared. Captain E.E. 'Ted' Fresson, a former Royal Flying Corps pilot, was barnstorming at fairs around the Moray Firth when, on 22 August 1931, he was hired to fly the first fare-paying air passenger from Wick to Kirkwall. Within two years, Fresson had established an airline, and in May 1933 initiated regular flights between Inverness and Kirkwall. Orkney is now well served by air, and many travellers prefer the short hop in an aircraft to the longer sea crossing.

Captain Swanson's worst voyage, he recalled once, was his first as a skipper when he sailed the *St Ola* against a 70-knot gale, taking five hours to cross from Scrabster to Stromness. In his and his ship's long career, many other incidents took place, and you can hear them yet by the street corners and firesides in Stromness. In 1908, the wife of a Wick cooper called Buchanan went into labour on the southward crossing; the engineer, James Wilson, attended to the mother as best he could and a little girl entered the world off Dunnet Head - she was named Asherola, after the doctor at Scrabster and the ship. Another event was tragic. The *St Ola* could carry one or two cars on deck and it was the practice to drive them on across planks when the tide brought pier and ship to the same level. Shortly before the Second World War, a woman failed to stop in time and drove over the side of the ship into the water in Stromness harbour; she was drowned, and after that the mate of the *St Ola* always did the driving himself.

In the late 1930s, the *St Ola* was used in the Michael Powell/Emeric Pressburger film *The Spy in Black* in which she was 'sunk'. Wartime brought new risks and in October 1942 she was almost sunk in earnest. The cruiser, HMS

163

Sussex, was carrying out 8-in. gun practice when the *St Ola* passed between her and her target. The cruiser captain decided that he could fire over the ferry, but unfortunately the cruiser's range-finding equipment locked on to the *St Ola* and the second salvo fell 'extremely close' behind her. On other occasions the *St Ola* was shelled by Ness Battery and almost hit a mine.

The most notorious incident in Swanson's career took place on a foggy Saturday morning, 4 July 1936. An hour after leaving Scapa and just before she was due to rendezvous with the mail launch from St Margaret's Hope, the *St Ola* struck the east side of Hunda. The passengers and the mail were taken off, and Swanson and his crew were left to try to refloat. William Banks, then mate and later to be captain himself, went over the side to inspect the hull. Swanson called down to him, asking if he could see any damage, and Banks replied, 'Ye've made a hell of a mess of the man's rocks.' In fact the *St Ola*'s hull was intact and she was refloated none the worse for her grounding. Swanson was understandably chagrined: the owners wrote him an impertinent 'must do better' letter, but possibly a more embarrassing reminder of his mistake came to him from an unexpected source some time later. The captain was showing the bridge to some important passengers, giving them his usual stories, when he noticed a small boy whom he knew to belong to South Ronaldsay tagging along. Swanson threw the youngster stern looks to scare him off but the little fellow stood his ground. Finally Swanson addressed him: 'I've sailed the Gulf of Carpentaria. Do you know where that is?' The boy thought for a moment and said, 'No, but I ken whar Hunda is.'

William Banks took over from Swanson as captain in January 1943 and stayed to become the captain of the second *St Ola*, launched from Hall's yard in Aberdeen in February 1951. *St Ola II* (the Roman numerals have never been part of the ships' names but they are useful to distinguish them) made her first Firth crossing on 31 May that year. The old ship was scrapped and with her went some other customs of the day. First-class passengers on *St Ola I* had a small coffee room for refreshment and could enjoy some warmth from the engine room; but second-class, or steerage, passengers were not allowed aft of the bridge. If they were lucky, tea was passed down to them, and a sign on the ship reminded them that they were less important than the livestock and the mails. In 1951 a first-class return was 25 shillings; steerage cost 16 shillings. With the new *St Ola*, classes were abolished and a flat return fare of one guinea (21 shillings) was introduced. At the end of the War the daily route became established to the west of Hoy, although bad weather could still lead the captain occasionally to choose the Scapa Flow route.

Walter Leask joined *St Ola I* as purser in 1949 and stayed to serve in the same office on her two successors until he retired in 1983. He came out of retirement briefly to paper the officers' and the crew's quarters on *St Ola III*, while she continued about her business, after the men complained about the botched, depressing decor; 'The messroom table was ideal for pasting,' Walter told me.

Shortly after *St Ola II* began service, excursions to Wick ceased; after one stormy voyage, it took the crew 25 minutes to scrub the ship clean of vomit before they could contemplate the return voyage. After that, it seemed more prudent to hire buses to connect with the Scrabster terminus.

St Ola II, a vessel of 640 tons, carried 360 passengers and around six vehicles. These were hoisted on and off by crane, and the owners of the smaller cars were unlucky in that their vehicles were first on and last off, the larger vehicles being slotted in above them. Unloading could take some time. *St Ola II* saw my first crossing of the Firth, on an excursion for the annual agricultural show at Kirkwall, a special day when many Caithnessians ventured to Orkney. Departure was early in the morning and the return voyage in the evening saw much business in the bars and soon after in the lavatories, for those who made them in time.

Jack Stevenson became captain after William Banks, and before he retired in 1974 he saw into service in February of that year the third *St Ola*. *St Ola II* went on to a new career as a North Sea survey vessel called the *Aqua Star*. Again built in Aberdeen by Hall Russell & Co., *St Ola III* reflected the increasing trans-Firth traffic; a ro-ro vessel, she could carry many more vehicles - up to ninety-eight cars and seven trucks - and 400 passengers. John Anderson took over briefly as captain after Jack Stevenson, until he too retired in 1975. These years also saw changes in the ownership of the ferry: first, in 1961, the North of Scotland company became part of Coast Lines and then, in 1971, was acquired by P & O. After a few changes, P & O Scottish Ferries emerged as the present name in 1987.

St Ola II and *St Ola III* enjoyed steady but fairly uneventful careers, though Walter Leask recalls one nasty day at Scrabster for the latter. The weather was bad and the ro-ro ramp jammed, preventing the ship from docking normally. She came alongside the pier to disembark the passengers and then withdrew to lie at anchor off Holborn Head lighthouse. The fierce westerly wind, however, broke both anchor chains, and she was forced to sail for Stromness at night. 'We climbed a few,' says Walter Leask in the understated way of seamen. After three hours, the ship was still only halfway home, and Captain David Pottinger decided to run east with the tide, rounding Cantick Head and at last finding relatively sheltered water in Scapa Flow.

The *St Ola* now operates under two captains. Captain Pottinger and his fellow master, Captain John Tulloch, have both retired recently, and their places have been taken by Captains Kevin Manson and Jim Winterburn. Captain Fred Johnston, also recently retired, carried out summer relief work on the *St Ola* in addition to his normal duties as master of the *St Sunniva*. The crew also now work shifts and the *St Ola*'s personnel are no longer exclusively Orcadian.

In the wake of the sinking of the *Herald of Free Enterprise* off Zeebrugge, when the ro-ro doors were left open when the ferry sailed, all British ferries had to be extensively refitted. *St Ola III* was included, although many considered the modifications to be inappropriate, as the ro-ro door on her opened upwards like a visor, and sailing with it unclosed could never have happened. New buoyancy tanks were added, spoiling her lines and affecting the performance of her stabilisers. She began to roll more in heavy weather and earned the unfortunate nickname of 'roly-poly Ola'.

The latest, the fourth, *St Ola* to ply the Firth came into service towards the end of March 1992. A German-built ship, she saw many years of service in the Baltic as the *Eckeroe* before being bought by P & O and adapted to her new life. She can carry twenty trucks, 180 cars and 500 passengers.

With the development of Scrabster as a ferry port, the ferry route between Huna and South Ronaldsay went into an eclipse. It remained, however, a much-frequented crossing as the people on the east side of Orkney came regularly to Duncansby in their own boats, and the term 'Orkney's back door' came into being.[47] Because of the lack of harbour facilities - there were only small piers at Huna and John o'Groats - the traffic was restricted to yoles, until 1971 when two enterprising Caithness men called Ian Thomas and Donnie Bews started a passenger crossing to Burwick in a launch called *Pentland Atom*.[48]

In the following year, Bill Banks started a ferry service between John o'Groats and St Margaret's Hope with the *Pentalina*, carrying first fifty and then seventy passengers. In 1973 Thomas and Bews began to operate with the *Pentland Spray*. They built their own landing places at Burwick and at John o'Groats from scaffolding pipes and angle irons, at John o'Groats attaching it as a floating pier with a walkway of sleepers to the existing harbour structure. This arrangement served well for a while, even though it did one day submerge to give some passengers a ducking.

167

The short sea crossing, as it has come to be called, has proved very popular with tourists, and bus tours of Orkney are arranged to coincide with the ferry so that a day trip is possible. After the 1974 season, Bill Banks took the *Pentalina* to Flotta where the oil terminal was being built. In 1976, Thomas and Bews bought a larger vessel, the *Souter's Lass,* which had previously been used to ferry workmen across the Cromarty Firth to the oil-platform construction yard at Nigg; and in the same year Lawrence Mowatt of South Ronaldsay ran a ferry launch called *Nina.*

The harbour facilities at John o'Groats and Burwick were upgraded in the early 1980s, and now the short-sea crossing is an established service every summer. Thomas and Bews had a new vessel, the *Pentland Venture,* built specially on Humberside for the route; she started in 1987, carrying up to 180 passengers, and in 1990-1 was enlarged to take 250. The ferry has had her share of rough days but the schedule has been kept regularly every year, between 1 May and 30 September. Ian Thomas acquired a new vessel, the *Hoy Lass,* formerly engaged on ferry work at Flotta, in the autumn of 1993, and revealed plans to begin operating with two vessels in 1994. Once in a while, the crossing is enlivened by an unusual incident: in June 1987, the *Pentland Venture* helped rescue the crew of the German trawler *Hessen* which sank off the Skerries, and in June 1992 she took in tow the lighthouse relief boat when the latter fouled her propeller, again off the Skerries.

The short sea crossing takes about 45 minutes and the route varies according to the tide. As the ferry leaves John o'Groats she may head to the north-west towards Stroma, passing along the east side of the island before striking across the main channel of the Firth to Swona and then turning eastward under the square-cut, black cliffs of the Wing to Burwick pier. This is the closest most visitors will come to Stroma and Swona: on the former the weathered, grey houses with their dark windows and doors and the smears of yellow lichen on the flagstone roofs do not look empty, although they have been deserted since the 1950s; and Swona's outline, from the surf

168

breaking white on the rocks of the Tarf Tail to the dipping strata of the higher east side with its dark green turf and the bright splash of flowering whin, lies like a dragon across the horizon. The south-bound crossing reaches the Duncansby side under the cliffs of Longgeo, and slips westward along the shore to the pier. Birds follow the ferry: solitary fulmars, stiff-winged and aloof; squadrons of guillemots streaking over the wavetops; and single terns, flapping and angular like origami constructions. If the passenger is lucky and the tide is right, the skipper may approach Burwick from the east, sliding by the Lother Rock where seals haul out to bask and snort in the sun.

God save Mrs Manson

Throughout the nineteenth century, visitors were becoming increasingly common in the summer months. Young and old people of means, imbued by the fashionable notions of romanticism, and looking for a sublime taste of the savage in the wilder parts of Britain, were taking advantage of improvements in roads and transport to discover their country.

In 1825 Alexander Sutherland, a veteran of Waterloo, brought his bride to Caithness on a honeymoon trip. They rode from Wick to Duncansby, Sutherland dutifully noting the countryside as they passed. Their first sight of the Pentland Firth, from the summit of Warth Hill, was 'magical': below them lay the 'silver' strip of ocean and near the Skerries 'a gallant vessel, in full sail, was stoutly breasting the tide'. They 'hailed the first peasant who crossed our path' to ask the way to John o'Groats.

The couple found their way down to the mound where the ferryman's house was supposed to have stood, sat down on the green grass and began to pick out landmarks with the help of their map. Two fishermen ambled up and pointed out what was to be seen.

'On all these objects,' wrote Sutherland, 'the beams of the declining sun, as it hung in glory over the broad   169

Atlantic, played with the brilliancy of a tropic summer.' They watched the sun distort into an egg-shape as it neared the horizon and in the afterlight went up to Duncansby Head. The crushed shells and worn rocks on the beach at Sannick reminded them that the Firth was not always as picturesquely calm as on this June evening. Impressed by the Gloup and what Sutherland's journal describes as 'the Stalks' of Duncansby, they returned to the inn at Huna - to a disappointment.

There were only two beds. Some drunken Stroma men offered the couple the exclusive use of one, maintaining that they all could manage fine in the other. Sutherland did not like this arrangement, and the couple found more agreeable accommodation in a neighbouring house. From here, on the following day, they rode to Thurso, accompanied by two handsome sons of their host. It was hot and calm, and long lines of foam marked the edges of the currents in the Firth. Sutherland could distinguish men working in the fields on Stroma, and white houses on Hoy and South Ronaldsay. Their guides explained how only a short time before a boat had been sucked into the Swelkie and lost.

'When we beheld the Merry Men of Mey,' recalled Sutherland,

all nature seemed to make a deathlike pause; so profound was the stillness that prevailed. The hollow moan of the tide leaping and foaming on that solitary reef was the only sound that broke the deep silence. That moan is never hushed ... It seems as if the Almighty had decreed that these guilty waters shall never know rest, till they yield up, at the last day, the bones of the innumerable victims whom they have engulphed.

Another traveller who found disappointment at Huna Inn was John MacCulloch. In a letter to Sir Walter Scott he described how he arrived at the place one day in 1821 and could hardly get across the ditch around it. 'If I was the Earl of Houna Inn,' he wrote, 'I would blow it up, for my own credit ... no species or variety of Highland midden that I ever saw can be compared to Houna Inn.'[49] Beriah Botfield reached Huna in 1829 and found the inn to be 'a long continuous range of low huts', sparsely furnished.[50]

Joseph Mitchell, the engineer, came to the Firth and crossed it for very practical reasons. Here is his account of an evening spent at Duncansby in May 1838:

I set out with Captain Campbell and his friend Captain Fraser, and Mr Rose the county clerk for Huna - the ferry house for Orkney - and the little inn 1½ miles from John o'Groat's house, and while potatoes and chops were being prepared, we walked to the extreme northern point of Great Britain. The foundation of the house is to be distinctly seen, but nothing else except the pure watery element on the one side, with the Orkney Islands in the distance and the dull flat heathy country on the other. The walk along the sea beach is invigorating and delightful. Nothing can exceed the exquisite purity of the shell sand which forms the beach. The shells seem perfect in form and the whole is of transparent whiteness caused I presume by the bubbling eddies of the Pentland tide, running to and fro at the rate of nine miles an hour. This walk with the strong sea air made us quite ready for dinner on our return to the inn.[51]

George Borrow, the author of *Lavengro*, unwisely chose November 1858 to visit John o'Groats. He was caught in a bad storm and the land was covered in ice and snow; unsurprisingly Borrow confessed in a letter to his wife to be suffering a little from depression.[52]

In September 1863, an observer on the Warth Hill would have seen walk by a lean, thin-faced man with a prominent jaw and curly hair. From his dress, the stranger would be obviously a gentleman - with his top hat, black silk tie and high collar, waterproof coat, umbrella and small bag. From his accent, should the stranger speak a greeting, as he probably would have done, he would have been instantly identifiable as an American. For this would have been Elihu Burritt, a journalist from

Connecticut, at the end of his walk from London to John o'Groats.[53]

Burritt was, above all else, an enthusiast. Full of praise for the genius of work and free enterprise, and adulatory towards life in what he saw as the mother country, he was a shrewd observer but, like many a tourist to come after him, a little naive. In Wick he had seen a newspaper being printed on an American 'Columbian' press, and had found sewing machines to be 'in all the towns and villages'; he hoped that if no American clock were to be at John o'Groats, some of his fellow-townsmen back home would send one.

It was a beautiful day. The sea was calm and 'blue as a lake'; a lark sang above him as he walked, and men and women were harvesting with sickles. At three o'clock, anxious for his first glimpse of Orkney, he crossed the Warth Hill. The islands 'burst into view'.

He was disappointed by the mound that marked John o'Groat's house - 'literally not one stone is left upon another' - but he recovered his spirits by filling his pockets with groatie buckies. At teatime 'there was a moaning of winds down the Pentland Firth - a clattering and chattering of window shutters, as if the unrestful spirits of the old Vikings and Norse heroes were walking up and down the scene of their wild histories and gibbering over their feats and fates.' Burritt had translated some of the Norse sagas; he regretted strongly not being able to visit Orkney.

In the evening he ate cakes and wrote letters to his friends in the States and England. Then he spent an hour poring over the visitors' book in the inn: 'there were names from all countries of Christendom and also impressions and observations in prose, poetry, English, French, Latin, German and other languages'. Burritt found that previous visitors shared his complaint about the nonexistence of the famous octagonal house, but that everyone equally testified to the hospitality they encountered. He noted one entry: 'Visited John o'Groat's House; found little to see; came back tired and hungry; walked into a couple of tender chickens and a good piece of bacon: God save Mrs Manson and all the Royal Family.'

Next day Burritt picked up his bag and his umbrella, walked to Wick, gave a lecture on his travels, and caught the coach to Inverness.

The Grave of Mariners

Robert Louis Stevenson called the Pentland Firth 'the grave of mariners',[54] and so it has sadly proved on many occasions. Two organisations work permanently to minimise the dangers: the Royal National Lifeboat Institution and the Coastguard Service. The present base for the Coastguard in the area of the Firth is the Pentland Maritime Rescue Sub-Centre in Kirkwall, which looks after the long, stormy coasts between Cape Wrath and the Ord as well as the Orkney islands. The Pentland Sub-Centre co-ordinates its work with the main East Coast centre in Aberdeen; at the same time, Coastguards keep a close eye on the area from mobile shore patrols, and several local men work as auxiliary Coastguards. The Caithness side of the Firth was supervised from a Sub-Centre in Wick but this was closed in 1984.

The Coastguard has its origins in the attempt to suppress smuggling in the seventeenth century.[55] The illegal import of liquor, tobacco, cloth and other commodities was practically an industry along the coasts of Britain. The term 'smuggling' was also applied to the illicit distilling of spirits and, despite the law, these activities were very widespread and involved all sections of society. Will Richan, the captain of the convoy escort *Norfolk*, took every advantage of his voyages to Scandinavia to stock his cabinets. Excise officers searched the *Norfolk* in July 1807, after she returned from Elsinore, and found, among other liquors, 560 gallons of rum. Richan was forced to quit his commission.[56] In the same period, the Revd James Hall thought it a shame that the clergy of Orkney and Shetland should 'so often wink at

173

their churches being repositories of smuggled goods', and, with his tongue firmly in his cheek, suggested that this was perhaps due to a misinterpretation of the Apostle Paul's exhortation to be filled with the spirit.[57]

In 1809 a body called the Preventive Water Guard was formed to complement the activities of revenue cruisers at sea and the so-called riding officers who patrolled the coasts. The Water Guard was eventually charged with assisting coastal shipping, their main aim being to protect cargoes although it inevitably also involved life-saving.

The Water Guard failed to stop smuggling and it was supplemented in 1817 by the Coast Blockade, a patrol set up by ships of the Royal Navy but which eventually became part of the Coastguard Service. Six ships were based in Leith in the 1820s to patrol the northern coasts - the *Nimrod*, *Driver*, *Cherokee*, *Swinger*, *Martial* and *Nimble*. As well as these, twelve revenue cruisers operated under the aegis of the Admiralty, and two further cruisers were under the control of the Board of Customs & Excise. This varied and expensive operation was set on a regional basis in 1822, when the Coastguard Service was established. In 1831 the Service was recognised as a valuable reserve for the Royal Navy, and in 1856 the Coastguard Service Act placed the organisation under Admiralty control.

Smuggling was rife along the Caithness and Orkney coastline.[58] In March 1837 a new preventive boat was based at Lybster where, it had been observed by the authorities, foreign vessels for months had been buying and selling goods in an 'open and mischievous manner'. It seems that local businesses were suffering greatly from their floating competitors: duty-free rum, gin, brandy and tobacco were openly changing hands for herring as well as money, and 'theft, drunkenness and an open violation of the Lord's Day were the baneful consequences.'[59]

Folklore is replete with tales of the outwitting of revenue officers. One story, undated but probably relating to the early 1800s, tells what happened when some officers in Stromness learned that an illicit cargo had recently been landed on Stroma.[60] Aware that every move they made was being closely watched, the officers tried to keep their destination a secret and hired a boatman in Scapa to take them ostensibly and urgently to St Margaret's Hope. Once at sea, they told the boatman to go instead to Stroma but he, probably guessing their purpose, refused to alter course, even to the extent of threatening to lay into them with the tiller should they attempt to take over his boat. The disgruntled revenue officers had no option but to proceed to the Hope. When they reached the village, they hired another boat to take them to Stroma. Their first boatman tipped the wink to their new helpers, and at the same time arranged for the news about the revenue officers to be carried by riders the length of South Ronaldsay; so that, while the officers were now being ferried at a deliberately slow pace to Stroma, another boat was able to cross quickly from Burwick to the islands to warn of their approach. By the time the officers reached Stroma, all the illicit goods had been expertly hidden.

Stroma was also a notorious centre for whisky distilling. At one time even the island's schoolmaster was reputed to be supplementing his income by selling whisky from the schoolhouse.[61] Men from the revenue cutter *Prince of Wales* raided the island in May 1816 and destroyed two stills and 40 bushels of malt.[62] At a later period, a Customs officer called Terence Macmahon became the open foe of the moonshiners and was in the habit of making dawn raids on the island under the shelter of fog. On one occasion in March 1837 he destroyed 150 bushels of malt and two stills in full swing; a smuggler called Peter Green and his wife were arrested and taken to Wick jail.[63] Macmahon wrought equal damage to the home brew industry of Swona and all in all, by 1838, was being hailed in the *John o'Groat Journal* as having put a complete stop to smuggling on Stroma, with the result that the natives had grown 'steady, sober and discreet'. He had found much hidden whisky by measuring the houses inside and outside and uncovering hiding places in the walls. His triumph seems, however, to have been short-lived for, 175 within months, the Stroma folk were reported to be distilling again.

Macmahon's zeal received a setback in 1840 when he and his revenue men were chased off Shapinsay by a gang of 'ruffians'.[64] Some eighteen months later he was transferred to Cumberland to be riding officer there; the press lauded him for his enforcement of the law, and it is perfectly likely that there were celebrations on Stroma too. Smuggling was to the Stroma folk an essential economic activity and its suppression led, according to a note by the 1841 census taker, to a decrease in the island's population.[65] Not long after this, the anti-smuggling campaign was hit by tragedy. The Coastguards seized spirits on the Skerries; the Stroma pilots were immediately suspected and four were summoned to Burwick for interrogation. On the way, the boat sank and the four men - Andrew, John and William Sinclair and Peter Green, whom we have already met - drowned. Peter Green left five children fatherless.[66]

In 1843 a Parliamentary committee reported on the cost of shipwrecks around the British coast. They calculated that at that time an average of two ships were being lost each day, an annual financial loss of about £7000 and amounting to a sizeable proportion of the national fleet.[67] The number of ships destroyed in and around the Firth staggers the imagination - W. Bremner and D.G. Sinclair have recently attempted to list all the wrecks and mishaps known on the Caithness coast;[68] for the period from 1830 to 1981 their catalogue fills forty-five pages. A single burst of bad weather could account for several vessels and lives. Early in October 1845 an exceptionally fierce storm occurred, and the sea raged to the extent that lobsters were driven ashore.[69] The schooner *Tom* was caught off Duncansby Head; she foundered and the crew of seven, including one woman, drowned. The captain's body was washed ashore at Huna after ten days. In all, the storm damaged or drove ashore twenty-three ships in Orkney and four in Caithness.[70] A sudden, terrible south-easterly on the morning of 19 August 1848 devastated the East Coast herring fleet; ninety-four men lost their lives, thirty-seven of thém at Wick within yards of the shore.[71]

The Coastguards did what little was in their power to protect shipping from disaster. In June 1837 they spotted a brig, the *Margaret* en route from Danzig to Londonderry, heading in a thick fog for the rocks at Freswick. They called to her but were unable to prevent her going aground; later, however, they managed to tow off the brig without damage.[72] The Aberdeen sloop *Ruby* came ashore at Freswick in March 1844 in heavy surf; John Mowat, a local pilot, and the Coastguard officers managed to save four of the crew.[73] Three Coastguards were rewarded in December 1845 for saving a man from a wrecked schooner at Scrabster.[74] In June 1887, Patrick Picot won a Board of Trade silver medal for repeatedly plunging into the surf of Murkle Bay to disentangle rocket lines to the wrecked *Flower of Olrig* and *James*.[75]

Life-saving equipment gradually came into use during the nineteenth century. One of the first pieces was Manby's mortar, whereby a line could be fired from shore to a stricken ship; this forerunner of the rocket line was named after its inventor, George Manby, a native of Norfolk and a boyhood friend of Nelson. The mortar was capable of firing a line 150 yards, and an extra charge could increase this distance to 500. Being made of brass mounted on a wooden stand, it weighed over 300 lb and could be used only as a permanent installation. Despite this drawback, from its introduction in 1807 until 1865, when it was replaced by the Boxer rocket, it saved over 1000 lives.[76] A Dennett's rocket apparatus arrived in Thurso in November 1847, thanks once again to the efforts of Lieutenant Medley of the Coastguards.[77] The Boxer rocket continued in use until the 1950s. Pistol-fired rockets were introduced in 1922 and the modern rocket for use with breeches-buoy equipment appeared in 1948.

Voluntary life-saving companies were formed at some places around the Firth. Apparatus was installed at Stromness in 1868 and fifteen men formed the first company there. Their first rescue was not until 1881, when

177

the *Arcturus* foundered 600 yards off shore. The rocket lines were fired but splashed hopelessly short; and volunteers with lifelines had to fight through the water to the ship to save fourteen lives.[78]

The record for the 'longest' ship-to-shore rescue by breeches-buoy belongs to the Stromness, Hoy and Longhope companies. On 23 October 1952, the Aberdeen trawler *Strathelliot* ran on to a reef, the Taing of Selwick, at the north end of Hoy, 400 yards from the island. The weather, fine when the grounding took place, turned overcast and wet, and the Force 6 wind was throwing in a heavy swell that defeated the Stromness lifeboat's attempts to draw close. The breeches-buoy was finally rigged up and the twelve-man crew pulled to safety.[79]

The Firth can boast its share of odd sea stories. Take, for instance, the strange behaviour of three men on the brigantine *Watchman* in 1855.[80] En route from Liverpool to Inverness, the *Watchman* found herself becalmed on a misty June morning to the north of Stroma with the tide carrying her towards the rocks. The mate and two men took to a small boat to tow her clear. A ground swell sprang up, and the men in the boat, refusing their skipper's order to return, slipped the towrope and rowed off into the mist. The *Watchman* drifted on through the Firth until, close to the Skerries, a breeze sprang up and provided enough way for the ship to work back to Scrabster. Meanwhile the three deserters had landed at Burwick, claiming that their ship had gone down stern first. The three went on to Wick, heard that the ship was safely in Scrabster, hurried there only to learn that she had sailed, returned to Wick and there had to face their skipper. He forgave them but docked their pay. This was not the only case of desertion: when, in November 1856, John Cormack's crew refused to sail with him in a leaking sloop from Thurso to Wick, he took her through the Firth by himself.[81]

A becalming sealed the fate of the schooner *Good Design* in June 1871. Drifting between the Skerries at the mercy of the tide, the captain ordered his crew to abandon the ship. Their small boat filled and turned turtle, and the captain and two men disappeared. A boy, George Alexander, kept himself afloat on two oars. The mate, a Freswick man called George Sinclair, clung to the capsized boat keel for a time until he lost his grip. Alexander drifted for an hour and a half on his oars until he came close enough to the lighthouse for one of the keepers to dive in to bring him ashore.[82]

The cargo of the Leith steamer *Copeland* which went aground on Langaton Point, Stroma, in fog in July 1888 included almost 500 Icelandic ponies, many of whom were raised from the hold and allowed to swim ashore; one of the *Copeland*'s passengers was the novelist H. Rider Haggard, the author of *King Solomon's Mines*.[83]

The people of Scarfskerry were puzzled one day in March 1891 to find a ship ashore but no sign of her crew. Their pondering was roughly interrupted by an explosion. The cargo of the steamer, the *Victoria* bound from Hamburg to New York, included dynamite detonators, and the villagers did not know that the Longhope lifeboat had already taken off the crew when the ship went out of control in the Firth.[84]

In February 1908, an Aberdeen trawler, the *Ben Aden*, ran down a yole from John o'Groats a little to the southeast of Duncansby Head. Three of the five Groats men were lost. The trawler's helmsman claimed that he had been dazzled by the sun.[85] Local knowledge could not always save the Firth fishermen. Sinclair Steven, sixty-eight years old and thoroughly acquainted with the sea, was lost with his son, John, in April 1932 when their boat was overcome in heavy seas near Duncansby Head.[86] A Keiss boat was lost off Auckengill in January 1907 in cruelly ironic circumstances. The village's fleet of eight boats were all out after the winter herring, and had begun to haul their nets in the evening darkness when a stiff gale sprang up. The fleet made for shelter, some back to Keiss, others to Freswick. John Henderson in the *Sarah* saw through the darkness and the rain the white sail he knew belonged to William Bain's boat. Bain's sail was new and 179 untanned, unlike all the others in the village. In the rip called the Rough of Auckengill, as Henderson was deciding to turn about to run for Freswick, the white sail disappeared and cries were heard. The crew of the *Sarah* waited in the vicinity for as long as they dared but saw nothing more. William Bain, his half-brother Donald and his brother-in-law Alex Cormack lost their lives; and the official inquiry concluded that their heavy catch of herring perhaps contributed to the swamping of their boat.[87]

In November 1918, Captain John Mackenzie was sailing his schooner *Isabella* home to Thurso on what was to have been his last trip before retirement. With him were his son and two others. A gale caught up with them somewhere off Freswick and nothing more was seen until a body and wreckage came ashore at Duncansby.[88] In July 1927 the Stromness schooner *Mary Grace* struck on Swona - on this occasion the crew got ashore in their own boat.[89] Another schooner, the *John H. Barrow*, drifted ashore on Swona in 1929 when she was becalmed and was later towed off by the Longhope lifeboat;[90] in 1934 the Danish schooner *Elizabeth* became stranded on Little Skerry but was later refloated.[91] The last incident involving a sailing vessel in the area of the Firth seems to have been the grounding of the Swedish three-masted schooner *Trinite* in November 1946. Homeward bound from Iceland with a cargo of salt herring, the *Trinite* struck a reef off Brims Ness early one Monday morning. The crew were unhurt and the schooner was later refloated and repaired in Scrabster.[92]

Dramatic rescues are remembered along with the tragedies and, among these, the saving of the crew of the *Ahti* must rank highly. This Finnish brig ran ashore at Ham in the early hours of 23 September 1856. The strong gale took her masts and the rocks pounded a hole in her bow. The crew gathered in the stern in a pitiful seeking for safety, but one after another the sea plucked them overboard. The local people gathered on the cliffs and could do nothing to help until three hours had passed and the surf abated a little. Donald Thompson, a Scarfskerry fisherman, rowed with four companions in a yole to save whom they could. The one mile from the pier to the wreck took them half an hour. They rescued the two survivors still clinging to the *Ahti* and rowed home again, this time taking an hour and a half to make progress against the ebb tide. The five men were awarded a medal and money by the Board of Trade; and a Coastguard who saw the incident was amazed that any boat could have survived the sea they faced, as at times their yole was completely lost to view.[93]

Another rescue took place from the Leith barque *Larne* in December 1863. Driven westward by a storm, her sails spent and her rigging useless, the *Larne* was forced into a geo between Ham and Brough shortly after darkness fell. The local people flocked to the cliff edge but the wind and the sea defeated their attempts to lower lines to the wreck until finally, by tying smouldering peats to the rope ends, contact with the crew was established;[94] seventeen men were saved. On Christmas Day 1866, a similar incident took place when Canisbay folk plunged into the surf of Gills Bay to drag to safety the crew of the brigantine *Scotia*. Blown eastward by a gale, the *Scotia* tried to anchor in Gills Bay but one cable snapped and the other anchor dragged. The five-man crew took to their dinghy as the brigantine was driven ashore but the little boat capsized.[95]

Some Fine Services[96]

The Royal National Lifeboat Institution must be one of the most highly regarded voluntary bodies in the country. The heroism and spirit of the men who crew the boats is belied by the understated language the Institution uses: a rescue, often of many lives under appalling conditions, is termed a 'service'. Lifeboatmen, of whom only the mechanic or sometimes coxswain/ mechanic is a full-time employee of the service, would not want it any other way; they are the archetypal stoical, tough heroes of the sea.[97]

Lionel Lukin, a coachbuilder in London, has a fair claim to have pioneered the modern lifeboat: in 1785 he converted a Norwegian yole by adding air chambers and an iron keel, and offered it to a Ramsgate pilot for testing, but it seems that his vessel was used for smuggling rather than its intended purpose. Lukin went on to convert or build other boats which found service at various points on the eastern English seaboard. In 1809 James Bremner, the minister of Walls and Flotta, brought out a pamphlet on how to convert a ship's boat into a lifeboat. Explaining that his forty years' experience among the 'dangerous tideways and rapid currents' of the Firth meant that he knew his subject, his idea was simple enough - to lash empty casks or cork into the boat to give it buoyancy. It seems, however, that Bremner had been sending his plan to Trinity House, London, for as long as fifteen years before he published it. Various bodies had given him awards for his contribution to maritime safety.[98]

The National Lifeboat Institution was founded in 1824 on the Isle of Man by Sir William Hillary but was hampered by a lack of funds in its early years. Royal designation was bestowed in 1853. This was not before James Bremner, the engineer and salvage expert himself, had come up with his own design in 1846 for use at Wick. Bremner's boat was powered by paddles worked through levers and cranks by the crew of eight. Trials revealed that this boat, although fast and manoeuvrable, was difficult to launch into surf and the idea died a quiet death.[99]

The first RNLI lifeboat in the area of the Pentland Firth was established at Thurso in 1860; her territory was, and is, the south side of the Firth and the western approaches as far as Cape Wrath. The lifeboat shed was built at Scrabster for £103; and the first coxswain was John Brims. The first boat, the *Polly*, was launched six times from her shed at Scrabster and saved forty-nine seamen.[100]

There has been a lifeboat, called the Longhope boat, stationed on South Walls since 1874, when the local landowner J. Moodie Heddle donated a site to the RNLI and provided £30 per year for the upkeep of the facility. The original shed stands at the head of Aith Hope; in 1906 a new shed was erected a half-mile seaward on the west side of the Hope, where its functional structure of dark-red corrugated iron and its latticed launching ramp still dominate the scene. The first boat, named *Dickinson Edleston* after the Yorkshireman who contributed to her building, was described as 'powerful'; she was 37 ft long, 9 ft wide and was propelled by twelve double-banked oars. At the first launch in September a strong wind 'accompanied by considerable seas' was blowing. The men were well pleased by their boat. Benjamin Stout was the first coxswain.[101]

Before the establishment of the Longhope station, the local pilot boat performed rescues when it could. Such an event happened on a dirty night in 1869 when the crew were saved from the *Canadian*, a Greenock vessel driven ashore near Tor Ness. The wreck of the *Saxon* with the loss of all on board in 1874, when the pilot boat was away, emphasised the need for a proper lifeboat station, and the local people wrote to the RNLI to request it. Orkney's first lifeboat, at Stromness, had been established only in 1867, in the wake of a similar tragedy when eleven people had drowned during the wreck of the *Albion* on Graemsay.[102]

A fierce storm hit the Caithness coast two days before Christmas in 1876. A German schooner, the *Emelie*, was driven shore two miles from Ackergill on the south side of Sinclair's Bay. The crew of six scrambled into the rigging to escape the sea pounding over the deck, but the gale defeated the rocket team's attempts to shoot a line to them. The local people dragged the salmon coble from the village to the scene and, under the leadership of John Cormack, volunteers launched it into the surf. By this time the rocket team had managed to fire a line on to the *Emelie* and the nine volunteers in the coble used it to assist their

183

efforts at the oars. Three crewmen from the *Emelie* were taken into the coble and, his vessel now dangerously overladen, Cormack decided to head back to the beach. The rocket line caught under the coble's hull as she left the schooner and capsized her. Only five of the volunteers struggled to safety. Of the six men on the *Emelie*, only one survived the wreck.[103]

This incident led to the establishment of a lifeboat station at Ackergill in 1878. The *George and Isabella*, as the new lifeboat was called, arrived in Wick by train in March and was led in procession to her new home by the Artillery brass band, the Freemasons, tradesmen with their banners, Royal Navy reservists, fishermen and 'numerous bagpipers'. The local rocket company, perhaps anxious not to have the show stolen entirely, also demonstrated their apparatus. William Thain was the first coxswain at Ackergill. In the same year, in response to fishermen who were 'desirous to have such a boat', a lifeboat station was also opened at Huna, with John Calder as the first coxswain. Thirty-four feet long and powered by ten oars, she was named the *WMC* after an anonymous donor in Manchester and was launched for the first time in December.[104]

The advent of motor lifeboats based at Wick and Thurso led to the closure of the Huna and Ackergill stations respectively in 1930 and 1932, but the old sheds are still on site with the impressive launching ramps sloping down into the sea. The people of Wick set up their own lifeboat service in 1846, using fishing boats and the harbour's pilot boat; this was supplanted by the British Fishery Society lifeboat in 1848. These 'private' boats did sterling service before the first RNLI lifeboat was formally inaugurated in 1895, and Alexander McKay, the last of the Fishery Society coxswains, continued in post on the new boat, the *John Avins*.[105]

The early lifeboats were powered by sail and oar - 'pu'in and sailin' boats', as they were called - and their range was limited. The Thurso boat carried out most of its rescues in the Scrabster roads. However, distance did not prevent some astonishing feats of endurance. Likewise, the time of day did not deter the lifeboatmen. The *WMC*'s first rescue took place at night in the Firth in a westerly gale. The Wick fishing boat *Margaret Gunn* was being sucked into breakers on the south side of the Firth, her mast broken. The *WMC* plunged into the rough sea at 1 am and brought the seven-man crew of the fishing boat to safety before their vessel sank. Just a few hours earlier, in the same gale, the Longhope lifeboat had gone to the assistance of an Aberdeen steamer who had lost her propeller and had anchored in a dangerous spot. Seeing that the steamer, the *Ben Avon*, was not in danger of sinking, the lifeboat returned to Longhope and telegraphed to Thurso for a steam-tug to take the casualty in tow.[106]

On 3 March 1891, the SS *Victoria*, outward bound from Hamburg to New York, found herself in trouble at the western end of the Firth, in the teeth of a snow-laden northwesterly gale, and sent up flares. The Longhope lifeboat went to her aid and found her sinking. The crew, twenty-two men, were taken off; the thunderous sea prevented the lifeboat making it back to Longhope and she had to take refuge in Widewall Bay until the gale abated on 5 March. For this service, the coxswain, Benjamin Stout, received the Institution's silver award; and an 'extra pecuniary reward' was made to his crew. Half of the rescued men were German: the Kaiser presented a gold watch to Stout and £24 to the lifeboat crew.[107]

The rescue of the *Manchester City* in 1898 is still regarded as an epic of the Firth. On 31 October, two days out from the Tyne on her maiden voyage, bound for Montreal in ballast, this freighter lost her rudder in a northwesterly gale when she was three miles south-south-west of Dunnet Head. Lifeboats from Huna, Thurso and Longhope answered her distress signals and found her anchored. Before long, however, the heavy seas snapped her cables and she began to drift eastwards, although her engines still enabled her to make way dead ahead and astern. The *St Ola* tried and failed to put a tow aboard her. Coxswain Stout laid the Longhope lifeboat along-side, and Bill Mowat scrambled up a swaying rope ladder to the deck of the *Manchester City*. Using his knowledge of the tides and the ship's ability to go ahead and astern, Mowat piloted her past Stroma and the Skerries until they reached the comparative safety of the east coast. A Grimsby trawler, the *Jamesia*, helped the freighter to limp south, and after more scrapes she won home to Jarrow on 7 November. The Longhope lifeboat left the *Manchester City* off Noss Head and struggled home, having been out without rest or change of dry clothing for around twenty hours. Bill Mowat stayed aboard the *Manchester City* until her arrival in England. The £1400 salvage money which the lifeboatmen were later awarded must have seemed very well earned.[108]

The schooner *Brazilian* bound from South Shields to Stornoway with a cargo of coal had been windbound in Longhope Bay for several days when she eventually poked her bow out into the Firth in January 1905. She did not get far. Off Cantick Head a north-westerly struck her and snapped her masts. The lighthouse keeper at Cantick Head saw her flares at two o'clock in the afternoon, by which time she was drifting helplessly down the Firth. When the Longhope lifeboat got to her a little later, she was tossing in fierce waves that prevented the rescuers coming alongside. They did the next best thing in the circumstances and led the schooner to South Ronaldsay where she beached safely. It was snowing and very cold, and the lifeboat crew were out for twenty-four hours. Three days later, with the wind still blowing a gale from the north-west, they were called out again to the steamer *Domino* who had had her rudderhead ripped out by the storm.[109]

As new types of lifeboat were developed, the RNLI tried to provide their stations with them as quickly as possible. When Thurso, Stromness and Stronsay were given new boats in 1909, the three, two with engines, sailed from the London docks to their new homes. They left on 15 April, under the command of Commander Howard

Rowley RN, Mr Small the motor surveyor of the RNLI, and two mechanics. Each of the lifeboats had a five-man crew. Two weeks later, on Friday 30 April, the little convoy left Wick on the last leg of the long trip. As if to provide the boats with a foretaste of what to expect on service, the sea was 'dirty' and the wind was blowing from the north. They rounded Duncansby Head at half past ten, the three roped in line astern. Here they picked up the ebb tide and made progress through the Inner Sound. The sails were up. The wind shifted to the north-west and, when they reached the Men of Mey, the force of the sea broke the tow rope on all three boats. Each was left to its 'individual merits', in the words of the report, and though the sea was a 'veritable churn' they all came through without a murmur. The Thurso boat was at times showing three-quarters of her keel in the tumbling sea. At last, at one o'clock, they gained the calmer waters off Scrabster. After a rest, the two boats destined for Orkney set off again. The Stronsay boat's engines failed and she had to turn back, but the Stromness one ploughed on and reached her haven at eight o'clock in the evening.[110]

The last pu'in and sailin' lifeboat at Longhope was the *Anne Miles*, more affectionately referred to still in Orkney as the '*Annie Miles*'. On 24 October 1926, crewed by Captain Porteous of Stromness, Bill Mowat, Charles Mowat and George Johnston, she set sail for her new station, Howth near Dublin. After leaving Tobermory on the morning of the 27th, the weather changed; in heavy seas and a south-easterly gale, it was unsafe to dock anywhere and the crew sailed on until they reached Dublin at eight o'clock in the morning of the 29th. They had completed 225 miles in forty-seven hours without rest or hot food, the longest single journey ever made by a sailing lifeboat.[111]

Over the years medal after medal was awarded to the men on the lifeboats. Coxswain John Swanson of Longhope earned his first decoration when he led the rescue of nine men from the Aberdeen trawler *Braconmoor* ashore on Tor Ness 'in very difficult circumstances' in 1930. He won a silver clasp for a second service two years later at the same spot, for saving eight men from the Hull trawler *Dorbie*. In the pitch darkness of a February night in 1936, Coxswain William Dass took his lifeboat in under the cliffs of Brims Ness to pluck forty-one men from the stranded French trawler *Neptunia*: he was awarded the bronze medal.[112] In February 1944, the Norwegian steamer *Freidig* foundered near Cape Wrath when her cargo of grain shifted. Coxswain John McLeod and his crew on the Thurso lifeboat answered the distress call and in a high sea in Melvich Bay found first a liferaft with five dead men aboard and then another with two survivors; the rest of the *Freidig*'s crew were never found. Coxswain McLeod was awarded the RNLI bronze medal and the British Empire Medal.[113] Coxswain Alfred Johnston of Longhope won the RNLI bronze medal for rescuing the crew of the tanker *Oljaren* when she went aground on Muckle Skerry in April 1951.

Details of many wrecks can be found in some of the books listed in the Bibliography. I have had to select only a few to tell the story of the Firth. One I could not have failed to include is that of the *Pennsylvania*, whose name has acquired something of a legendary status. For once, humour rather than tragedy quickens the tale.[114]

The evening of 25 July 1931 was calm and lovely in the Firth, with hardly a whisper of wind. On Swona, James Rosie told his family that there would be fog before morning and, sure enough, when his daughter Eva woke at 5 am on the 26th, the island was wrapped in a muffling, thick blanket. To her amazement, she saw outside the house a handsome seaman wearing a foreign uniform. He asked her if this was Stroma. James Rosie, following his maxim that one should always be fully clothed before getting involved in an emergency, dressed and put on his hat before telling the seaman where he really was. The fog cleared sufficiently to reveal the masts of a ship. The *Pennsylvania*, a Danish steamer eastward bound from New York, had struck fast on Swona with a falling tide.

The Longhope lifeboat came to the scene, but the crew of the steamer refused any offer of help and landed on

Swona in their own boats. A Dutch tug came to remove as much of the cargo as she could carry, after attempts to refloat the hapless steamer failed and her back broke. The Danes abandoned her. With no hope of salvaging the ship, the insurance underwriters wrote her off and she was sold for only £100 to a group of local people who formed a consortium for the purpose. The *Pennsylvania's* general cargo included an amazing array of goods - office equipment, clothing, motorbikes, footwear, food, even motor cars and a truck, tyres, tools, galvanised pipes and sheets, cigarettes. As much as possible was taken off the wreck, an escapade of salvage in which the Stroma men played a leading and ingenious role. The *Pennsylvania* lasted another three weeks, as the buyers laboured to save every item of value, before she finally broke to pieces.

The *Pennsylvania* episode was virtually repeated four years later when the *Gunnaren*, a handsome Swedish ship heading for Goteborg from New York, struck the coast of Swona in fog in August 1935. Her general cargo contained a large amount of apples; and suddenly all the housewives on Stroma were making apple jelly, and their children enjoyed an abundance of chewing gum and crisps.[115] The *Gunnaren* was cut in two, in an attempt to save the stern section, but this salvage effort failed and the halves of the ship ended up ashore a quarter of a mile apart.

The equipment available now to the rescue services has reduced although not eliminated the risk to life involved in shipwreck. At four o'clock in the morning on 3 February 1956, a Norwegian cargo vessel, the *Dovrefjell*, struck on the south side of Little Skerry. A southerly gale prevented the Longhope and Wick lifeboats from getting close enough to take off the crew, and helicopters were called in. The seas were breaking over the trapped ship and the crew took refuge on the bridge. The three helicopters, an RAF Sycamore from Leuchars and two Navy Dragonflies from Lossiemouth, shuttled back and fore for some three hours, lifting the crew of forty to safety in twos and threes. This was the first time helicopters were used in civilian rescue in Britain.[116]

189

Two wrecks are remembered for their attendant tragedy. The *Johanna Thorden* sailed from New York on her return maiden voyage to Finland in January 1937.[117] I have been told that her captain was in a hurry to get home before the Baltic ice finally formed and left without an updated chart of the Pentland Firth. This was to have fatal consequences. Unknown to him, the Tor Ness light had been brought into use on 6 January and, when the *Johanna Thorden* passed through the Firth on the dark, rough night of the 12th, he mistook Tor Ness for Swona and failed to alter his course to avoid the island. Just before six o'clock in the morning, the *Johanna Thorden* ripped open her port bilge on the Tarf Tail. The impact swung the bow towards the shore, and the ship went aground. The radio was also put out of action. The crew were unsure of their location and assumed wrongly that they had hit the Skerries.

They took to their boats. The first boat, with twenty-five aboard, including two women and two children, was carried eastward into the darkness. The captain, the wireless operator and some others, thirteen in all, waited for a little while until the angle of the sinking stern allowed them to cast off in the second boat. When dawn crept over the Firth, James Rosie discovered the wreck on his doorstep. He thought that all the crew had been lost, and he and his family searched the shore for bodies. They found none. Meanwhile, the second boat came ashore on South Ronaldsay near St Peter's kirk; it capsized in the surf and five of those aboard were lost. A farm worker, John Peace, was the first to meet the eight survivors but, as the wireless operator was the only one with any English, communication was extremely difficult. The Longhope lifeboat joined the search around Swona but it, too, found no one and was recalled. Finally, after about two hours, the existence of the first boat to leave the *Johanna Thorden* was made clear to the Orkney folk. It was too late. The southerly wind had driven the boat up the eastern side of South Ronaldsay, and before it was located on the morning of the 13th it had reached the Deerness coast. It was clear that it must have capsized and the twenty-five people aboard were drowned. A chilling tale I heard on Orkney adds a supernatural footnote to this story: on the night the *Johanna Thorden* went ashore, a woman on South Ronaldsay dreamed she saw a fair-haired woman with gold earrings lying on the beach - and next day such a body was found.

The second wreck still recalled with particular sadness is that of the *George Robb*, an Aberdeen trawler.[118] Outward bound to the North Atlantic fishing grounds, the *George Robb* was caught against the cliffs near the Stacks of Duncansby at close to midnight on 6 December 1959. The weather was ferocious, with the wind at Force 10 gusting to Force 11, the worst in the memories of many of the local people. The Longhope lifeboat was thrown on to her beam ends at one point near Duncansby Head, and even on the following day, when the hurricane had abated a little, the journalist Jim Henderson was blown off his feet five times on the clifftop. The trawler's distress signal, indicating where they were ashore, was picked up by William Ham, who set off with his wife and some of his friends and neighbours to render what help they could. Struggling over the Duncansby moors in the teeth of the wind, the party heard the wrecked ship's siren blast a few times and then fall silent. They saw a light in the wheelhouse but they could not get close to the vessel, trapped on a reef some yards offshore and being pounded by smashing seas. The Coastguards and life-saving teams from Scarfskerry and Wick arrived, and the Longhope lifeboat stood offshore, but the storm likewise thwarted their efforts to reach the trawler. The would-be rescuers fought against the wind to carry gear over the moor from Duncansby Head. In the course of the struggle, Eric Campbell, a Wick Coastguard, collapsed and later died. A searchlight pinpointed the *George Robb* but no sign of life could be seen on board. When dawn came, she was lying on her port side, her back broken in several places, and the beach was strewn with wreckage and gear. When local people made their way   191 down a cliff path to the shore they found the body of one of the trawlermen, who is thought to have come ashore alive and to have perished from exposure. All the twelve men aboard the trawler were lost.

The coxswain at the helm of the Longhope lifeboat on the night the *George Robb* was wrecked was Daniel Kirkpatrick, a man of experience and courage. A few months before, he had been awarded a silver medal for rescuing the fourteen-man crew of another trawler, the *Strathcoe*. The *Strathcoe* hit the cliffs of Hoy between The Sneuk and Rackwick sometime before three o'clock on the morning of 4 February 1959.[119] On this occasion the weather was fairly good, with a light north-easterly breeze, but a heavy ground-sea was breaking on the island and pounding the trapped vessel mercilessly. High water was due at 6 am. Steering the lifeboat, the *Thomas McCunn*, through flying spray and drifting fog patches, Coxswain Kirkpatrick and his crew found the *Strathcoe* rammed fast in the Geo of the Lame. The red wall of Hoy's west coast is 500 feet of sheer rock at this point, and the sea was breaking 15 feet above the funnel of the trawler.

The motion of the surf, thundering in on the cliffs and rising higher as the flood advanced, prevented Kirkpatrick bringing the *Thomas McCunn* into the *Strathcoe*'s quarter. At five o'clock he threw his engines into reverse and backed away from the cliff to anchor offshore in 10 fathoms. He allowed the lifeboat to swing on the anchor until she was clear of the starboard quarter of the trawler, and fired three lines towards her. Two of the rocket-powered lines fell short, but the third caught and was made fast to the *Strathcoe*'s winch by the skipper. Kirkpatrick waited for dawn, and at 6.20 took the first man off the trawler through the wheelhouse window by breeches-buoy. The lines dipped and twisted and the man was nearly drowned before he was dragged into the lifeboat. Knowing that the ebb tide would set in along the shore and quieten the swell, Kirkpatrick decided to wait. Finally, at 7.45, the tailblock of the breeches-buoy was resecured and the thirteen men still on the *Strathcoe* were pulled to safety.

In 1964, Coxswain Kirkpatrick received a second-service clasp for plucking nine men from the trawler *Ben Barvas* by breeches buoy when she was driven ashore on the Skerries. A third-service clasp was awarded to him for saving men from the *Ross Puma* in April 1968, wrecked on the Little Rackwick shoals in a wild gale and snow.[120] There is a rider to the *Ross Puma* story that illustrates how much seamen rely on local knowledge. The trawler had signalled that she was ashore on the south side of Stroma. If this was so, the sea conditions would not have been a grave threat to her and there would have been plenty of time in which to reach her; but Jackie Groat, the secretary of the Longhope lifeboat and in shore command of her operations, had the hunch that the *Ross Puma* may not have known her true position, and asked the lifeboat to search first to the west of Tor Ness. The *Ross Puma* was, indeed, ashore west of Tor Ness.

One lifeboat story dominates the recent annals of the service in the Firth - the loss of the *TGB*.[121] It began on the night of 17 March 1969. A south-easterly gale of Force 9 had been blowing for three days, and the sea was a maelstrom, with flurries of snow and sleet reducing visibility to yards. A freighter, the 2300-ton Liberian-registered but Greek-owned *Irene*, signalled that she was in distress east of South Ronaldsay and drifting out of control. At 7.40 pm, the maroons went up, and twenty minutes later the *TGB* slid into the sea with eight men on board. With Dan Kirkpatrick were two of his sons, Daniel and John. The other members of the crew were Robert Johnston, the mechanic, and his sons, James and Robert, and James Swanson and Eric McFadyen.

Sydney Peace, the former secretary of the Longhope station, was in Edinburgh at the time. Two days before, he had flown over the Firth from Kirkwall airport and had noticed, he recorded later in *The Scottish Lifeboat*, how the spray was breaking over the 200-foot cliffs of Copinsay: 193

'The whole eastern seaboard of Scotland was being ham-
mered,' he wrote. On the morning of Tuesday the 18th, a
telephone call summoned him from his breakfast to say
that the *TGB* was missing.

Piecing together the various reports of events of that
night, we can follow the *TGB* on her last trip east past
South Ronaldsay. The flood tide was making through the
Firth at nine knots at this time; the wind was
south-easterly Force 9 and high water at the Skerries was
about three hours away. These conditions could produce
what Dr Peace called liquid cliffs, 60 feet high. Signifi-
cantly it was one of the strongest tides of the year, the 'top
o' the stream' as the local men call it.

The *TGB* rounded Brough Ness, and was last seen on
a north-easterly course towards where the *Irene* had reported herself to be in trouble. The last radio signal from
the lifeboat had been picked up at Coastguard Headquarters in Wick a few minutes before. Coxswain Kirkpatrick
was now steering his boat through the area where the flood
tide coming south along the South Ronaldsay coast met
in the Liddel Eddy the flood boiling down the Firth itself.

The Kirkwall lifeboat, the *Grace Paterson Ritchie*,
bigger and faster than the *TGB*, was also trying to reach
the *Irene*, but from the north. At about 9.20 pm she
recorded climbing the largest wave encountered that night:
it may have been 80 ft, and it is possible that the same
lump of water overcame the *TGB*. At 11.05 pm, the *Grace
Paterson Ritchie* received a message from the Kirkwall
Coastguard Headquarters instructing her to break off
trying to approach the cargo ship and instead to search
for the Longhope lifeboat. Ten minutes later, the Kirkwall
boat put up a parachute flare but got no answering signal.

Dawn. There was still no sign of the *TGB*. Shackleton
aircraft, a helicopter and three other lifeboats - from Wick,
Thurso and Stronsay - began to search for her. Meanwhile,
the hapless *Irene* had been driven ashore near Grim Ness
at the north end of South Ronaldsay and the seventeen on
board rescued by breeches-buoy.

Jackie Groat detailed the search areas. He knew that

the ebb tide could carry any floating object back through the Firth and asked the Thurso lifeboat to search west of Swona. They found the capsized hull of the *TGB* on Tuesday afternoon, floating not far from Tor Ness and only two miles or so from home. She was towed into Scrabster and righted. The port wheelhouse door was open and the hull was burst along the starboard side - it looked as if the *TGB* had been lifted and dropped by the sea. The bodies of the crew, except that of James Swanson, which has never been found, were inside. Six were in the cabin; the body of Coxswain Kirkpatrick was at the wheel.

The RNLI's inquiry forwarded its report to the Board of Trade: it concluded that the *TGB* had been overwhelmed by the very high seas and maelstrom conditions. The crew left seven widows, one widowed mother and eight children. The Lord Lieutenant of Orkney launched a special appeal fund to supplement the modest RNLI pensions and it quickly reached £100,000. In December 1969, the Greek Academy of Arts made posthumous awards for gallantry to the lost men. Everybody in the north was affected by the tragedy; the community of the sea grieved. James Swanson had been born in Dunnet and had been at school with my mother; and a memorial font to him now stands in Dunnet kirk. It is twenty-five years since the event but I can remember, although I was in Aberdeen at the time, waiting for news as the search for the missing boat went on.

At Longhope, for a short time, it seemed there might not be a lifeboat there again but, as preparations for the funeral service went ahead, the men in the community quietly let it be known that they were willing to form a new crew. It was clear to Jackie Groat that the tradition of life-saving would continue. The *Grace Paterson Ritchie* moved to Scapa to train the new crew; Jack Leslie came from the Stromness lifeboat to be the new coxswain, and Ian McFadyen, whose brother was lost on the *TGB*, was appointed mechanic. For a time the *Hilton Briggs*, formerly in Aberdeen, served at Longhope, and in 1970 the station welcomed a new Solent-class boat, the *David and Elizabeth*   195

King & EB. It was not long before she carried out an award-winning service.

The Grimsby trawler *Ross Tern* struck on the Tarf Tails on Swona on the night of 10 February 1973.[122] As the vessel started to break apart, six men abandoned her on a liferaft, leaving five others aboard. The weather was calm at this point. The alerted lifeboat slipped out of Aith Hope shortly after midnight and headed east. The wind freshened, throwing a heavy swell through the Firth. Using parachute flares, the *David and Elizabeth King & EB* located the drifting liferaft and, rolling fiercely in the swell, came alongside and pulled the trawler-men to safety. Coxswain Leslie now turned his attention to the *Ross Tern* herself. More flares revealed that the trawler was stuck fast on the rocks and listing to starboard. Reefs on either side prevented the lifeboat coming along-side, and Coxswain Leslie decided to steer in to the trawler's stern. The swell was rising and falling through 10 feet at this point. The lifeboat inched in, feeling her way and in serious danger of falling off on to the reefs beside her. Their only chance of rescue was to pluck the trawlermen from the *Ross Tern*'s superstructure on to the bow of the lifeboat. One man was pulled to safety before Coxswain Leslie had to go astern and realign the lifeboat. Then the remaining four were pulled aboard. It began to snow as the *David and Elizabeth King & EB* headed for St Margaret's Hope. Coxswain Leslie won the RNLI bronze medal and the crew received medal service certificates.

In her eighteen years of service at Longhope, the *David and Elizabeth King & EB* was launched on seventy-seven emergencies and saved thirty-three lives. She was replaced by another new lifeboat, the *Lord Saltoun*, in March 1988, and in December of that year Billy Budge became the new coxswain.

The seven men recovered from the *TGB* are buried side by side in the cemetery of Kirkhope in the south-east corner of South Walls. The sea laps gently to the sheltered sands beyond the cemetery wall and the striking, almost awesome bronze figure of a man in lifeboat gear, sculpted by Ian Scott of North Ronaldsay and unveiled by the Queen Mother in August 1970, looks down the Hope towards Switha and the Firth beyond.

A Natural Roadsted called Scapa Flow

No book about the Pentland Firth would be complete without mention of the great naval anchorage in Scapa Flow.[123] An uncle of mine served during the First World War on one of the fishing boats that serviced the Fleet and performed defence duties; and during my childhood I heard many stories of how my relatives watched the air battles over the Flow in 1940 from the Caithness side, when the night was lit by fires and the streaks of tracer.

Graeme Spence, a nephew of Murdoch Mackenzie and himself a surveyor for the Admiralty, was the first to propose the Flow as a base. In June 1812, he wrote to his employers suggesting they establish 'a Temporary rendezvous for Line-of-Battle Ships, in a Natural Roadsted called Scapa Flow'. He enclosed with his letter a chart of the southern isles of Orkney, coloured to show the varying nature of the coastline, and a report in minute, clear handwriting.[124]

Spence admitted that there could be objections to using the place because of the dangers of navigation, but he went on to say that, though the tides and currents might be a problem for strangers, the locals 'would think light of it' and that with their knowledge, 'a fair wind' and a few buoys and beacons, everything would be fine. In other words, if the Orkney fishermen could sail in the Firth, surely the captains of His Majesty's Navy could follow.

Spence went on to quote his uncle: 'The passage along the North Coast of Scotland has hitherto been thought so dangerous that to avoid it Ships have gone South-about Britain ... whereas by inspecting my Survey of Orkney there is ... perhaps less foundation to apprehend danger   197

on the coast of Orkney than on any other part of Britain.'
A light that his uncle had recommended to be erected on
North Ronaldsay was in place and functioning, as was
another on the Skerries, he added.

One month later, the Admiralty thanked their surveyor
for his proposal;[125] and thereafter seem to have forgotten
it - or at least for a time. In the same year, but this time
from the other side of the Firth, John Henderson sent a
memorandum to the Admiralty, asking their lordships to
investigate the advantages of Scrabster as an assembly
point for the merchant convoys sailing for the Baltic.
Scrabster was 'much better calculated' for the purpose than
any harbour in Orkney, ran the argument: it had room for
200-300 sail, it was well sheltered from all quarters, there
was little trouble with tides, good ground for anchors, up
to 10 fathoms of water, and 'sufficient room to work out
with any wind that blows' - and, to crown all, Thurso was
nearby.[126] No doubt Henderson was thinking of how the
town's merchants would benefit. At the time these
proposals were being made, Longhope was already
established as a gathering place for convoys, and it is
without doubt the better anchorage.

It was not until the outbreak of the First World War
that Spence's idea of Scapa Flow as a naval base was fully
realised.[127] In August 1914, the British Grand Fleet under
the command of Admiral Jellicoe appeared in the Flow,
and Orkney was placed under strict security.[128] The
defences of the Flow were not complete and the capital
ships kept on the move, sliding between the islands at dusk
and dawn, their coiling plumes of smoke mingling with
the mist and spray. Later, blockships were sunk in some
of the entrances, and boom-defence boats, commandeered
drifters on one of which my uncle served, guarded the
larger channels against U-boats. Four- and six-inch gun
batteries were set up.

Of the Grand Fleet itself, much has been written. It
sailed out to battle only once - to Jutland. The great fear
of the Navy in the Flow was submarine attack. The effort
to guard the entrances was continuous and the defences

were gradually strengthened as the War went on. Very early in the hostilities, on 1 September 1914, a U-boat was reported to be inside the Flow but this proved to be a false alarm. Almost two months later, *U 18*, under the command of Heinrich von Hennig, crept through Hoxa Sound. Von Hennig saw only a few smaller vessels through his periscope - the capital ships were off the west coast of Scotland at the time - but he resolved to lurk to the south of Flotta to pick off two approaching destroyers. The German periscope, however, had been spotted and the destroyers von Hennig had pinpointed as targets were in fact the first of several vessels searching for him. *U 18* dived, the destroyers passed over her, and thereafter for a time she dodged about, occasionally raising the periscope for a quick look. Meanwhile a Peterhead trawler, the *Dorothy Gray* under skipper Alexander Youngson, had also joined the search for the intruder and was struggling to keep up with her faster colleagues. Von Hennig's equipment failed to pick up the lumbering engine noise of the *Dorothy Gray* and he surfaced almost under her bows. The trawler ran into the U-boat, disabling her and putting her periscope out of action. Von Hennig made an escape to the east while the trawler blasted her siren to attract the destroyers. Diving quickly, *U 18* hit a rock on the sea-bed, surfaced, was rammed again by the trawler *Kaphedra*, dived again and finally ran smack into the Skerries. Von Hennig gave up at this point, his ship plates sprung and leaking, but he had almost escaped, as when he surfaced and broke out a white flag the pursuing destroyers were still three miles away.[129]

By the end of the War, anti-submarine defences were formidable. On 28 October 1918, *UB 116* under Lieutenant J. Emsmann gave her position away as she tried to penetrate Hoxa Sound when she activated a loop system of galvanometers laid on the sea-bed. Mines were fired in response and *UB 116* was destroyed.[130]

An incident often recalled with strong feelings on the west coast of the Orkney mainland took place on the night of 5 June 1916. In a terrible northerly gale, the cruiser HMS

Hampshire, with Lord Kitchener on board, went down off Marwick Head. The balance of the evidence points to her having struck a mine, although this explanation is still not accepted by all who are interested in this tragedy. Only twelve of the crew survived, but many more perhaps could have been saved if the local people had been alerted in time to the disaster or, in some cases, not actively prevented from helping the crowded liferafts swept inshore.

The analysis of the Battle of Jutland led the Naval high command to seek to use aircraft for intelligence gathering. The cruiser, HMS *Furious*, was adapted as an aircraft carrier and was commissioned in June 1917. On 2 August that year, Squadron Commander Ernest Dunning became the first man to land on a carrier when he touched down in a Sopwith Pup on the *Furious* in the Flow. A second trial, on 7 August, sadly ended in tragedy when the Pup fell overboard, and Dunning, probably knocked unconscious, drowned before he could be rescued.

Very late on the evening of 9 July 1917, the battleship HMS *Vanguard* blew up in an explosion caused probably by spontaneous combustion in the cordite in her magazine; over 700 men were killed. On a January night in 1918 two destroyers, HMS *Opal* and HMS *Narborough*, turned back from a patrol to the east of the Firth in a blinding blizzard and tumultuous sea. Losing their course, they ran aground on Hesta Head on South Ronaldsay and from the two crews only one man made it ashore.

Perhaps the most notable event of all took place after the War ended, when the German fleet scuttled itself in the Flow. Under the command of Admiral von Reuter, the interned German ships spent the winter of 1918-19 in the Flow. Morale fell among the imprisoned sailors - they were not allowed ashore, although some sympathetic Orcadians made contact with them - and the Admiral finally resolved on a last daring act to redeem some honour and to take his ships out of the victor's hands. At 11 am on the morning of 21 June 1919, the German seamen began to scuttle all their ships. The Royal Navy force guarding them panicked; firing took place and some

Germans were wounded or killed. Within the space of a few hours, five battlecruisers, eleven battleships and numerous cruisers and destroyers slipped to the bottom of Scapa Flow. One vessel, however, survived and still performs sterling service: Admiral von Reuter's barge was bought by Jackie Groat's father at Longhope, and her speed enabled her to become an ambulance vessel in the years after the War, taking several patients from Longhope to Scapa.

Then, for a while, the Flow was quiet, the main activity being the efforts to salvage some of the sunken German vessels. When the Second World War began, the Fleet returned. This time it appeared that the main threat was from the air. The Flow was repeatedly bombed in the early years of the War. The *Iron Duke* was bombed and beached in Ore Bay in October 1939. Indeed, the first British civilian to lose his life in an air raid was an Orkneyman, James Isbister, at the Brig o' Waithe, who came to his door to watch the planes attacking Scapa. Ships in the Firth also were targets and once a Stroma fishing boat had to make a hasty return to harbour when she found herself in danger from above. On other occasions the lighthouses were strafed. The last full-scale raid on the Flow took place on 10 April 1941 when about sixty German aircraft came over - seven were shot down.[131]

A flood of seamen and soldiers descended on the quiet islands in both wars. Many of them came north by train to Thurso and then crossed the Firth in a flock of transports. The trains were nicknamed 'Jellicoes' - what the troops called the Firth was less affectionate. Sometimes the rail journey took three days and the soldiers, laden with kit, gas mask, tin hat and rifle, must have thought they had reached the end of the world as they stumbled wearily on to the Thurso platform in some grey dawn. Malcolm Brown and Patricia Meehan have collected the reminiscences of some in their book *Scapa Flow*. On one occasion, a man was lost overboard from a ferry, and often half of the wretched passengers had to be carried ashore on stretchers after the crossing. The *St Ola* and the

St Ninian served as troop-carriers; they were bad enough but neither matched the reputation the *Earl of Zetland*, who was such a lively sailor that she was said to be torpedo-proof because her bottom was never in the water long enough to take a hit.

A considerable feat of seamanship occurred on the night of 13 October 1939 when *U 47*, under the command of Kapitänleutnant Günther Prien, nosed in through Kirk Sound between Mainland and Lamb Holm, and torpedoed the *Royal Oak*. Prien waited until just after high water when the slack tide would allow him some steerage way, and manoeuvred past the blockships in the Sound with only yards to spare. At one point the U-boat went aground, but Prien worked her clear; and just as she won into the Flow the headlights of a car at St Mary's caught her in their beam, but with no resulting alarm. As the Navy's luck would have it, most of the Fleet was not in the Flow that night but at anchor in Loch Ewe, which was considered to be safer from submarine attack. *U 47* slipped back and fore for a while until at last Prien spotted the *Royal Oak*. Seven torpedoes were fired at the battle-ship, four hit, and she went down with 833 of her complement. Prien escaped through Kirk Sound with the ebb tide helping him along; he was killed later in the War, depth-charged in his *U 47* on 8 March 1941 by HMS *Wolverine*.

The site of the *Royal Oak's* last resting place is marked by a buoy off the coast of Deepdale in the north-east corner of the Flow. It is an official war grave and off limits to the divers who explore other vessels. A little smear of oil from the battleship's innards still makes its way to the surface.

To prevent further incursions by submarine through the channels to the east of the Flow, a series of four causeways were built - the Churchill Barriers. They took four years to complete, cost £2 million, and consisted of giant blocks of concrete. Five hundred work-men and 1200 Italian prisoners of war worked on the causeways, defined as road links to the South Isles so that

POW labour, forbidden on military or defence projects, could be used. The Italians converted two Nissen huts into a tiny chapel, decorated by Domenico Chiochetti and others, on the deserted island of Lamb Holm, a sad and beautiful reminder of savage years of conflict. Now the causeways have allowed pleasant little beaches to grow in their lee, and the blocked egress from the Flow has increased the southward tide through Hoxa Sound by two knots.

Censorship prevented the publishing of details about wrecks and rescues, even those caused only by natural storms, until after the War. The blackout - lighthouses were switched off - resulted in an increased number of maritime accidents and, with vessels also being torpedoed and bombed, the lifeboats and the other rescue services had a busy and dangerous time of it. On occasion, it was not until bodies and wreckage drifted ashore that the public became aware of a tragedy.

In January 1940 a Norwegian steamer, the *Faro*, hit a mine off South Ronaldsay and drifted ashore; seven of her crew were drowned. Another mine accounted for the Danish ship, *Christians Borg*, to the east of the Skerries in the following April. In the same month, the crew of the *Giralda*, a Leith steamer, took to their lifeboats when their ship was bombed off Old Head but lost their lives in the coastal surf. The 10,000-ton tanker *Gretafield* was torpedoed nine miles to the south-east of Wick one night in February 1940. Oil leaked from her tanks and caught fire as it spread over the sea. Amazingly most of the crew escaped through the inferno in their lifeboats to be picked up on other vessels, but eleven men died.

The weather and tides took their toll of the increased shipping. In dense fog in July 1940, the destroyer HMS *Imogen* was cut in half by another destroyer while off Duncansby; the stern section was carried west by the ebb tide until it sank to the north-west of Stroma with eighteen men on board. The *Empire Parsons*, one of a convoy westbound in January 1942, went ashore in the darkness on the east side of Stroma; the crew were rescued and, on 203 this occasion, the other ships in the convoy were warned off in time.

Charles McAra, who joined the Royal Navy in 1940, recalls:

However attractive Orkney may seem in peacetime to summer holidaymakers, in 1942 Scapa was a grim and sombre place for seamen, stokers, signalmen, far from the companionable pleasures of Pompey or the delights of Devonport and, for most of them, unimaginably remote from their homes. For my own part I found that the bleakness of the setting only served to make all the more moving the sight of all the grey ships of Scapa. Destroyers, cruisers, great capital ships, this was their home, the place from which they set out westwards to the Atlantic or north to Iceland and then on the PQ convoys north-east to the fringe of the pack-ice beyond Bear Island and then on to Murmansk or Archangel. And, if they were lucky, this was the place to which they returned. Bleak as it was, Scapa was still home to those ships.[132]

In May 1945, in a faint reprise of the end of the First World War, German U-boats sailed into Longhope to surrender *en masse*. Scapa Flow was finally and formally closed as a Home Fleet base at the end of March 1957, but relics of its wartime role still abound. Above Lyness the walls of the former signal station crumble on the hill like a Crusader castle, and one day recently on the beach at Aith Hope I picked up a fragment of a NAAFI mug. Such is the interest in the Flow's life as a base that a Visitor Centre has been opened at Lyness.

The War coloured the childhood of all who grew up in the decade or so after hostilities had ceased. The sand dunes backing Sinclair's Bay had been heavily mined for fear of invasion, and the removal of the buried weaponry and booby traps took a long time. Poles erected in the bay and the dunes to deter parachute landing quickly disappeared, but lines of concrete obstacles and tank traps like squat, square teeth delineated the beach, and provided us with a convenient adventure playground, although our parents reminded us often of the risk of stepping on a lost mine. As far as I am aware, no one ever suffered. An army blockhouse stood until quite recently above the harbour at Keiss and gave fine shelter for sitting overlooking the harbour; other blockhouses were used by beachcombers for storing their findings.

The most poignant reminders, however, are to be found in the cemeteries by the Firth among the standard-issue gravestones, each with its anchor and cross, many with names but several reading only 'A Sailor of the Great War - Known unto God'.

Weather and Tides, which no man can control

One of our great-grandfathers was called James Miller: he was born in 1798 and grew up when Wick was poised on the threshold of the herring boom. He became a stonemason and lived at Stain to the south of Keiss. Probably he worked on the building of the harbour under James Bremner, whom he must have known, and on the houses that were put up as the village grew. He seems to have married twice; his second wife, Margaret Ganson, gave him six children to add to the four from his first marriage, and the second youngest, James, was born in November 1855.

I can remember our grandfather quite well, although he died twelve days before my fifth birthday. He had reached his ninety-seventh year. Gradually going blind, he continued to weave fishing nets until his fingers grew too feeble. Photographs let us see him in his younger days - stoutly-built, white-bearded, wearing a hat with a faintly Scandinavian look.

As I have mentioned before, James had a yole called the *Pansy*, and in 1911, when he was fourteen, our father left school to join his father and his brother at the fishing. 205

By this time Keiss had given up the effort to be a herring port, although herring were still fished for in the autumn, and the fishermen concentrated on catching crabs and lobsters.

Keiss became renowned for crabs, and in some years caught as much as or more than any other village in Scotland. It was seasonal work. *Cancer pagurus*, the edible crab or partan, as it is sometimes named in the word borrowed from Gaelic, spends the winter months well off shore. Around Easter they begin to move towards shallow water. Ruled by the same migration, the fishermen then put away the cod lines and got their creels ready.

Our mother's family came from the western end of the Firth, from the township of Westside in Dunnet, under the lee of Dwarwick Head and the mansion called the House of the Northern Gate. They earned their livelihoods by mingling crofting with fishing and other trades, and sometimes the men left home to be merchant seamen: our grandfather's brother, Edward, became a captain.

Donald Calder, our grandfather, had a croft at Ness, the seaward end of Westside; it belongs today to a cousin, but during my childhood it was our normal resort during school holidays. In the summer Donald Calder worked at the salmon fishing. At the start of the 1926 season, towards noon on 14 April, he and three others were docking the salmon coble in the natural inlet we called the 'boat peel'. The bowman jumped ashore, the mooring rope in his hands - when he looked round again, his three companions had disappeared, swept from the coble by a freak wave. The three were drowned and the bowman never recovered from the shock of this eerie accident. Our uncle later found our grandfather's body on the shore.

There are many roosts and tides flowing from the past, and many changes. Stroma and Swona are now deserted. I was lucky in that, in the early 1950s when a fund-raising drive was in progress to collect money to modernise Stroma's harbour, I was taken to the island to a sale of work. We crossed in a yole from Huna. I remember the islanders thronging in the school, and prominent among them Jock Sinclair.[133]

Crooked Jock, to give him his nickname, had only one leg. He lost his other during childhood. He used a crutch and was as nimble on a boat as other men. When Stroma lost all its inhabitants, Crooked Jock and his wife and his father, Andrew, settled in Keiss. Andrew frequently came to our house; he was a small man, with a cheeky twinkle about his face, and he predicted that one day I would be a minister. Crooked Jock himself was more belligerent, reputed to use his crutch as a weapon if his lost his temper; and he had a friendship with a one-legged seagull that he fed regularly at the harbour with pieces of bread. He had a detailed knowledge of the Firth's roosts: once, coming blindly from Dunnet Head to Stroma in thick weather, he established his position by recognising the boiling water of the Rip, a race that develops off the west of the island with the flood tide.

Around the turn of the century Stroma and Swona enjoyed an unusual service - floating shops.[134] Robert Garden of Kirkwall extended his floating shop service to the South Isles of Orkney and Stroma in 1889, and other operators followed. These enterprising little vessels brought regular supplies of life's modern comforts to many isolated communities. Before the First World War, the *Gleaner*, the best known of the seaborne emporia, called at Swona and Stroma every fortnight. There is a story that, motorised and taken over by Joe Smith before 1913, she once came face to face with a U-boat in the Firth, and the vessels ignored each other, each passing on her way. The trade fell away after the War, and with the decline went the *Star of Bethlehem*, the *Summer Cloud*, the *Star of Hope* and the *Endeavour*, until by 1930 only the *Gleaner* was still in business. In 1932 she was sold to a Thurso man and her unique work came to an end although, in 1934, rerigged and renamed *Pathfinder*, she went back to her native islands.

The Stroma folk campaigned long and strenuously in the early 1950s for a new harbour. Caithness County

Council was divided over the wisdom of investing in an island that since the turn of the century had been steadily suffering from emigration but, fortified by a grant from the Scottish Home Department, they agreed to support the scheme. Work on the harbour started in 1954, and it was finally ready in May 1956. During the construction the engineers complained about their difficulties in getting their local labour force always to turn out at low tide; the Stroma men, having crofts and creels to tend, had their own notion of timekeeping. Finally, however, the lack of amenity on the island and the better wages on offer on the mainland led to the last families leaving. Today Stroma belongs to a farmer, James Simpson, who commutes by boat to see his livestock.

Another community of the Firth has declined during this century. The people of Rackwick lived on the doorstep of the Atlantic.[135] Separated from their fellows on the northern side of Hoy by five miles of craggy moorland rising to over 1500 feet, and with their bay enclosed by the sheer faces of the Too of the Head and Craig Gate, they were an island in all but name. Around twenty families, nearly 100 individuals, lived here in the mid-1800s, growing some crops on small crofts no more than four acres. Some of the men worked at trades and the women carded wool or knitted stockings, but the sea was their lifeblood. Launching their yoles through the surf thundering in from the ocean, they were expert line fishermen, hauling harvests of cod from the waters around Hoy. The community thrived until the end of the nineteenth century, by which time there was an elementary school for the children. The cod shoals grew thinner after that, and the blame was attributed to poaching by Caithness seine-net boats. In the early 1950s, three lobster boats operated from Rackwick. The school closed in 1953[136] and by 1961 there were only fourteen people left, most of them elderly. Rackwick has, however, acquired a new lease of life in recent years: at the time of writing, there are four 'permanent' homes, and the beautiful solitude of the hills and the sea has attracted some new residents if only to holiday homes. In summer, tourists come in increasing numbers to view the cliffs and the birds and taste the serenity of the place.

Swona lost its last permanent residents in March 1974, when James and Violet Rosie, the son and daughter of the James mentioned earlier several times, closed the door of their house and moved to South Ronaldsay. They left behind their cattle, and Swona now has a feral herd, grazing and fertilising its green sward. They also left blankets, heaters and some basic food supplies, a thoughtful act whose generosity was soon to find its reward.[137]

In the darkness of the night of January 1975 a German trawler, the *Thunfisch*, came too close to the Skerries and ripped her hull on a reef.[138] The crew barely had time to fire two red distress flares and broadcast a mayday before the vessel foundered two and a half miles north-east of Duncansby Head. The alerted Longhope lifeboat was launched at 6.42. Coming east against the Force 7 wind and ebb tide, the lifeboat-men saw red flares beyond Swona, made all speed and picked up three men in a liferaft. The story of the *Thunfisch*'s last moments became known, and the survivors reported that their seventeen companions had abandoned ship in four other rafts. Where were they? As dawn slowly spread over the Firth, two helicopters, a Nimrod aircraft, the Wick and Thurso lifeboats and other vessels began to search the area, and finally spotted the missing rafts in a narrow geo on the east side of Swona. Alex Annal told me that at certain states of the tide anything adrift in the eastern end of the Firth was almost certain to end up in this geo. Helicopters lifted away the ten men found here. Meanwhile, the Longhope lifeboat, acting on a hunch of Jackie Groat, landed four of her crew on Swona. When they searched the island on foot, they found the remaining seven men from the *Thunfisch*, some naked, all exhausted by their experience, sheltering in the Rosies' former home where the stockpiled supplies had saved their lives.

The handling of large tankers in the Firth has given rise to concern about the risks of spillage.[139] The Orkney Islands Harbour Authority is fully equipped to deal with oil spills and there have been a number of minor spills, although these comprise only a very tiny percentage of the volume of oil handled at Flotta.[140] In 1979, two tanker captains were fined for releasing quantities of oil.[141] The loss of the tanker *Braer*, laden with 85,000 tonnes of crude oil, off Shetland in January 1993 increased concern that a similar accident could take place in the Firth, where any vessel losing power as the *Braer* had done could be quickly thrust off course and driven ashore. It was suggested by Councillor Bill Mowat of John o'Groats that the pilotage service for tanker owners calling at Flotta should be extended to all vessels with hazardous cargoes. A 24-hour radar cover of the Firth is operated by the Orkney Harbour Authority from Scapa; and, in March 1993, tankers agreed to adopt a voluntary code of practice whereby they would avoid sailing through environmentally sensitive areas such as the Firth whenever tidal conditions, weather and visibility are adverse.[143]

In the wake of the *Braer* disaster, Lord Donaldson was commissioned by the Government to review the environmental dangers from commercial shipping around the British coast. His report, entitled *Safer Ships, Cleaner Seas* looked at many aspects of the operation of merchant fleets and paid particular attention to the Pentland Firth, among other busy shipping lanes. The report observed that the Firth is subject to 'right of innocent passage', a concept enshrined in international agreements, as the only practicable route for large vessels using Scapa Flow and Flotta and as the shortest route around the northern Scottish mainland. The report concluded that the Firth is too narrow to allow a traffic separation scheme but offered guidance for masters, noting especially that laden tankers not bound to or from Flotta should not use the Firth against the tide or in conditions of reduced visibility or adverse weather. It also suggested that a deep-sea pilotage scheme could be considered for

210

northern waters if a demand for it could be established. In November 1993, the International Maritime Organisation approved the extension of the reporting scheme in operation in the English Channel to the Firth; under this scheme ships voluntarily report their presence to the Coastguard HQ.

The Norwegian tanker *Nyhval*[144] found herself in difficulties between the Skerries and South Ronaldsay in the middle of the day on 24 July 1993. The tanker, which had just left Flotta for Gdansk with 70,600 tonnes of crude oil aboard, refused to answer the helm in a tidal current. She veered out of control to port and had to be allowed to complete a full circle before steerage was regained and she was able to resume her eastward course out of the Firth. The incident lasted 35 minutes.

It is interesting to note in this context, a couple of incidents from last century. In June 1873 in fog, the *Martha*, a barque carrying 4000 barrels of refined petroleum from Philadelphia to Kaliningrad, mistook Dunnet Head for Stroma and became a total wreck on Dunnet Sands - the crew were saved.[145] In a similar accident in July 1892, the Russian barque, *Anna Mathilde*, went ashore almost under the doors of Huna lifeboat shed with a cargo of 2000 barrels of petroleum; in this case, the locals unloaded 400 barrels to lighten the ship and towed her off. An addendum to the reports of this incident is worth quoting in full:

This is the first time in the memory of the oldest inhabitant that a vessel stranded on that part of the coast has escaped becoming a wreck. It was taken for granted by most people in the Huna district that the Anna Mathilde would share the ordinary fate and great was their surprise, and no doubt equally great was their joy, when it was found that the Russian was once more afloat, little the worse for her mishap. The pious opinion nevertheless was expressed by some that the steps which were taken to save the vessel amounted to something like flying in the face of Providence, for if she was not decreed to remain where she was, why

211

did weather and tides, which no man can control, land
her there?[146]

Regard for Providence may not be what it was, but
the Firth remains the same. There have been proposals to
tunnel under it, and to harness its energy with power
stations.[147] The scheme of the mid-Victorian political
candidate, Edmund Lockyer, to bypass it by cutting
a canal between Sinclair's Bay and Dunnet Bay has
been sensibly forgotten.[148] In April 1993, an Inverness-
based group began to look for a site to test a wave energy
device called OSPREY (Ocean Swell-Powered Renewable
Energy) in the Firth;[149] and more or less at the same time
a government report stated that the Firth had the
potential to supply three times the output of all the hydro
stations in Scotland, and that existing offshore technology could be adapted to harness the power of the
currents.[150]

In 1984, a major survey of the channel, the first since
Victorian times, was undertaken.[151] And sport has
joined the more traditional activities: rowing races are
held between Stroma and the mainland, two Caithness
men have water-skied from Scrabster to Stromness, and
a canoeist has made a solo passage of the Firth in a kayak.[152]
The cliffs attract climbers: the Old Man of Hoy was
first scaled in July 1966 by Chris Bonnington, Tom
Patey and Rusty Baillie; and the first ascent of St John's
Head was accomplished by a team from Sheffield led by
Jack Street and Ed Ward-Drummond in July 1969.

A scheme to open a new vehicle ferry between Burwick
and Gills Bay went ahead in 1988. Although a Gills ferry
has been dreamed of since 1905 when the Gills pier was
built, and contemplated before then - meetings in 1892
were held about the possibility of extending the railway
to Gills Bay[153] - some always counselled against its suit-
ability for larger vessels and its security in bad weather -
'the worst harbour between here and Hell,' an Orcadian
told me once. Others, equally experienced in crossing the
Firth, maintain that the east end of the channel is the best

place for a ferry and that if harbours could be provided the ideal route would be St Mary's - Gills Bay. Stromness to Gills Bay is a shorter distance than Stromness to Scrabster, and it was the opening of Scrabster harbour and the subsequent arrival of the railway that set the ferry pattern last century. The proponents of the east-end crossing point to the wicked swell in the west end of the Firth in winter in support of their case.

Orkney Islands Council backed the new ferry company with a £2 million grant and a further loan. Work started on the building of new piers at Gills and Burwick. After further funding, and numerous setbacks and delays, the new ferry, called the *Varagen*, completed her trials and made her maiden crossing on 15 August 1989. The terminals were not yet fully finished when a gale on 16 September tore a steel linkspan away from the Gills terminal and made it impossible for the ferry to dock. The scheme is now in abeyance, and discussions about its future continue, while the *Varagen* is providing good service to Orkney's North Isles.[154]

The Firth continues to show its darker nature, adding more names to the long list of vessels which have met grief in its confines. The fully equipped rescue services now ensure that fatalities are rare, but incidents begin in time-honoured fashion when men make errors and wind and tide overcome the power of engines.

On Sunday 30 July 1979, a fractured fuel pipe in the engine room of the ore carrier *Vida* put her at the mercy of the sea two miles from the Swelkie. The crew radioed for help and then abandoned ship. The tanker *BP Springer* was on the scene within minutes and picked up the *Vida's* crew from their lifeboat. This left the freighter with her cargo of 30,000 tons of iron ore heading eastward out of control. Kenneth Pirie, a deckhand on the Orkney Harbours Authority launch, went aboard the *Vida*, found her electrical power system and consequently her radar still operating, and played a key role in the subsequent successful salvage operation by the three Orkney tugs, *Kessock*, *Kinloch* and *Keston*. The *Kessock* towed the *Vida*   213 first to Sinclair's Bay; the *Keston* then took her to Kirkwall, through fog, arriving late on Sunday evening. The rescuers of the *Vida* later shared a handsome salvage reward of £35,890.[155]

The 1000-ton German trawler *Hessen* struck the Beacon rocks on Stroma on the evening of 25 June 1987 and began to take water. As she drifted eastward it became clear that she could not be saved. Two Sea King helicopters from HMS *Ark Royal*, by chance exercising off Cape Wrath, two fishing boats, the ferry *Pentland Venture*, and the Longhope lifeboat, co-operated to lift off the twenty-one people on board before the *Hessen* finally slipped beneath the surface to the east of Duncansby Head. For one of the rescued crew, it was a repeat experience: he had been on board the *Thunfisch* when she had sunk almost in the same area in 1975.[156]

A severe storm on 19 September 1990 threw the sea over the harbour walls at John o'Groats: the moored ferry broke loose and four small boats were sunk; on that day a total of twenty-two boats were said to have been sunk between John o'Groats and Thurso. The ferry *St Rognvald* was butting through a gale to the east of Duncansby Head, en route from Shetland to Aberdeen, close to midnight on 4 March 1991, when a wave smashed through the window of the bridge, injuring the captain and another man, and putting the steering out of action. By the time emergency gear was brought into operation the *St Rognvald* had come close to striking the cliffs near the Stacks of Duncansby. Helicopters from Lossiemouth and Sumburgh were able to lift some of the crew to safety as the Wick lifeboat, the *Norman Salvesen*, stood by. After seven hours and some moderation of the gale, the lifeboat guided the ferry to a safe anchorage in Sinclair's Bay. The courage and skill of Walter McPhee, the Wick coxswain, and his crew were recognised with an award by the RNLI.[157]

So the story of the Firth goes on. In this book I have had to select only a few of the episodes in its long history, and others can be found in the various publications listed in the Bibliography. There is no end, as long as the folk living on its shores continue to look on its waters with an eye sharp for marvels and to show the courage that takes us down to the sea in ships.

At the time of writing, Stroma claimed another victim. The Danish coaster *Bettina Danica* went ashore close to Mell Head at the south-west corner of the island at four o'clock in the morning of 13 February 1993. On this occasion the weather was not to blame: a Danish Board of Inquiry found that the first mate, the officer on watch, had erred in trying to navigate the channel on autopilot. The crew were taken off by helicopter, but attempts to refloat the vessel failed and she was abandoned where she had come to rest - one more victim of a wild and open sea.[158]

Acknowledgements

Many people have contributed to the writing of this book, giving their time and their knowledge freely. I hope I have let none of them down and to them all I owe a debt of gratitude. My brother and my sister have long put up with having a writer in the family. Particularly I wish to thank them and also Alex Annal of South Ronaldsay; Jackie Groat MBE, Billy Budge and Billy Mowat in Longhope; James Henderson of the *Northern Times*; Captain Fred Johnston of P & O Scottish Ferries; Walter Leask of Stromness; Sutherland Manson of Thurso; William Ham and Peter Matheson of Scarfskerry; Kenneth Michie of North Walls; Walter Mowat of John o'Groats; Captain Robert Sclater, Director of Orkney Harbours; the late Peter Sinclair of Keiss; Brian Sinclair in Paisley; Jim Stanger of P & O Scottish Ferries, Stromness; Capt. Billy Sinclair; Cllr Norman Smith of South Ronaldsay; and Dr Paul Thompson of the University of Aberdeen.

In Kirkwall, Elma Wilson and Gordon Linklater gave hospitality, and Howie and Sidsel Firth also made me feel at home. Bryce Wilson of Stromness Museum was tirelessly patient in answering questions, and he and William Rosie of John o'Groats offered the use of their extensive collections of illustrations.

I also would like to pay tribute to the help and time given to me by the staff of many libraries and institutions, particularly the National Maritime Museum, Greenwich; Public Record Office, Kew; Scottish Record Office and the National Library of Scotland, Edinburgh; Guildhall Library, London; Aberdeen University Library; Northern Lighthouse Board, Edinburgh; P & O Library, London; and the public libraries in Inverness, Wick and Kirkwall.

I am grateful to my literary agent and editor, Duncan McAra, and to my publisher, Howie Firth, for their continual advice, encouragement and support; and to Corina Knight for her tireless typing.

None of the above is responsible for any errors; these are mine.

216

Appendix 1

Place-names and Place-name Elements

Most of the place-names in Orkney and northern Caithness are of Norse origin. Many incorporate one or more elements from a series of descriptive terms which were used by the Norse seafarers and mariners, including:

ayre	*cauceroy*
berry	*berg*, a rock
brim	*brim*, surf
brough, broch	*borg*, a fortified place
clett	*klettr*, an upstanding rock
geo, goe	*gjá*, a rift, chasm or opening in a cliff
gloup	probably *gloppa*, a steep-sided depression, but suggested by some as deriving from *gljúfr*, a chasm
hope	*hóp*, a bay
kame	*kambr*, ridge of land
ness	*nes*, a headland
roost	*röst*, a tidal race
skerry	*sker*, a low-lying rock, usually tidal
stack	*stakkr*, a sea stack
tang, teing	*tangi*, a point of land, often found as a tidal reef
wick	*vík*, a bay

The two suffixes commonly found in settlement names, *-ster* and *-bister*, are both derived from *bólstaðr*, a settlement or farmstead.

Thirl or tirl (door) is Scots and derives from Anglo-Saxon *þyrel*, hole, opening, or *þyrlian*, to bore.

The following glossary offers explanation of some of the place-names around the Firth. The precise origin of all the names is uncertain. Hugh Marwick's volume *Orkney Farm Names* (Kirkwall, 1952) is the major source of Orkney names; no comparable work has been published for Caithness.

Aith Hope	Aith is from *eið*, an isthmus.
Burray	*Borgar-ey*, broch island.
Burwick	*Borgar-vík*, broch bay.
Canisbay	The second element in the name is *bær*, a farmstead, but the origin of the first element has never been established. Suggestions range from the personal names, Cano or Conan, to *konungr*, king.
Cantick Head	The origin of this name has defeated scholars. There is possibly a link with the Gaelic *ceann*, head, in this case in the sense of headland, but Gaelic names are rare on both sides of the Firth. Could Cantick be a survivor from the pre-Norse Pictish names?
Creès, Head of	Possibly from *kró*, a corner of land.
Duncansby	In the sagas it appears as *Dungalsbær*, the farmstead of Dungal, a Celtic chieftain whose daughter married a Norseman.
Dunnet	The origin is obscure but it may well be a relict Celtic name from pre-Norse times. The earliest recorded form of the name is *Donotf*.
Dunnet Head	The name is of fairly recent date. Older maps refer to the tip of the peninsula as Quinicnap, Windieknop or similar variants, all of which point to an original Norse name, perhaps *kvernan*, a quern, from the shape of the high ground.
Flotta	*Flatey*, flat island.
Gills	*Gil*, a ravine.
Ham	*Hofn*, a haven.
Hamnavoe	*Hofn*, a haven of the bay, *vágr*.

Hoy — *Háey*, high island.

Hoxa — From *haugr*, a mound. The name is *Haugseið* in the sagas.

Huna — *Hofn*, haven, is the obvious derivation but there remains the possibility that it is derived from a man's name; compare Huney in Shetland, from *Huni-ey*, Huni's island.

Rackwick — *Rekavík*, the bay of wreckage or flotsam.

Ronaldsay — *Rognvalds-ey*, Rognvald's island.

Rora Head — The origin of Rora is uncertain but it could be from the Norse *reyrr*, a cairn.

Scapa — From *skalpr*, a long depression dividing areas of higher ground.

Scarfskerry — *Skarfr*, a shag or cormorant, with *sker*.

Scotland's Haven — The most intriguing of the Firth's place-names; no clear derivation for this shallow inlet beside St John's Point has been established. The obvious meaning of the English words remains a possibility but, apart from the words 'Orkney ferry' appearing beside the place-name in a map of Caithness published in Edinburgh by John Thomson & Co. in 1822, there is no evidence that the inlet was ever used as a regular landing-place for travellers from Orkney before the islands passed to Scotland; and the inlet itself is now shallow and hardly attractive as a harbour. It has been suggested, though not convincingly, that the first word may derive from *skat*, a Norse form of tax, or from the

219

	Gaelic *sgot*, a plot of land.
Sneuk	The most obvious origin is *snokr*, a snout.
St Margaret's Hope	The St Margaret to whom the bay is dedicated has been linked to Margaret, the three-year-old daughter of the King of Norway, who died on her way to Scotland in 1290 to inherit the Scottish throne from her grandfather, Alexander III; but this is simply a coincidence.
Stroma	*Straum-ey*, island in the tide.
Stromness	*Straum-nes*, headland of the tide.
Swelkie	*Svelgr*, whirlpool.
Switha	The name is Norse but its exact derivation is unknown.
Swona	*Svin-ey*, swine island.
Tarf Tail	The origin of Tarf is obscure but *torf*, turf, or perhaps þari, sea weed, are possibilities.
Too of the Head	'Too' is possibly from þufa, a mound, or *to*, a plot of grass.
Tor Ness	'Tor' could be derived from *torf*, turf or peat.
Walls	From the Norse *vágar*, bays or voes. Through the generations since the Norse settlement, as Norse declined and was influenced by Scots, the word changed to *waas*, which the mapmakers then thought to be short for 'walls'.

Appendix 2

Shipping in the Firth

For one year until 31 January 1994, the Department of Harbours of the Orkney Islands Council monitored in detail traffic through the Pentland Firth. The table shows the number of vessels passing through in a typical week (in this instance, 30 May to 5 June 1993) as well as the total number of vessels in each category recorded. Many vessels do not reply to enquiries.

Type of vessel		Total
Motor tankers	8	443
Coastal tankers	8	218
General cargo	21	734
Bulk cargo	20	520
Coasters	2	260
Container ships	-	107
Fishing vessels	9	663
Offshore vessels	-	50
Passenger ships	3	25
Warships	12	177
Ro-ro vessels	6	330
Liquid gas carriers	-	339
Chemical carriers	-	123
Survey vessels	-	9
Lighthouse tenders	-	60
Tugs	1	52
Others	1	137
No replies	38	1669
Total		5816

This was the first official, detailed survey. It is certain that Firth traffic was considerably higher in the 1950s and '60s.

All the authors referred to are listed in the Bibliography. The following abbreviations are used in the Notes:

ADM	Admiralty papers, in the Public Record Office, London.
CC	*Caithness Courier*
INA	*Inverness Advertiser*
JoG	*John o'Groat Journal*
LL	*Lloyd's List*
OLM	*Old Lore Miscellany*
OSA	*Statistical Account of Scotland*
	This was originally published in a series of twenty volumes in the 1790s. The descriptions of the five Firth parishes are: South Ronaldsay and Burray, Revd James Watson, vol. 15, 1793; Hoy and Graemsay, Revd Robert Sands, vol. 16, 1794-95; Walls and Flotta, Revd James Bremner, vol. 17, 1794; Dunnet, Revd Thomas Jolly, vol.11, 1791; Canisbay, Revd John Morison, vol. 8, 1791.
NSA	*New Statistical Account of Scotland*
	Unlike its predecessor, the parish accounts in this series were published in a logical grouping, with all the Firth parishes being in vol. 15, 1845. The authors were: Walls and Flotta, Revd Walter Weir; Hoy and Graemsay, Revd Gavin Hamilton; South Ronaldsay, Revd John Gerard; Canisbay, Revd Peter Jolly; Dunnet, Revd Thomas Jolly.

The numbers in the text refer to the Notes and Sources below. Where the author of a particular source is clear in the main text, the reader should refer directly to the Bibliography for details of the work.

Introduction

1 Charles Calder's obituary, *JoG*, 2 Feb. 1934.
2 Information from Jackie Groat.
3 Information from Billy Mowat.
4 Conrad's novel *The Nigger of the Narcissus* was published in 1897.

I Slackwater

1 Technical descriptions of waves and other oceanographic phenomena can be found in many textbooks. I have drawn mainly on King, 1959.
2 One of the best 'fog stories' concerns the ferry, the *St Rognvald*. In August 1931, northbound from Leith to Stromness, she was trapped in a thick fog for three days off the Caithness coast. The 200 passengers passed the time with concerts, games and dances; the cargo was broken into for food, and fish were bought from a drifter. A coaster nearly collided with the waiting ship. Finally the *St Rognvald* was able to slip north, reaching her destination after seventy hours at sea.
3 The writings of John of Fordun and Bishop Leslie are included in Hume Brown, 1893. See also Leslie's *Historie*.
4 Sydney Peace, '18th March 1969', in *The Scottish Lifeboat*, 1970.
5 There is a good discussion of the age of the Firth in Berry, 1985. See also Bailey, 1971.
6 The archaeology of Orkney is described in many books; see especially Hedges, 1984, and Renfrew, 1985.
7 An excellent summary of early voyages by Pytheas and others is given in Carpenter, 1973.
8 A full discussion of past climates is in Lamb, 1977.
9 The Ferriby plank boats are on display in the National Maritime Museum, Greenwich. These and other early craft are described in Greenhill, 1982.
10 The replica Bronze Age boats are described in Johnstone, 1980.
11 Johnstone, 1980.
12 Extracts from the *Irish Annals* are given in Anderson, 1922.
13 Information from Jackie Groat.
14 Mackay's voyage is described in Calder, 1887.
15 The HMS *Barham* episode is described in *Tidal Streams*. The logbook of The *Barham* reads more prosaically for the same event:
> 0400 steering S 06 W, wind NNW Force 8-10, weather blue sky in patches,

squally sea very high to tremendous, air temp 40ºF
0500 Auskerry Light abeam
0613 Pentland Skerries abeam
0745 course altered to S 45 W, both engines slowed
Noss Hd abeam.
(Logbook ADM 53/17620)

16 Dave Worral, the engineer of the *Commodity*, is quoted in JoG, 5 Oct 1984.
17 Information from Sutherland Manson.
18 See page 173.
19 For more details, see Andrews, 1990.
20 Admiralty Chart *Pentland Firth and Approaches*, 1981.
21 Two editions of *Orkneyinga Saga* are readily available. Both are listed in the Bibliography.
22 Snorri Sturluson's *Heimskringla*.
23 The *Historia Norvegiae* passage is quoted in Anderson, 1922, and Crawford, 1987.
24 The Grotti and the Wells of Swona legends are retold in *OLM*, vol. 3, 1910.
25 Mackenzie, 1750.
26 Calder, 1887.
27 Wilson, 1842.
28 JoG, 15 Sept. 1843.
29 Information from Sutherland Manson.
30 The location of Rauðabjorg is uncertain: Rattar, Roeberry on South Walls, and Red Head on the west side of Stroma have all been suggested.
31 Anderson, 1922.
32 Anderson, 1922.
33 Norse ships - see, for example, Graham-Campbell & Kidd, 1980; Klindt-Jensen, 1970; Foote & Wilson, 1980.
34 See, for example, Wernick, 1979.
35 OSA, Thurso, 1798. 'Wood of all sorts' is the second item on the list of imports, after dressed flax and before fishery salt.
36 Fenton, 1978.
37 Sandison, 1981.
38 Anson, 1950; Wilson, 1965.
39 Information from Alex Annal.
40 Walter Green, JoG, 24 May 1918, 'Boatbuilding in the early days of Pulteneytown'.
41 Stromness Museum, and also in Newman, 1987.
42 My main sources of information on the Firth yoles are our late father, Dave Miller of Keiss, Peter Matheson, Sutherland Manson and Brian Sinclair.
43 Wildy Sinclair, 'The Building of a Stroma yole', in Marshall, 1987. **225**

44 Alex Annal told me of James Rosie's fast sailing yole, the *Falcon*, which outraced all her rivals.

45 The most comprehensive account of the Sinclair voyage to America is the book by Frederick Pohl, 1974.

46 See Andrew Sinclair, *The Sword and the Grail*, 1993.

47 The link between Robert the Bruce and South Ronaldsay is argued for by, for example, Evan Barron in *OLM*, vol. 2, 1909. I also heard the story on South Ronaldsay.

48 Lindsay's Rutter - see Taylor, 1981.

49 An excellent summary of the development of shipping in this period is given in Marcus, 1980.

50 Leslie, 1895.

51 Accounts of the Lord High Treasurer of Scotland, vol. 7, 1540.

52 *Ibid*, vol. 1, 1496;

53 *Ibid*, vol. 1, 1526;

54 *Ibid*, vol. 5, 1531;

55 *Ibid*, vol. 9, 1550;

56 *Ibid*, vol. 10, 1552.

57 In Bain (ed.), 1890.

58 Buchanan, 1862, vol. 2; also in Hossack, 1900.

59 Martin, 1975.

60 Marcus, 1980, states that English fishermen began to work Icelandic waters in 1408-9 and that English traders started sailing to Iceland in 1413. We can be sure that Orkney was a stopping place from these early times.

61 The voyages of John Knight, William Baffin and others are given in Purchas, 1625.

62 The word 'portolan' is derived from *portolano*, the medieval Mediterranean word for pilot book or written sailing directions. According to Moir, 1973, the oldest chart to show Scotland was produced in Majorca in 1325. The first printed map of Scotland on its own was published in Italy in about 1560.

63 Homem's and Fornani's work is on display in the National Maritime Museum.

64 Early globes are also on display in the National Maritime Museum.

65 Editions of Ptolemy's work can be seen in various museums. With regard to the interpretation of the headlands, for example Moir, 1973, suggests that the three are Holborn Head or Strathy Point, Dunnet Head or Holborn Head or St John's Point, and Duncansby Head. Taking the most easterly as Noss Head seems neatly to sort out this conundrum. It all depends, of course, on Ptolemy having reliable information to work from in the first instance.

66 Nicolay's map appears in Adair's *The Description of the Sea-Coast and Islands of Scotland*.

67 The full story of Pont and Blaeu, as far as it is known, is in
   Moir, 1973, and Stone, 1991. Some extant 16th-century maps
   of the north of Scotland may include information made
   available by a Caithness-born cleric called John Elder who,
   in 1543, sent a map of Scotland to Henry VIII. Elder's map
   has been lost but he was probably the source for some later
   mapmakers' knowledge of such features of the Firth as the
   Swilkie and the Bores. Elder had a curious career: for a long
   time he was in the pay of the English and he may well have
   acted as a spy.

68 Pont's and Gordon's maps were published in vol. 5 of the
   Atlas Novus and in vol. 6 of the *Atlas Major* by Blaeu.

69 Van Keulen's chart is in his 1714 atlas in the National Maritime
   Museum. His first charts of Scotland were published in
   Amsterdam in 1682 and went through various changes and
   editions in the succeeding decades.

70 Greenville Collins's chart - National Maritime Museum,
   G218.14/4 (i).

71 Adair's death is given as 1722 in *Bannatyne Club Misc.*, 1836;
   and by Moir, 1973, as having taken place on 15 May 1718.
   The MS of Adair's chart of the Pentland Firth (c. 1715) is in
   the Admiralty Library, London. His *Description of the
   Sea Coast and Islands of Scotland* was published in 1703 as
   an atlas with a general chart of Scotland and five charts of
   the east coast as far north as Aberdeen.

II Roost

1 *OSA*, South Ronaldsay and Burray.
2 Information from Alex Annal.
3 *JoG*, 4 Nov. 1989.
4 Information from Billy Mowat.
5 The work of Bryce and Mackenzie is described in, for
   example, Robinson's *Marine Cartography in Britain*.
6 The various activities of the lairds of Orkney in the
   eighteenth century are fully explored in Fereday, 1983.
7 See, for example, the *Dictionary of National Biography*.
8 Bellin, 1757.
9 It is not entirely clear which birds Low refers to. Taisties
   (guillemots), lyres (shearwaters) and Tommy Nodies
   (puffins) are clear; Scoutiaulin is most likely the Arctic skua,
   and scout may be the razorbill.
10 Forbes's journal is published in Craven, 1908.
11 The details of the *Crown* disaster are given in the Kirkwall
   proclamation issued at the time. It is reproduced in
   Ferguson, 1988.

12 *LL*, 27 Oct. 1741.
13 *Lloyd's List* is available in bound volumes in the Guildhall Library, London. Until the appearance of local newspapers in the 1800s, it is the main source of information about wrecks in the north.
14 *LL*, 8 Aug. 1749.
15 *LL*, 23 Jan. 1747.
16 *LL*, 14 Jun. 1750.
17 *LL*, 5 Nov. 1762.
18 *LL*, 10 Feb. 1830.
19 *LL*, 2 Nov. 1830.
20 *LL*, 10 Apr. 1830.
21 *LL*, 12 Apr. 1830.
22 *JoG*, 29 Dec. 1848.
23 *LL*, 6 Nov. 1753.
24 *LL*, 11 Jan. 1830.
25 *Ll*, 8 Sept. 1747.
26 Thomson, 1987.
27 Hossack, 1900.
28 Watson, 1978.
29 For a general account of privateering, see Macintyre, 1975.
30 Donaldson, 1984.
31 *LL*, 10 July 1744.
32 *LL*, 18 July 1760.
33 *LL*, 5 May 1761.
34 *LL*, 18 Sept. 1747.
35 *LL*, 28 Jan. 1757.
36 *LL*, 19 July 1957.
37 Fereday, 1980, gives an excellent account of activity around the Firth during the Jacobite Rising in 1745-6. I am also grateful to J.S. Gibson, Edinburgh, who has done a special study of the role of the French Navy in the Rising, for information on how the French saw the Firth.
38 *LL*, 18 July 1780.
39 *LL*, 22 Aug. 1780.
40 *LL*, 8 Aug. 1758.
41 ADM 1/696, 3 July 1813 (see Vashon, Note 43).
42 *LL*, 15 Sept. 1747.
43 Vashon's correspondence, and the letters to his successors at Leith, on which I have drawn heavily in this section, the so-called 'Leith in-letters', are available in the Public Record Office - Refs ADM 1/689 to ADM 1/708. Leith was an independent command from 1803 to 1824. Before and after this period, Scottish waters came under the aegis of the North Sea or Nore command - ADM 1/709 to 735, and ADM 1/762 to 794.
44 Elliott's letter - ADM 1/692, 13 Oct. 1809.

45 Fereday, 1971. The remains of what could be a gun emplacement from the same period have been found at Harrow on the Caithness side of the Firth - *Press and Journal* 2 Nov. 1991; and personal communication from R. Gourlay, Highland Regional Archaeologist.

46 Scott, new edn, 1982.

47 ADM 1/697.

48 The early days of Stromness are well described in the collections of the Stromness Museum, and in many books, for example, Thomson, 1987. See also the parish accounts in *OSA* and *NSA*.

49 Wilson, 1842.

50 Bailey, 1971.

51 *OSA*, Sandwick and Stromness.

52 *NSA*, Sandwick and Stromness.

53 Government census returns. Examples of the Hudson's Bay connection here include Margaret Manson, living at Rackwick in 1851 and born at Hudson's Bay; and Jane Simpson, the daughter of an innkeeper in St Margaret's Hope in 1891, who was born at Fort Churchill.

54 Marcus, 1980.

55 Thomson, 1987. Lubbock, 1937, gives an excellent history of the Arctic whalers.

56 Cormack & Cormack, 1971.

57 Ayton & Daniell, 1818.

58 *OSA*, South Ronaldshay and Burray.

59 *JoG*, 3 May 1837.

60 *JoG*, 30 June 1837.

61 *LL*, 6 Dec. 1831.

62 Government census returns, 1841.

63 *OSA*, Sandwick and Stromness.

64 Baldwin, 1982.

65 *OLM*, vol. 9, 1929.

66 *OSA*, Canisbay.

67 *OSA*, Birsay and Harray.

68 *OSA*, Wick.

69 Thomson, 1987.

70 Canisbay Kirk Session records - in Craven, 1908.

71 *OSA*, Walls and Flotta.

72 *OSA*, Canisbay.

73 Information from family members.

74 *OSA*, South Ronaldshay and Burray.

75 The story of Wick's herring boom is well told by Iain Sutherland, 1984. Contemporary accounts of Wick in the mid-nineteenth century are in Wilson, 1842, and Bertram, 1865.

76 Telford's survey - Scottish Record Office, GD9/32/2.
77 The detailed story of Herston's rapid rise is in 'Herston Village' by Alex Annal, *The Orkney View* vol. 29. Burray: Miller, 1985.
78 Gibson, 1984.
79 *OSA*, Canisbay.
80 *OSA*, Dunnet.
81 Thom, 1986, estimates that Hoy, Dunnet Head and Duncansby Head, the three main sites for breeding seabirds in the Firth, are each home to 10,000-100,000 breeding pairs. This does not count wading birds and seafowl who breed on the islands or only feed from the sea.
82 *OSA*, Dunnet.
83 *OSA*, Dunnet.
84 Fenton, 1978, has a good general account of fowling in Caithness, Orkney and Shetland.
85 *OSA*, Canisbay.
86 *JoG*, 18 July 1845.
87 *JoG*, 17 Nov. 1843.
88 *JoG*, 7 Aug. 1846.89 Munro, 1978.
90 *JoG*, 14 July 1848.
91 *JoG*, 26 Sept. 1845.
92 *Press and Journal*, 23 Dec. 1986. In Feb. 1993, six sperm whales found their way into Scapa Flow and remained there for a month until a determined effort to drive them back to the open sea succeeded. The whales were herded out through Hoxa Sound from where they moved west to the Atlantic.
93 Booth & Reynolds, 1988.
94 Information from Paul Thompson.
95 Harwood *et al*, 1991.
96 The historical exploitation of seals is described in the *OSA* and Fenton, 1978.
97 *OSA*, Dunnet and Canisbay.
98 Esther Richan's breakfast is described in Thomson, 1987.
99 Donaldson, 1984. The letters of the Sinclair lairds of Mey give a vivid picture of their way of life in the 18th century.
100 Simper, 1974.
101 Fenton, 1978.
102 *OSA*, Thurso.
103 *OSA*, Sandwick and Stromness.
104 Taylor, 1991.
105 *Orkney Herald*, 4 May 1927.
106 The story of Bews and the other press-ganged men is in Admiral Vashon's correspondence, which also contains much of the other press-gang information in this section - ADM 1/689 *et seq*.

107 A good general history of the Royal Navy during the time of Nelson is given by Marcus, 1971. (Scots should not be deterred by the book's title.)

108 Muster book, HMS *Victory*, Aug. 1804 to Jan. 1805 - ADM 36/15898.

109 General information about the conditions of the British seaman can be found in Lloyd, 1968; and a general account of the press-gang in Hutchinson, 1913. The monthly wage of 23s 6d was paid to ordinary seamen, the rank most pressed men could aspire to, in 1797, and represented a rise of 4s 6d over the previous rate. Able seamen received 29s 6d per month after 1797. Occasionally, the taking of a prize brought large windfalls to seamen.

110 Pope, 1963.

111 'two apprentices' - ADM 1/697. The apprentices' master wrote to petition for their release; I do not know if this was successful.

112 *NSA*, Orphir.

113 Mackintosh, 1975.

114 *Ibid*.

III Tiderip

1 James Bremner's life has been the subject of only one short booklet, that by Mowat. Other information about him is given in the weekly columns of the Caithness papers of the time, and in his obituary, published in the *Northern Ensign* and copied in the *Inverness Courier*, 21 Aug. 1856.

2 Bremner, 1845.

3 Mitchell, 1883.

4 A general account of the *Great Britain* can be found in Corlett, 1775, and Vaughan, 1991.

5 The *Illustrated London News* devoted a three-page spread to the refloating of the *Great Britain* on 21 Aug. 1847.

6 A very good general account of the folklore of fishing communities can be found in Anson, 1950. A brief description of some Caithness customs, with the added bonus of knitting patterns, is in Munro & Compton, 1983.

7 Horne, 1907.

8 *Rival* - CC, 18 Oct. 1989. The construction date is given as 1918, which would conflict with Wildy Sinclair's assertion that the last Stroma yole was built in 1913.

9 Sutherland, 1937.

10 *Traveller's Guide*, 1798.

11 Canisbay Kirk Session minutes, in Craven, 1908.

12 Sutherland, 1937.

13 *Moby Dick*, Ch. 58.
14 Gorrie mentions in 1869 in regard to South Ronaldsay that 'the fantastic notion ... that drowned people were changed into seals has passed away'. A general account of selkie legends around the Atlantic seaboard can be found in Thomson, 1965. A Caithness legend, 'E Silkie Man' was first published in *OLM*, vols. 2, 1909, and 3, 1910; and was later reissued by Caithness Books - see Houston.
15 Horne, 1907.
16 Eliza Mackay's sighting of a mermaid and subsequent correspondence is recorded in Henderson, 1812.
17 The *Campbells*'s encounter is in *JoG*, 29 March 1895. Bill Hutchison - recorded in the Orkney Sound Archive, Kirkwall Public Library.
18 *JoG* Old Files, 12 Sept. 1980.
19 Wilson, 1975.
20 Picken, 1972.
21 Calder, 1887. The loss of a vessel called the *John* 'in the Orkneys' mentioned in *LL*, 12 Nov. 1771, probably refers to the same incident.
22 Picken, 1972.
23 Canisbay Kirk Session minutes, in Craven, 1908.
24 *JoG*, 18 Sept. 1840.
25 *INA*, 2 June 1857.
26 *INA*, 6 July 1880.
27 Information from Alex Annal.
28 Information from James Henderson.
29 Aitken, 1988.
30 OSA, Canisbay.
31 Another version of this story, in which the snakes originate on Stroma but die when taken over to Orkney, is given in Morrison, 1883, and in Calder, 1887.
32 Craven, 1911.
33 Craven, 1911.
34 Government census returns, 1871.
35 Young, 1992.
36 Gorrie, 1869.
37 General books about lighthouses in Britain include Stevenson, 1959; Beaver, 1971; Hague & Christie, 1975; Wilson, 1975; and the Admiralty Hydrographic Office volumes, 1832-90. I have also obtained information from the Commissioners of Northern Lighthouses.
38 *OSA*, Thurso.
39 Stevenson, 1851.
40 Wilson, 1975.
41 Stevenson, 1851.

42 Scott, new edn, 1982.
43 Information from the Commissioners of Northern Lighthouses.
44 Government census returns, 1841.
45 Government census returns, 1851.
46 *JoG*, 20 June 1845.
47 *Northern Ensign*, 24 July and 7 Aug. 1884.
48 *LL*, 13 Dec. 1811, and Calder, 1887.
49 *JoG*, 20 Mar. 1981.
50 Banks, 1972, recalls the lighthouse keepers' account of the loss of the first foghorn. With a roar and a tremble that woke the sleeping men, the foghorn and the portion of the cliff on which it stood fell away in the night.
51 *JoG*, 16 Apr. and 7 May 1847.
52 Anderson, in *JoG*, 6 Oct. 1989.
53 ADM 1/3522.
54 Hossack, 1900.
55 Donnelly's chart was published in 1802 in Laurie & Whittle.
56 Dawson's *Memoirs* is a general survey of British marine cartography. A general history of marine surveying is given by Sir Archibald Day, 1967.
57 Kemp, 1976.
58 Logbook - ADM 52/4514.
59 Logbook - ADM 53/2803.
60 The results of these Victorian surveys were published in 1850 and can be seen, for example, in the National Maritime Museum - *Survey of the Pentland Firth* by Cmmdrs Thomas & Becher, NMM G218:14/9 and 14/13.
61 Details of the lives of Otter and Slater are in Dawson. The curious allegations surrounding Slater's death are in Stephen, 1891.
62 There are many books about the search for the North-west Passage. I have used Lehane, 1981.
63 *JoG*, 20 June 1845.
64 Lehane, 1981.
65 Bremner, 1861.
66 '2000 up to...10,000': *OSA*, Canisbay, gives 2000 while the figure of 10,000 is given in Calder, 1887. Watson (*OSA* South Ronaldshay and Burray) gives an average of nine ships per day passing through the Firth, making an annual total of around 3000.
67 *JoG*, 13 Sept. 1844.
68 A general account of the Scottish coastal sailing traffic is given in Simper, 1974.
69 *OSA*, South Ronaldshay and Burray.
70 Banks, 1972.

71 Nicolson, 1925.

72 Obituary, JoG, 14 Feb. 1936.

73 *JoG* Old Files, 1 Nov. 1991. A fuller version of this episode is recalled by W.A. Bremner in Young, 1992, where the vessel . is named *Cupid*. David Banks with two other Stroma men, John Mowat and Stewart Allan, lost their lives in the Firth in October 1918 when their boat was overcome in the Western Bores off Duncansby.

74 *NSA*, Walls and Flotta.

75 Government census returns, 1841.

76 Government census returns, 1851.

77 *JoG*, 2 Mar. 1836.

78 *JoG*, 20 Apr. 1838.

79 *JoG*, 8 Dec. 1843.

80 *INA*, 19 Feb. and 26 Feb. 1856.

81 *JoG*, 11 May 1838.

82 *JoG*, 17 Apr. 1840.

83 *JoG*, 13 Jan. 1843.

84 *JoG*, 23 May 1845.

85 Information from Alex Annal.

86 *JoG*, 31 Mar. 1843.

87 Nicolson, 1925.

88 *JoG*, 10 Jan. 1845.

89 *JoG*, 2 Mar. 1836.

90 *JoG*, 24 Sept. 1841.

91 *JoG*, 7 Apr. 1843.

92 *JoG*, 29 Sept. 1843.

93 *JoG*, 21 July 1843.

94 Edward Medley has no biography. The details of his life given here are assembled from reports in local papers, including his death and funeral notice - *JoG*, 27 Apr. 1849 - and his obituary - *JoG*, 18 May 1849. Medley's complaints about how pilots were treated are summarised in his letter to *JoG*, 16 Dec. 1842. His approach to the House of Commons is described in *JoG*, 4 Aug. 1848, where his recommendations are reprinted in full. Medley's welfare work for seamen and their families is also recorded in *JoG*.

95 *JoG*, 20 Mar. and 3 Apr. 1846.

96 *JoG*, 26 Oct. 1838.

97 *JoG*, 1 May 1840.

98 *JoG*, 18 Mar. 1842.

99 *JoG*, 3 Dec. 1847.

100 *JoG*, 28 Apr. 1848.

101 *INA*, 21 June 1853.

102 *JoG*, 18 Feb. 1842.

103 *JoG*, 9 June 1848.

104 *JoG*, 15 Dec. 1848.

105 Horne, 1907.

106 *JoG*, 26 Jan. 1838.

107 Government census returns, 1861-81.

108 Information from Alex Annal. Young, 1992, states that Malcolm Simpson was the last Stroma pilot to operate under sail; he died in 1965, aged ninety-four.

109 Nicolson, 1925.

110 Obituary, *JoG*, 18 Sept. 1925.

111 *Press and Journal*, supplement, 12 Jan. 1977.

112 Information from Captain Robert Sclater.

IV Flood

1 The mention of the Brims ferry in 1603 comes in a letter by Zachary Pont, the minister of Bower and the brother of Timothy the mapmaker. While waiting for the ferry, Zachary was attacked and wounded by Francis Moodie of Breckness. The reason for this assault is unknown. Pont's complaint is in Craven, 1908.

2 Ayton, 1818.

3 *A Journey to the South* - this anonymous manuscript is quoted in Horne, 1907.

4 Picken, 1972.

5 Graeme's diary - quoted in 'Jouneying to Orkney' by Betty Walthew, *Scots Magazine*, May 1982.

6 The Groats in Fife are mentioned in G.F. Black, *The Surnames of Scotland*, New York 1946. Gregor Lamb in *Orkney Surnames*, Edinburgh, 1981, argues for the surname being derived from a nickname to do with milling and points to the Old Norse word *grautr* (porridge) as an origin. Iain Sutherland (letter, *CC*, 10 Dec. 1986) derives the name from Norse *gróttr* (mill). The evidence for Dutch origin is not fully conclusive but carries the weight of tradition and is further supported by the recent discovery by Joyce Poole, International Blood Group Reference Laboratory, of a rare blood group in the Groat family in Orkney which was previously found only in a few Dutch families.

7 *OSA*, Canisbay.

8 Early Groat family charters are summarised in Calder, 1887, including the first ferry record in 1549.

9 The Grote tombstone reads: Donald Grot, sone to Johne Grot laid me heir April XIII day 1568 M.D.L. Lewys and Donald Grot and his gonaield lad and thaar faorbears of Donald whouse God cald me ye XIII day of April. Anno Dominy MDL 1568.

10 Gilbert Grote. The protocol book of this notary public was published in 1914 by the Scottish Record Society. One item is a memo about the puchase of Caithness fish in July 1554 by an Edinburgh trader.

11 *Accounts of the Lord High Treasurer*, vol. 7, 1540. This John Grote may have been a native of Fife rather than a member of the Caithness family, as he is stated to have sailed from Saint Andrews to Orkney.

12 Buchanan, *History of Scotland*, vol. 1.

13 Bayne, 1735.

14 The notes with Eunson's chart of 1800 state 'Johnny Groats House is situated on a high rock and may be seen in fine weather 5 leagues off'. In Imray and Son's *Sailing Directions*, 1854, appears 'Duncansby Head ... distinguished by the large rock called John o'Groat's House, or the Castle of Duncansby, which lies about one mile S of the Head and and appears over the land like a house upon a hill'.

15 Sibbald MS, Ref 15.1.1, ff.37, 183-4, National Library of Scotland.

16 In the Mercat Press facsimile edition, 1975, of Barry.

17 Macfarlane, *Geographical Collections*, Cannesbay. The rate of exchange between Scots and English currency fluctuated until the Scots currency was officially abolished in 1707. The exchange rate I have used is that current towards 1707, when Scots coins were one-twelfth the value of their English equivalents.

18 Henderson, 1812.

19 *OSA*, Canisbay.

20 *JoG*, 13 June 1845.

21 *OSA*; and Henderson, 1812.

22 Thomson, 1987.

23 Thomson, 1987.

24 Thomson, 1987.

25 Wilson, 1842.

26 Thomson, 1987.

27 *JoG*, 29 Dec. 1837.

28 *JoG*, 18 Oct. 1839.

29 *NSA*, Canisbay.

30 *JoG*, 6 Dec. 1839 and 11 Dec. 1840.

31 *JoG*, 11 Dec. 1840. The ferrymen received one shilling per trip, and if bad weather benighted them on the wrong side of the Firth they found themselves out of pocket. The Huna ferry owner received 1s 3d - not enough, he argued, to keep the boats in order.

32 Cormack & Cormack, 1971.

33 The story of steam or oil-powered ferries across the Pentland

Firth is well recorded in a number of books - for example, Donaldson, 1966; Cormack & Cormack, 1971.
34 Passage times in the days of sail could vary greatly, a a voyage from Orkney to Edinburgh taking weeks if winds and tides were adverse. An early fast voyage, recorded in Donaldson 1984, tells how a ship sailed from Staxigoe to the Firth of Forth in 48 hours. A contender for one of the fastest passages must, however, be the schooner *Cairnduna* which sailed from Thurso at 2.00 pm on 27 December 1867 and reached Aberdeen at 3.30 am on the 28th, despite losing her foreyard and some sail. The steamer passage between Kirkwall and Leith in the late 1830s took 34-40 hours.
35 *JoG*, 15 Apr. 1842.
36 *JoG*, 3 Mar. 1843.
37 *JoG*, 22 Nov. 1844; denied - *JoG*, 18 Sept. 1846.
38 *JoG*, 4 Apr. 1845.
39 *JoG*, 11 Apr. 1845.
40 *JoG*, 13 June 1845.
41 *JoG*, 9 Jan. 1846.
42 *JoG*, 1 Dec. 1848.
43 *JoG*, 2 June 1848.
44 Brief accounts of some aspects of the *St Ola* story are given in Burnet Leys's and McRobb's booklets. My main sources here are Stromness Museum and Walter Leask.
45 Miller, 1985.
46 *Northern Ensign*, 3 May 1892.
47 See, for example, Ernest Marwick in *Scots Magazine*, Feb. 1967.
48 Information from Walter Mowat.
49 MacCulloch, 1824.
50 Botfield, 1830.
51 Mitchell, 1883.
52 Borrow's visit is mentioned in *OLM*, vol. 10, 1935.
53 Burritt, 1864.
54 Stevenson's 'grave of mariners' comment is in his essay 'The Education of an Engineer', reprinted in Jeremy Treglown (ed.) *The Lantern-Bearers and other essays*, London, 1988.
55 A general history of the Coastguard service is given by Webb, 1976; and an account of the Service in Orkney in Allan Taylor's articles in *The Orcadian*, 12 Oct. and 19 Oct. 1972.
56 The Board of Excise report on Richan's smuggling is quoted in Vashon's correspondence to the Admiralty, ADM 1/690.
57 Hall, 1807.
58 Trading between ships has always been the practice of seamen. It continues to this day. Banks, 1972, recalls French fishing smacks en route through the Firth to the

Newfoundland banks giving local fishermen letters to post
and paying for this service with brandy and tobacco.

59 *Northern Star*, 8 & 16 Mar. 1837.
60 Mackintosh, 1975.
61 Bob MacCallum, 'Early education in Caithness', *JoG*, 25 Mar. 1977.
62 ADM 1/698.
63 *Northern Star*, 16 Mar. 1837; *JoG*, 12 Jan. 1838.
64 *JoG*, 24 Jan. 1840.
65 Government census returns, 1841.
66 *JoG*, 26 Nov. 1841.
67 *JoG*, 22 Dec. 1843.
68 W. Bremner and D.G. Sinclair's list of wrecks, *Caithness Field Club Bulletin*, 1984, and unpublished material. See also Ferguson, 1988; his graph of shipping losses between 1651 and 1960 totals some 450 casualties for Orkney and the Firth. The peak came between 1820 and 1850.
69 *JoG*, 24 Oct. 1845.
70 *JoG*, 24 & 31 Oct. 1845.
71 *JoG*, 1 Sept. 1848.
72 *JoG*, 23 June 1837.
73 *JoG*, 1 Mar. 1844.
74 *JoG*, 26 Dec. 1845.
75 *JoG* Old Files, 19 June 1987.
76 Webb, 1976.
77 *JoG*, 26 Nov. 1847.
78 Webb, 1976.
79 Taylor, *Orcadian*, 12 & 19 Oct. 1972.
80 *INA*, 19 June 1855.
81 *INA*, 11 Nov. 1856.
82 INA, 9 June 1871.
83 Ferguson, 1988.
84 Ferguson, 1988; and *JoG* Old Files, 8 Mar. 1991.
85 *JoG*, 21 Feb. 1908. The master, mate and helmsman of the *Ben Aden* were charged with causing the deaths of the fishermen and, in the ensuing trial, the mate was found guilty and imprisoned for two months - *JoG*, 15 May 1908.
86 *JoG*, 29 Apr.1932.
87 *JoG*, 11 Jan. and 1 Feb. 1907.
88 *JoG*, 8 Nov. 1918.
89 *JoG*, July 1927.
90 Bremner & Sinclair, 1984.
91 Bremner & Sinclair, 1984.
92 *JoG*, 25 Nov. 1946.
93 *INA*, 30 Sept. and 28 Oct. 1856.

94 *INA*, 15 Dec. 1866. The tale of the burning peat is in Alex Shearer's booklet, *The Fair Side o the San*, Thurso, 1954.
95 *INA*, 28 Dec. 1866.
96 The title phrase is from the RNLI Station History of the Longhope lifeboat.
97 The history of the RNLI in and around the Firth has been generously recorded. As well as the accounts kept in the Station Histories at RNLI Headquarters, London, see for example the back issues of *The Lifeboat* and *The Scottish Lifeboat* magazines, and the books or articles by Anderson 1989, Davies 1985-6, Kipling 1982, Jeff Morris and Stromness Museum. The story of the early decades of the Longhope lifeboat has also been recorded by Charlie Rioch for the Orkney Sound Archive, Kirkwall Library. I am also grateful to Jackie Groat for many details of various incidents.
98 Bremner, 1809.
99 *JoG*, 4 Sept. 1846.
100 RNLI Station History, Thurso.
101 *Lifeboat*, vol. 9, 1875.
102 *INA*, 9 Jan. 1866.
103 Morris, 1984.
104 *Lifeboat*, vol. 10, 1878.
105 Morris, 1984.
106 *Lifeboat*, vol. 12, 1883.
107 *Lifeboat*, vol. 14, 1891.
108 The story of the *Manchester City* is given in various sources but I have used principally Morris, 1990; Charlie Rioch's taped reminiscences in the Orkney Sound Archive; and *The Orcadian*, 28 Jan. 1899.
109 *Lifeboat*, vol. 19, 1905.
110 *Lifeboat*, vol. 20, 1909.
111 Morris, 1990; with information from Jackie Groat.
112 RNLI Station History, Longhope.
113 Morris, 1980.
114 The wreck of the *Pennsylvania* has been the subject of several written accounts. My main source has been the taped account by Alex Annal, recorded for BBC Radio Orkney, with additional information from Sutherland Manson.
115 Information from Peter Sinclair.
116 *JoG*, 10 Feb. 1956.
117 Information from Alex Annal and from written accounts by Bill Sinclair in *The Orkney View*, Feb.-Mar. 1992, and by one of the survivors from the wreck, Olof Pehkonen, in *The Orkney View*, Oct.-Nov. 1992.
118 *JoG*, 11 Dec. 1959. Reminiscences of the *George Robb*

tragedy have been published in *JoG*, 15 Dec. 1989, and *The Press and Journal*, 11 Apr. 1980. James Henderson also gave me information. Controversy still surrounds the rescue attempts over whether the rescuers could have descended the cliffs sooner and saved the man who came ashore.

119 RNLI Annual Report, 1959.

120 RNLI Station History, Longhope.

121 My main sources are the RNLI Annual Report, 1969; Dr Sydney Peace's article in *The Scottish Lifeboat*, 1970; and Jackie Groat.

122 Morris, 1990; with information from Alex Annal.

123 For a good general history of the Scapa Flow base, see Hewison, 1985. The remains of the German Fleet now attract scuba divers, and detailed handbooks are available on these - see, for example, Smith, 1989.

124 National Maritime Museum, ref G212: 14/5 MS.

125 ADM 12/155.

126 Henderson, 1812.

127 Admiralty papers - Spithead conference, July 1914, on the fortification of Scapa Flow - ADM 1/8380/150.

128 Correspondence on martial law - ADM 1/8389/240.

129 Bennett, 1968. Iain Sutherland, 1985, focuses on the lucky role of the *Dorothy Gray*.

130 Bennett, 1968.

131 The best book, indeed the only book, on Caithness's role in the Second World War, which also contains many references to the air raids on Scapa Flow and to shipping incidents, is by N. Glass. An unusual account of one man's war effort ferrying dangerous cargoes across the Firth is given in Bridges, 1957.

132 McAra, 1991.

133 For a full account of Stroma's last years, see Young, 1992.

134 Aitken, 1988; and *JoG*, 27 July 1934.

135 Billy Mowat, who was born at Rackwick, told me about the community's past. Kenneth Michie and some of his pupils at North Walls School also gave valuable information.

136 The closure of the school was attended by tragedy. Two of its three pupils, all from the Mowat famiy, were drowned in the burn near their home.

137 Information from Alex Annal.

138 Information from Jackie Groat.

139 Articles expressing concern about the use of the Firth by oil tankers appeared in *JoG*, 10 & 17 Nov. 1978. Oil spills are recorded in *JoG*, 24 Dec. 1982 and *Press and Journal*, 11 Dec. 1987.

140 Information from Captain Robert Sclater.
141 *The Orcadian*, Oct. 1979.
142 *JoG*, 15 Jan. 1993.
143 *JoG*, 26 Mar. 1993.
144 *JoG*, 13 Aug. 1993.
145 *INA*, 13 June 1873.
146 *Northern Ensign*, 2 & 9 Aug. 1892.
147 Tunnel - *JoG*, 9 Dec. 1983; *CC*, 2 May 1990. Power - *CC*, 3 Dec. 1986.
148 Horne, 1907.
149 *JoG*, 2 Apr. 1993.
150 *JoG*, 16 Apr. 1993.
151 *CC*, 4 July 1984. The survey was carried out by BUE SubSea for the Ministry of Defence, using three survey vessels with sidescan sonar. This was the first survey of some parts of the Firth and adjoining waters since last century.
152 The water-skiers were Gordon Stewart and David Barnes, *CC*, 17 Apr. 1985. The canoeist was Brian Wilson, *CC*, 14 Aug. 1985. In the summer of 1993, Frank Hornby and Jimmy Jewell, two engineers from the Royal Navy base, HMS *Vulcan*, crossed the Firth in a standard Searider inflatable dinghy in 1 hour 40 minutes 40 seconds. They claimed a record but two Orcadians, Norman and George Brass, cut 27 minutes off their time ten days later with a speedboat called *Snow Queen*.
153 *Northern Ensign*, 9 Aug. 1892.
154 I have drawn on personal knowledge and newspaper reports throughout 1988 and 1989. This story is not yet finished, but see, for example, *JoG*, 30 June 1989; *CC*, 20 Sept. 1989; *CC*, 21 July 1993; *CC*, 15 Dec. 1993; *The Orcadian*, 23 Dec. 1993.
155 *The Orcadian*, 2 Aug. 1979.
156 *CC*, 1 July 1987.
157 *CC*, 6 Mar. 1991; and *JoG*, 5 July 1991.
158 *JoG*, 26 Feb. 1993.

Accounts of the Lord High Treasurer of Scotland, Edinburgh, 1877-1970.

Adair, John, T*he Description of the Sea-Coast and Islands of Scotland with Large and Exact Maps, for the Use of Seamen*, Part 1, Edinburgh, 1703.

Adair, John, *A Chart of the Pentland Firth with the Islands of Orkney and Shetland*, Edinburgh, c. 1715.

Admiralty Hydrographic Office, *The Light-houses of the British Islands*, London, 1832 to 1890.

Aitken, Margaret, *The Island of Stroma*, Thurso, nd.

Aitken, Margaret, *Twelve Light Years*, Edinburgh, 1988.

Anderson, A.O. (ed.), *Early Sources of Scottish History*, Edinburgh, 1922.

Anderson, A., 'Selfless duty to sailors in distress' (Huna lifeboat history), *JoG*, 6 Oct. 1989; 'When Ackergill responded to the call' (Ackergill lifeboat history), *JoG*, 13 Oct. 1989.

Anson, Peter F., *Fishing Boats and Fisher Folk on the East Coast of Scotland*, London, 1930.

Anson, Peter F., *Scots Fisherfolk*, Banff, 1950.

Ayton, Richard & Daniell, William, *A Voyage round Great Britain Undertaken in the Summer of the Year 1813*, London, 1818.

Bailey, Patrick, *Orkney*, Newton Abbot, 1971.

Bain, Joseph (ed.), *The Hamilton Papers*, Edinburgh, 1890.

Baldwin, J.R., 'Fishing the Sellag', in *Caithness: A Cultural Crossroads*, J.R. Baldwin (ed.), Edinburgh, 1982.

Banks, John S., *The Heather Blooms at John o'Groats*, John o'Groats, 1972.

Bannatyne Club Miscellany, vol. 2, Edinburgh, 1836. Papers relating to John Adair FRS, Geographer for the Kingdom of Scotland.

Barry, George, *The History of the Orkney Islands*, Edinburgh, 1805.

Bayne, Aeneas, *A Short Geographical Survey of the County of Caithness*, 1735, MS Wick Library.

Beaver, Patrick, *A History of Lighthouses*, London, 1971.

Bellin, Jacques N., *Essai Geographique sur les Iles Britanniques*, Paris, 1757.

Bennett, G., *Naval Battles of the First World War*, London, 1968.

Berry, R.J., *The Natural History of Orkney*, London, 1985.

Bertram, James, *The Harvest of the Sea*, London, 1985.

Blaeu, Wilhelm, *Theatrum Orbis Terrarum, sive Atlas Novus*, vol. 5, Amsterdam, 1654. *Atlas Major*, vol. 6, Amsterdam, 1662.

Booth, C.J. & Reynolds, P., 'Whales and Dolphins in Orkney', *The Orkney View*, vol. 20, 1988.

Botfield, Beriah, *Journal of a Tour through the Highlands of Scotland during the Summer of 1829*, Edinburgh, 1830.

Brand, John, *A Brief Description of Orkney, Zetland, Pightland Firth and Caithness*, London, 1701.

Bremner, James, *Plan for Converting Every Ship Her Own boat into a Temporary Lifeboat*, London, 1809.

Bremner, James, *Treatise on the Planning and Construction of Harbours*, Wick, 1845.

Bremner, W. & Sinclair, D.G., 'Wrecks of the Pentland Firth', *Caithness Field Club Bulletin*, 1984.

Bremner, W.L., *The Pilot of the Pentland Frith, and Other Poems*, Guildford, 1861.

Bridges, Antony, *Scapa Ferry*, London, 1957.

Brown, M. & Meehan, P., *Scapa Flow*, London, 1968.

Buchanan, George, *The History of Scotland* (trans. Aikman), Glasgow, 1862.

Burgher, Leslie, *Orkney: An Illustrated Architectural Guide*, Edinburgh, 1991.

Burritt, Elihu, *A Walk from London to John o'Groats*, New York, 1864.

Caesar, Julius, *The Conquest of Gaul*, S.A. Handford (trans.), London, 1951.

Calder, James T., *Sketch of the Civil and Traditional History of Caithness since the Tenth Century*, 2nd edn, Wick, 1887.

Carpenter, Rhys, *Beyond the Pillars of Hercules*, London, 1973.

Collins, Greenville, *Chart of the Orkneys and the Pentland Firth*, London, 1686.

Collins, Greenville, *Great Britain's Coasting Pilot*, London, 1693.

Corlett, Ewen, *The Iron Ship*, London, 1975.

Cormack, A. & A., *Days of Orkney Steam*, Kirkwall, 1971.

Craven, J.B., *A History of the Episcopal Church in the Dioceseof Caithness*, Kirkwall, 1908.

Craven, J.B., *Church Life in South Ronaldshay and Burray*, Kirkwall, 1911.

Crawford, Barbara E., *Scandinavian Scotland*, Leicester, 1987.

Davies, Joan, 'Rugged in the extreme: Caithness lifeboat stations', *The Lifeboat Journal*, Winter 1985-6.

Dawson, L.S., *Memoirs of Hydrography*, Eastbourne, 1885.

Day, Sir Archibald, *The Admiralty Hydrographic Service 1795-1919*, London, 1967.

Defoe, Daniel, *A Tour thro' that part of Great Britain called Scotland*, London, 1746.

Donaldson, Gordon, *Northwards by Sea*, Edinburgh, 1966.

Donaldson, J.E., *The Mey Letters*, Sydney, 1984.

Downie, Murdoch, *The New Pilot for the East Coast of Scotland*, London, 1792.

Eunson, George, *A Chart of the Islands of Orkney*, London, 1800.

Fenton, Alexander, *The Northern Isles: Orkney and Shetland*, Edinburgh, 1978.

Fereday, R.P., *The Longhope Battery and Towers*, Stromness, 1971.

Fereday, R.P., *Orkney Feuds and the '45*, Kirkwall, 1980.

Fereday, R.P., *The Lairds of 18th-Century Orkney*, PhD thesis, Aberdeen

243

University, 1983.

Ferguson, D.M., *Shipwrecks of Orkney, Shetland and Pentland Firth*, Newton Abbot, 1988.

Foote, P.G. & Wilson, D.M., *The Viking Achievement*, London, 1980.

Gibson, W.M., *Stronsay: The Herring Fishing*, Edinburgh, 1984.

Glass, N.M., *Caithness and the War 1939-1945: A Record*, Wick, 1948.

Gorrie, Daniel, *Summers and Winters in the Orkneys*, London, 1869.

Graham-Campbell, J. & Kidd, D., *The Vikings*, London, 1980.

Grant, David, *Yarns of the Pentland Firth*, Wick, 1931.

Greenhill, Basil (ed.), *The National Maritime Museum*, London, 1982.

Gunn, Neil M., *The Silver Darlings*, London, 1941.

Hague, D.B. & Christie, R., *Lighthouses: Their Architecture, History and Archaeology*, London, 1975.

Hall, James, *Travels in Scotland*, London, 1807.

Harwood, J., Hiby, L., Thompson, D. & Ward, A. 'Seal Stocks in Great Britain', *NERC News*, Jan. & July 1991.

Heather, William, *The Marine Atlas*, London, 1808.

Hedges, John W., *Tomb of the Eagles: A Window on Stone Age Tribal Britain*, London, 1984.

Henderson, John, *General View of the Agriculture of the County of Caithness*, London, 1812.

Hewison, W.S., *This Great Harbour: Scapa Flow*, Kirkwall, 1985.

Horne, John (ed.), *The County of Caithness*, Wick, 1907.

Hossack, B.H., *Kirkwall in the Orkneys*, Kirkwall, 1900.

Houston, David, *E Silkie Man*, Thurso, nd.

Hume Brown, P., *Scotland before 1700 from Contemporary Documents*, Edinburgh, 1893.

Hutchinson, J.R., *The Press Gang Afloat and Ashore*, London, 1913.

Imray & Son, *Sailing Directions for the East Coasts of England and Scotland*, 4th edn, London, 1854.

Johnstone, Paul, *The Sea-Craft of Prehistory*, London, 1980.

Kemp, Peter (ed.), *The Oxford Companion to Ships and the Sea*, Oxford, 1976.

King, C.A.M., *Beaches and Coasts*, London, 1959.

Kipling, Ray, *Rescue by Sail and Oar*, Sulhamstead, 1982.

Klindt-Jensen, O., *The World of the Vikings*, London, 1970.

Knox, John, *A Tour through the Highlands of Scotland and the Hebride Isles in 1786*, London, 1787.

Lamb, H.H., *Climate: Past, Present and Future*, London, 1977.

Laurie, Robert & Whittle, James, *A Pilot for the Greenland Whale Fishery*, London, 1802.

Laxdaela Saga, M. Magnusson & H. Palsson (eds), London, 1969.

Lehane, Brendan, *The Northwest Passage*, Time-Life Books, Amsterdam, 1981.

Leslie, John, *The Historie of Scotland*, J. Dalrymple (trans.), Edinburgh, 1895.

Leys, A. Burnett, *St Ola to Orkney*, Thurso, nd.

Lithgow, William, *A Most Delectable and True Discourse*, London, 1614.

Lithgow, William, *The Totall Discourse of the Rare Aduentures and painfull Peregrinations of long nineteene Years*, London, 1628.

Lloyd, Christopher, *The British Seaman*, London, 1968.

Low, George, *A Tour through the Islands of Orkney and Schetland*, Kirkwall, 1879.

Lubbock, Basil, *The Arctic Whalers*, Glasgow, 1937.

McAra, Charles, *Mainly in Minesweepers: A Scot at Sea*, London, 1991.

MacCulloch, John, *The Highlands and Western Isles of Scotland*, London, 1824.

Macfarlane, W., *Geographical Collections*, Sir Arthur Mitchell (ed.), Edinburgh, 1906.

Macintyre, D., *The Privateers*, London, 1975.

Mackenzie, Murdoch, 'The State of the Tides in Orkney', *Philosophical Transactions of the Royal Society*, vol. 46, London, 1749.

Mackenzie, Murdoch, *Orcades: or a geographic and hydrographic survey of the Orkney and Lewis islands in eight maps*, London, 1750. (National Maritime Museum - Atlas MMU 01)

Mackintosh, W.R., *Around the Orkney Peat-Fires*, Kirkwall, 1975.

McRobb, A.W., *The Second St Ola*, Lerwick, 1977.

Marcus, G.J., *A Naval History of England 2: The Age of Nelson*, London, 1971.

Marcus, G.J., *The Conquest of the North Atlantic*, London, 1980.

Marshall, M.W., *Fishing: The Coastal Tradition*, London, 1987.

Martin, Colin, *Full Fathom Five: Wrecks of the Spanish Armada*, London, 1975.

Miller, James, *Caithness*, London, 1979.

Miller, James, *Portrait of Caithness and Sutherland*, London, 1985.

Miller, Ronald (ed.), *The Third Statistical Account of Scotland, Vol. 20A - the County of Orkney*, Edinburgh, 1985.

Mitchell, Joseph, *Reminiscences of My Life in the Highlands*, London, 1883.

Moir, D.G. (ed.), *The Early Maps of Scotland*, Edinburgh, 1973.

Monteith, Robert, *Description of the Islands of Orkney and Zetland*, Edinburgh, 1711.

Morris, Jeff, *The Story of the Thurso Lifeboats*, Thurso, 1980.

Morris, Jeff, *The Story of the Wick and Ackergill Lifeboats*, Wick, 1984.

Morris, Jeff, *The History of the Longhope Lifeboats*, Coventry, 1990.

Morrison, Hew, *Tourist's Guide to Sutherland and Caithness*, Wick, 1883.

Mowat, Bill, *John o'Groats*, John o'Groats, 1962.

Mowat, Helen, 'Caithness Lighthouses', *Caithness Field Club Bulletin*, vol. 4, 1986.

Mowat, John, *James Bremner - Wreck Raiser*, Thurso, nd.

Munro, Henrietta, *Pictures of Old Thurso and District*, Thurso, 1978.

Munro, Henrietta & Compton, Rae, *They Lived by the Sea: Folklore and*

Ganseys of the Pentland Firth, Thurso, 1983.

Neill, Patrick, *A Tour through Some of the Islands of Orkney and Shetland*, Edinburgh, 1806.

Newman, P.C., *Caesars of the Wilderness*, London, 1987.

New Statistical Account of Scotland, Edinburgh, 1845.

Nicolson, John, 'The Old Pilots of the Pentland Firth.' *JoG Christmas Number*, 25 Dec. 1925.

Norman, Robert, *The Safegarde of Saylers*, London, 1584.

North Coast of Scotland Pilot, London, 1975.

Orkneyinga Saga, J. Anderson (ed.), Edinburgh 1873.

Orkneyinga Saga, H. Palsson & P. Edwards (eds), London, 1978.

Pennant, Thomas, *A Tour in Scotland*, 3rd edn, London, 1774.

Picken, Stuart D.B., *The Soul of an Orkney Parish*, Kirkwall, 1972.

Ployen, Christian, *Reminiscences of a Voyage to Shetland, Orkney and Scotland in the Summer of 1839*, C. Spence (trans.), Lerwick, 1896.

Pococke, Richard, *The Tour of Dr Pococke through Sutherland and Caithness*, D.W. Kemp (ed.), Edinburgh, 1887.

Pohl, Frederick J., *Prince Henry Sinclair: His Expedition to the New World in 1398*, London, 1974.

Pope, Dudley, *The Black Ship*, London, 1963.

Purchas, Samuel, *Purchas His Pilgrimes, contayning a History of the World in Sea Voyages and Land Travells by Englishmen and others*, London, 1625.

Renfrew, Colin (ed.), *The Prehistory of Orkney*, Edinburgh, 1985.

Robinson, A., 'Murdoch Mackenzie and His Orcades Sea Atlas', *Map Collector*, 16, 1961.

Robinson, A.H.W., *Marine Cartography in Britain*, Leicester, 1962.

Safer Ships, Cleaner Seas. Report of Lord Donaldson's Inquiry into the Prevention of Pollution from Merchant Shipping, London, 1994.

Sandison, Charles, *The Sixareen and Her Racing Descendants*, Lerwick, 1981.

Scott, Sir Walter, *Northern Lights*, W.F. Laughton (ed.), Hawick, 1982.

Settle, Dionyse, *A True Reporte of the Laste Voyage into the West and Northwest Regions*, London, 1577.

Severin, Tim, *The Brendan Voyage*, London, 1978.

Simper, Robert, *Scottish Sail: A Forgotten Era*, Newton Abbot, 1974.

Sinclair, Sir John (ed.), *Statistical Account of Scotland*, 1791-9.

Smith, Peter L., *The Naval Wrecks of Scapa Flow*, Kirkwall, 1989.

Snyder, Gerald, *The Royal Oak Disaster*, London, 1976.

Stephen, David, *Gleanings in the North*, Haddington, 1891.

Stevenson, Alan, *Biographical Sketch of the Late R. Stevenson*, Edinburgh, 1851.

Stevenson, David Alan, *The World's Lighthouses before 1820*, Oxford, 1959.

Stone, Jeffrey, *Illustrated Maps of Scotland from Blaeu's Atlas Novus of the 17th Century*, London, 1991.

Stromness Museum, *'For those in peril'*: *Orkney Lifeboat History*, Stromness, 1977.

Sturluson, Snorri, *Heimskringla: Sagas of the Norse Kings*, S. Laing (trans.), rev. P. Foote, London, 1961.

Sutherland, Alexander, *A Summer Ramble in the North Highlands*, Edinburgh, 1825.

Sutherland, George, *Folk-Lore Gleanings and Character Sketches from the Far North*, Wick, 1937.

Sutherland, Iain, *Wick Harbour and the Herring Fishing*, Wick, 1984.

Sutherland, Iain, *From Herring to Seine Net Fishing*, Wick, 1985.

Tacitus, *The Agricola and the Germania*, H. Mattingley (trans.), rev. S.A. Handford, London, 1970.

Tapp, John, *The Sea-Mans Kalendar*, London, 1669.

Taylor, A.B., *Alexander Lindsay: A Rutter of the Scottish Seas*, I.H. Adams & G. Fortune (eds), London, 1981.

Taylor, H.S.M., 'When the merchant fleet was at its peak', *JoG*, 6 Dec. 1991.

Telford, Thomas, *Report concerning the North East Coast of Scotland*, 1790, Scottish Record Office GD 9/32/2.

Thom, V.M., *Birds in Scotland*, Calton, 1986.

Thomson, D., *The People of the Sea*, London, 1965.

Thomson, W.P.L., *History of Orkney*, Edinburgh, 1987.

Tidal Streams of the Waters Surrounding the British Islands, 2nd edn, London, 1945.

Traveller's Guide: or, a Topographical Description of Scotland, Edinburgh, 1798.

Van Keulen, Johannes, *De Nieuwe Groote Lichtende Zee-Fakkel*, Amsterdam, 1682.

Vaughan, Adrian, *Isambard Kingdom Brunel: Engineering Knight-Errant*, London, 1991.

Wallace, James, *A Description of the Isles of Orkney*, Edinburgh, 1693.

Watson, George, *John Gow: The Orkney Pirate*, Thurso, 1978.

Webb, William, *Coastguard!*, London, 1976.

Wernick, Robert, *The Vikings*, Amsterdam, 1979.

Wilson, Bryce, *The Lighthouses of Orkney*, Stromness, 1975.

Wilson, Gloria, *Scottish Fishing Craft*, London, 1965.

Wilson, James, *A Voyage round the Coasts of Scotland and the Isles*, Edinburgh, 1842.

Windwick, John P., 'The Ladykirk Stone', *Proceedings of the Orkney Antiquarian Society*, vol. 6, 1928.

Young, David (ed.), *Stroma*, Wick, 1992.

Index

Vessel Names